PENGUIN BOOKS

WILD WISDOM: LIFE LESSONS FROM LEADING TEAMS TO SOME OF THE MOST INHOSPITABLE PLACES IN THE WORLD

Christine Amour-Levar is a French-Swiss-Filipina philanthropist, adventurer, author and human rights advocate. She has built a global career as a marketing and communications expert and social entrepreneur intent on solving some of the world's most pressing issues. A passionate champion of female empowerment and environmental conservation, Christine co-founded Women on a Mission (WOAM) and founded HER Planet Earth, two award-wining, not-for-profit organizations that take all-female teams on pioneering expeditions as a way to support worthy causes. HER Planet Earth's primary objective is to raise awareness and funds for underprivileged women affected by climate change, while WOAM aims to empower women who have been subjected to violence and abuse.

Christine is also an active board member and advisor to several purpose-led organizations in the Social Impact, Fintech and Cellular Agriculture spaces. As a writer she has published *The Smart Girl's Handbook to Being Mummylicious* in 2012 and contributed to international publications such as *Forbes*, the *HuffPost*, the *Straits Times of Singapore*, the *Manila Bulletin Newspaper of the Philippines*, etc., and has had speaking engagements with INSEAD, Nike, TBWA, Microsoft, Unilever, Credit Suisse, TEDx and more.

Being included on *Tatler Asia's* Most Influential Impact List 2020, Christine has won multiple awards including the United Women Singapore Gender Equality Impact Changemaker Award, a Women of the Future Kindness and Leadership Southeast Asia Leading Lights 2020 and the '100 Most Influential Filipina Women in the World' Award™. She is currently based in Singapore, where she lives with her husband and four children. www.christineamourlevar.com

ADVANCE PRAISE FOR *WILD WISDOM*

'Prepare to be fascinated and inspired! Christine's life story and adventures provide valuable life lessons on purpose and compassion that can be applied anywhere from the Arctic Circle to the corporate boardroom.'

—Claire Lim Moore, CEO of TransUnion HK and
best-selling author of *Don't Forget the Soap*

'Christine has always had a magical way of inspiring others to join her on incredible life-changing expeditions. This is a must read for anyone wanting to explore the world and learn from the lessons that adventure can teach us.'

—Annabelle Bond OBE, Mountaineer and Fastest Woman
Climber—7 Summits in 360 days

'It's not often you meet people that have been so transformational in what they do but Christine never accepted the status quo and started a journey of making a real difference. Through the work of her NGOs, HER Planet Earth and Women on a Mission, and the expeditions she has led, she is not only transforming the lives of thousands of disadvantaged women around the world but also disrupting many boardrooms with the need for increased empathy in all we do. Christine is a wonderful storyteller and a true disruptor.'

—Dan Paris, Regional Business Development Director,
TBWA/Group Asia Pacific

'Christine is one of our Kindness and Leadership Leading Lights. Over the years, she has used the power of compassion and empathy to make a massive difference in business, in her community and to inspire others to build a better world. In *Wild Wisdom*, Christine has recast adventure as a positive and deeply transformational experience that has the power to make us grow and impact the world for the better.'

—Pinky Lilani CBE DL, Founder and Chairman of
Women of the Future

'When asked about what keeps me hopeful in the face of the challenges we are facing as a planet, it is the incredible humans who are using their time and energy to make the world a better place. Christine Amour-Levar is one such person—a powerhouse, unwaveringly positive and down to earth. This book will inspire you to step into adventure and do more for humanity and for the planet.'

—Stephanie Dickson, Founder, Green is the New Black

Wild Wisdom

Life Lessons from Leading Teams to Some of the Most Inhospitable Places in the World

Christine Amour-Levar

PENGUIN BOOKS

An imprint of Penguin Random House

PENGUIN BOOKS

USA | Canada | UK | Ireland | Australia
New Zealand | India | South Africa | China | Southeast Asia

Penguin Books is part of the Penguin Random House group of companies
whose addresses can be found at global.penguinrandomhouse.com

Published by Penguin Random House SEA Pvt. Ltd
9, Changi South Street 3, Level 08-01,
Singapore 486361

First published in Penguin Books by Penguin Random House SEA 2022
Copyright © Christine Amour-Levar 2022

ISBN 9789815017076

Typeset in Garamond by MAP Systems, Bengaluru, India

www.penguin.sg

This book is dedicated to the women who show courage and resilience in the face of hardships and challenges.

Contents

FOREWORD   xi

INTRODUCTION   xv

CHAPTER 1: Learning to Stand Strong   1

CHAPTER 2: Spreading my Wings   20

WOMEN ON A MISSION   37

CHAPTER 3: Women on a Mission to Reach
Higher Ground—Everest Base Camp,
Nepal, 2012   38

CHAPTER 4: Footprints on the Sands of Time,
Wadi Rum, Jordan—2013   53

CHAPTER 5: Retracing the Ancient Trade Route
to Tibet—Tsum Valley, Nepal—2014   65

CHAPTER 6: 36°C Below Zero with the Nenets
Reindeer Herders of Siberia, Russia—2015   74

CHAPTER 7: The Cycle of Life, Biking for a
Cause in Cambodia—2016   87

CHAPTER 8: Into the Eye of the Lut Desert
of Iran—2016   94

CHAPTER 9: Turning the Tide in the Land
of the Thunder Dragon, Bhutan—2017   105

CHAPTER 10: Cycling Through the Gates
of Hell, Ethiopia—2017   114

CHAPTER 11: Rwanda: A Success Story
of Female Empowerment—2017   126

CHAPTER 12: Fly Like an Eagle Across
Mongolia's Altai Mountains—2018   134

HER Planet Earth   143

CHAPTER 13: Surfing in Siargao—Asia's
Newest Resort Destination—2017   145

CHAPTER 14: Scaling Antarctica's
Vertical Limits—2018   151

CHAPTER 15: Sailing for Conservation in the
Philippine Islands—2018   160

CHAPTER 16: A Journey to the Lost World—
Vietnam's Son Doong Cave—2019   168

CHAPTER 17: In the Land of Fire and Ice,
Iceland—2019   176

CHAPTER 18: On the Trail of the
Samburu People of Northern Kenya—2019   185

CHAPTER 19: Fat Tyres in the Frozen
Lands—Greenland—2020   192

CONCLUSION: The Wisdom of the Wild   203

AFTERWORD   217

ACKNOWLEDGEMENTS   223

REFERENCES   227

FOREWORD

by
Explorer Robert Swan, OBE,
The first person in history to walk to both the North and
South Poles.

I believe that our thoughts, actions and words have the power to effect great change far beyond ourselves. When you cast a stone in the water, the impact sends ripples across the surface, far beyond where the stone entered. Similarly, the decisions we make every day have an effect that spread far and wide, impacting much more than our own lives. When purpose meets compassion, this triggers a unifying intentional force centred on how to help others, which encourages attitudes of altruism and inspires collaboration, trust and team loyalty. Christine lives this philosophy, driven by the intent to solve some of the world's most pressing issues by empowering women.

I first met Christine in Antarctica's Union Glacier Camp in January 2018. She was there with her all-female crew in search of new peaks in the Heritage Range. I was with my son, Barney, on our way to the South Pole to complete the first-ever expedition powered solely by clean-energy technology. We got chatting about why we were there, and she shared her ideas around the connection between women and Nature, and the fact that climate change is not just an environmental catastrophe, but also a human rights issue. Christine spoke passionately about her desire to use adventure to empower and support women around the world in order to build a healthier and more sustainable future. This resonated with me completely. Indeed, people need inspiration and hope, rather than negativity surrounding the whole issue of climate change. Christine's purpose, optimism and vision of service inspires hope. It shows that action with compassion is contagious and can motivate other people to care for the world and for the communities beyond their reach.

I don't believe women are better than men or that men are better than women. There are simply no jobs that a woman cannot do. My own mother, who is 106 years old, has been my greatest inspiration. Ever since I was a young boy, she taught me to recycle, and my determination to protect the environment was deeply inspired by her love of nature. It's true that women and Nature are intrinsically linked, and this nurturing relationship is as old as time, reinforced via religion, philosophy and other cultural norms.

As a passionate champion of female empowerment and environmental conservation, Christine founded not one, but two award-winning non-profit organizations, Women on a Mission and HER Planet Earth, to bridge these two passions. As you will discover in this book, both take all-female teams on pioneering expeditions —with Women on a Mission empowering and supporting women who have been subjected to violence and abuse, and HER Planet Earth raising funds for underprivileged women affected by climate change. As a result, she has directly impacted the lives of thousands of women around the world. Over the past decade, in order to raise funds for these worthy causes, Christine has also taken hundreds of women of all nationalities, ages and backgrounds, on challenging expeditions to some of the most remote and far-flung places on the planet.

In *Wild Wisdom*, she shares her life story and lessons learnt from growing up in the Philippines, living and working across multiple continents, the challenges of entrepreneurship and how adversity has forced her to step far outside of her comfort zone on many occasions. She will also touch on the vital importance of knowing and understanding your values, the meaning of having grit, the courage to speak up for those who have no voice and why we must all fight for a more inclusive, compassionate and diverse world. Christine embodies what women supporting women can achieve, and her story will inspire you to tap into your own power and take positive action for humanity and for the planet.

Robert Swan, OBE, Founder 2041 Foundation
www.2041Foundation.org

INTRODUCTION

The Wild Imparts Wisdom

If someone had told me years ago, when I left university, that I would one day find myself in the middle of the Lut Desert of Iran, one of the largest and hottest deserts in the world, with a team of women, having to deal with the fact that our expedition guide had gone missing; or that, when on another expedition to the Arctic Circle, without warning, the ice would suddenly crack and our vehicle would plunge head first into the freezing Ob River, resulting in my teammates and me being stranded for hours on end in −36° Celsius temperatures; and that this would be followed by a seven-day migration with Nenets reindeer herders of Siberia, during which time we would live off raw reindeer meat and blood—I would never have believed it.

Incidentally, if you have not yet tasted raw reindeer blood, let me tell you, it's actually not that bad. It's salty, a little tangy and has a way of hitting the back of your throat when you swallow it. It's quite good, especially when it's fresh and still warm, or when you drink it in sub-zero temperatures—but I digress . . . and I will come back to these stories a little later in the book.

Indeed, these past few years, thanks to my work with my two NGOs, Women on a Mission and HER Planet Earth, I've had the great privilege of taking hundreds women of all nationalities, ages and backgrounds, to off-the-beaten-track locations around the world on challenging, often pioneering, expeditions that really push them outside of their comfort zone.

We've run expeditions to some incredible places, from regions of the Arctic circle to the coldest, windiest and most remote continent on earth, Antarctica. We've traversed the largest caves in the world in Vietnam, so big in parts you could fly a 747 through them. We've sailed around remote islands in Asia and experienced real Robinson Crusoe-like moments.

My teammates and I became the first all-female team to fatbike across the frozen Arctic Circle Trail of Greenland, the first group to stand-up-paddle board down rivers in the Kingdom of Bhutan and bike across the Danakil Depression of Ethiopia—the hottest place on earth. We've migrated with reindeer herders in the middle of the Siberian winter, ridden semi-wild horses near the Altai region and climbed many mountains in the Himalayas, Iceland and Africa. All these expeditions have had as their mission to raise awareness and funds for vulnerable women.

As you can imagine, these unique experiences with teams of women to some of the most inhospitable and remote places in the world have truly been incredibly humbling and formative experiences for me personally. They have forced me to push my limits on multiple occasions—really testing my mental, physical and emotional resilience—while allowing me to grow, succeed and fail in countless ways.

Throughout these travels, I've also spent precious moments with many indigenous peoples such as the Kazakh eagle hunters of Mongolia, the Samburu and Maasai tribes of Kenya, the Inuit people of Greenland, the Bedouins of Jordan, the Afar of Ethiopia and many other fascinating individuals in Siberia, Nepal, Bhutan and the Philippines. Time with them has been incredibly eye-opening and has made me realize that their ancient wisdom and unique ways of interacting with their environment can help us discover more about everything from mitigating climate change to leading in times of crisis. As I take stock of these past few years and plan the next stage of my career in this post-pandemic world, I realize that I've learnt more about myself and about what really matters in life, through these experiences, than in my twenty years in the corporate world, and as a result, I've found my own brand of leadership. I call it Wild Wisdom—the knowledge, self-awareness and perspective you gain from spending time exploring the natural world and from having a full spectrum of life experiences. Wild Wisdom allows you to understand yourself better, makes you a more courageous and compassionate leader, and sheds light on the relationship between Nature and humans.

Without a doubt, one of the most important lessons from this unusual journey has been that our mission in life should be about empowering and advancing others, not about wielding power or accumulating wealth but about lifting others up and helping them progress.

I've come to realize that good leaders inspire their team, their tribe, their pack—whatever you want to call it—to be a part of something bigger than themselves, something more meaningful and ultimately, more fulfiling. Put simply, I believe that we should all aspire to help others grow closer to who they are meant to be, and our real value as human beings ought not to be measured by how much we have achieved in life, but by how well we advance the lives of others along the way.

Every single one of us has the capacity to be a leader and can impact the world for the better. But how we learn to harness that power and influence, can be a real journey in itself. These expeditions that I have been fortunate to lead and organize over the years, were trials by fire. They taught me unforgettable lessons of humility and gave me a depth of maturity that I would never have gotten in any other way.

I learnt time and time again how vital it was to be authentic, aligning actions with values—and not the other way around. This is the first and crucial step for anyone to gain respect and inspire others to join them on challenging endeavours. I became a better listener, realizing the importance of really trying to understand people's aspirations and motivations. This resulted in a stronger sense of loyalty and commitment to our greater mission as a team.

I came to understand that the experiences that at the time felt most unpleasant and challenging were in fact the most formative and fulfiling. I learnt that you could empower others by highlighting their strengths and potential contributions. The key is to be attentive and identify those qualities and skills, then, invite them to lead and contribute in their areas of strength. Everyone wants to feel like they are growing and contributing to the bigger vision.

Having the courage to take responsibility when things don't go as planned or when mistakes are made, are also important qualities for any team leader. Leadership is not about being perfect or being the strongest. It is about being better together and crediting the team when objectives and milestones are successfully achieved.

Another big lesson for me was the significance of empathy and compassion. Our future is a world where technology and automation are on the rise, and because of this there will be an equally massive swell in the demand for people who have these valuable skills of empathy and compassion. They will continue to be some of the most critical workplace skills of the future because of their power to boost quantifiable business results and increase employee satisfaction.

Last but not least, having the courage to show vulnerability is probably one of the most difficult skills to implement. It takes guts to show our authentic self in a way that exposes our vulnerabilities. Most of us are brought up to believe that showing those deep wounds is a sign of weakness. In reality, the opposite is true and showing vulnerability is an incredible superpower. It creates an atmosphere of safety and trust, which in turn, increases productivity and well-being within the team.

The COVID-19 pandemic has also shown me how vulnerable we all are in times of crisis. It has made me realize that to drive change moving forward, corporate social responsibility needs to be at the heart of corporations, embedded in their business model, aligned with their values, and not merely part of a separate initiative. Indeed, research says purpose-driven firms—the ones that place their commitment to something other than generating profits—are more profitable for their investors in the long run. However, theories and good intentions can get tossed aside when stock prices or profit outlooks tip the wrong way. I believe most companies do not lack purpose, they lack the courage, commitment and follow-through to actually live their stated mission. In truth, we all need to support sustainable initiatives and champion them passionately because of their intrinsic value for humanity, the planet and for our organizations in the long term.

Leadership for the greater good, the likes of which we haven't seen for years, has been one of the great advantages of the coronavirus pandemic. And while it may be intuitive to return to the way things were as soon as possible, what we actually need to focus on now, is not how things were, but what needs to change moving forward. As economics Nobel laureate Paul Romer famously noted in 2004,

A crisis is a terrible thing to waste.

During a pandemic, priorities come into focus, trends accelerate, rules and regulations suddenly become more flexible, leaders pay attention and real change is finally possible. Perhaps the most important lesson now unravelling is one of human empathy and the urgent need, today more than ever, is for more purpose-driven leadership, focused on empowering and advancing others.

By sharing my personal story and highlighting my life lessons from leading teams on expeditions, I hope to set the stage for a new approach to experiential learning that transcends the traditional measures of organizational performance, to take care of the human condition and the planet, at a deeper, more intrinsic, heart level.

This is a journey that begins with my early years growing up in Philippines and France, living through the political upheaval of the People Power Revolution in Manila, attending university in Tokyo and working on multiple continents as a young professional. It touches on my learnings from navigating the heartache of my divorce from my ex-husband and finding love again as a single mother of two young children and being blessed with two more healthy children. The story retraces how I came about founding two NGOs that have as core mission raising awareness and funds for female empowerment and environmental conservation via challenging, expeditionary travel, which in turn has led me to explore some of the most beautiful and inhospitable places in the world.

Writing this book has been a wonderful exercise in introspection and has made me realize that everyone should write their story, whether for publication, to just to keep in a drawer or beam up to the universe. There is drama and value in every life. I am convinced that the energy it takes to write and reflect on our opportunities and life choices is, for all of us, an endeavour well worth attempting. Ultimately, this is a story about roots and values, sisterhood and adventure, pushing limits and lessons learnt and the power of our common humanity and compassion to drive change and impact the world for the better.

CHAPTER 1

Learning to Stand Strong

Be strong enough to stand alone, be yourself enough to stand
apart, but be wise enough to stand together when the time comes.

—Mark Amend

Early Years, Values and Origins

One of my earliest and happiest memories as a child was an Easter-egg
hunt in our family's garden in the Philippines. The morning tropical
sun was warm and welcoming as my little sister, Nathalie, and I ran
around excitedly in our matching batik dresses, looking for the hand-
painted eggs and chocolate treats that we could collect in our wicker
baskets. The exotic flowers that populated my mother's garden
were in full bloom, from hanging white orchids and star-shaped
frangipani bouquets, to blood-red hibiscuses and multicoloured
birds of paradise. Standing majestically in the middle of the garden
was a gigantic avocado tree that spread its cooling shade from
large branches heavy with fruit. At its base was our green and blue
treehouse on stilts, or *bahay kubo* as we say in Tagalog or in Filipino,
made of wood, dried nipa palm leaves and bamboo slats, where we
would play at being little madams for hours on end.

Life was good. I often reminisce about these happy early years
and feel extremely lucky to have grown up in a safe and loving
home. It was also a multiracial, multilingual and multicultural home.

1

Indeed, my parents both have rich life stories and backgrounds, which brought much texture and colour to our family life as I grew up.

My mother, Eloisa Araneta Huni, is a proud Filipina who was born in Manila in 1944 at a time when the capital was being razed to the ground by the Japanese during World War II. The family escaped to the province as the war raged on, carrying baby Eloisa in their arms, and only returned to Manila when things settled down at the end of the war.

My mother grew up in a close-knit family and taught me the value of being proud of my origins. She made me understand, early on, how important it was for me to know where I came from and the story of our family. She knew this would give me a sense of identity. Learning about our ancestors, celebrating family traditions, embracing our culture and understanding my roots would open my eyes to how special and unique I was.

My maternal grandmother, Luisa Del Rosario or Dada to us, had a strong influence on me growing up. She came from a wealthy Chinese-Filipino family that owned the country's largest funeral services company, La Funeraria Paz—still in existence today. It is a company that has enjoyed a thriving business for the last 100 years, in a country that is deeply religious and where no cost is too great to bid farewell to the dearly departed. Dada was the matriarch of our family and had seven children, my mother was her fourth. She was a kind and loving grandmother to me, quietly confident, always elegant and deeply religious. Dada was a constant and calming presence in our home when I was growing up. She visited us often, always discreet, but attentive to her grandchildren's well-being. In my eyes, she embodied grace and resilience, having survived the Japanese invasion of Manila, and the loss of two of her children in infancy. Widowed at sixty, she went on to live a long and fruitful life, travelling often, devoted to the poor, always cooking delicious meals for those she loved, until she finally died in her sleep, at home, surrounded by family, at the ripe old age of 101. When I am sometimes faced with life's ups and downs, I often ask myself, 'What would Dada have done in this particular situation?' and it comforts me to know that I have a part of her essence in me.

My maternal grandfather, Pablo, was a very different kind of person. Proud and flamboyant, he made it a point to enjoy the good things in life. Part of the prestigious Araneta clan, a name that still means something in the Philippines today, he grew up a child of privilege and inherited a plantation. Mum would regale us with stories of the Araneta ancestors, who originated from Guipúzcoa, the Basque region of northern Spain, in 1723, during the Galleon Trade. 'There were two brothers named Baltazar de Araneta and Don Jose de Araneta who arrived in Manila aboard the Spanish fleet, La Sacra Familia, from Spain by way of Acapulco, Mexico—Christine, you have the blood of Spanish conquistadors and adventurers in your veins, don't you ever forget that!' she would say. Sometimes, I would daydream about these brothers arriving on our Philippine shores, after a long and treacherous voyage across the seas and what it would have been like being a stowaway on their ship. Without a doubt, these colourful stories of my ancestors awoke in me the desire to travel and explore the world far and wide one day.

Many generations later, the Aranetas grew into one of the wealthiest families of the Philippines, known as Sugar Barons, investing in sugar cane plantations near Bago City, in the province of Negros Occidental. My grandfather's older brother, Amado Araneta, who made the family into a household name, established the real estate empire of Cubao, the commercial heart of Quezon City near Manila. His most prominent achievement is building the Araneta Centre. Its landmark structure, the Araneta Coliseum, was the world's largest indoor stadium. It still remains one of the largest in Asia. This is where my parents watched 'The Thrilla in Manila', the third and final boxing match between Muhammad Ali and Joe Frazier in 1975, and where I saw my first concert as a teenager, with Duran Duran, even getting to meet the band at the home of my uncle right after the show.

Mum grew up educated by Catholic Benedictine nuns, attending the exclusive girls' college of Saint Scholastica in Manila and later moved to Paris in the late 1960s to study French at the Sorbonne

University. While there, she lived in a small flat on the Boulevard St-Germain, which still had cobblestones in the day, and experienced the 1968 student revolutions first-hand. It was an exciting time to be in Paris.

From there, she travelled the world, often alone, visiting friends in far flung places like Santiago de Chile, Rio de Janeiro and even spent a couple of months on the island of Santorini, way before it became internationally famous as a holiday destination. When I first heard about my mother's stories travelling the world on her own in the 1960s and 1970s, living the life in Paris and cultivating fascinating friends from all four corners of the world, I realized what a delightful maverick and free spirit she really was. And in telling my story and writing this book, I finally understood how much of my adventurous spirit and thirst for exploration was deeply inspired and shaped by my mum's rich stories of our family and her defiant, unconventional and generous attitude to life. Indeed, she has always, throughout the years and even till today, chosen to live life on her own terms.

When Mum finally returned to the Philippines after a few years abroad, she moved right back in with her parents—as was the custom for unmarried women in those days—and that, I'm sure, must have taken some getting used to. Soon after, she started working for Air France as part of their ground staff, which was still considered a glamorous role in the day. A year later, at a party, she met a tall, dark and handsome Franco-Swiss stranger, my father, Bernard Henri Huni.

Papa was a towering influence on my life. Born in Bordeaux in 1938, the eldest of three boys, he grew up in France and Africa, became a naval commando during the Algerian War of Independence, and subsequently had a successful international career as a shipping executive. Papa was a highly intelligent, deeply loving and devoted family man, who was truly larger than life. Charismatic, full of energy and a bon vivant at the core, he made a lasting impression on anyone who crossed his path. I like to think that my ability to connect and bond with people from all walks of life comes from some of the charm and sense of empathy I inherited from him.

Growing up in occupied France during the World War II, Papa was marked by the Nazi occupation. He never forgot the German soldiers patrolling the streets near his home and the clicking of their big black boots as they shouted the Nazi military salute. His mother, my paternal grandmother, Marcelle Begole, was French but grew up in Tahiti in French Polynesia, the daughter of a French sea captain and a French-Tahitian mother. She married Jean-Jacques Huni, my paternal grandfather, who was a well-to-do business man of Swiss descent. His family had immigrated from the town of Horgen, in the canton of Zürich, Switzerland, a generation earlier, and settled in Bordeaux where they set up a successful shipping business. My paternal grandparents were well travelled and cultured people. They spoke many languages, read extensively and had friends and acquaintances from all four corners of the globe. They shared with me many stories about the adventurous years they spent living in North Africa when my father was a young boy, and how they even adopted two Fennec foxes, the small crepuscular fox native to the Sahara Desert, and brought them back with them to Europe.

When my father became an adult, he joined the French navy and became a Naval Fusilier, a type of commando specialized in amphibious warfare and trained for special operations on land and coastal regions. He was then deployed to Algeria to fight in the Algerian War, also known as the Algerian War of Independence from France (1954–62). He never spoke about the war because it had scarred him so deeply, but I have always been proud of the courage and strength he must have had to muster during those dark and terrible years. The Algerian War was a very bloody and brutal conflict because of the guerrilla tactics and civilians involved. Some say it was France's equivalent to the Vietnam War in terms of violence and carnage. And for many years after the war, Papa used to wake up with nightmares, screaming in terror, 'Where are the bayonets?!' The experience was so traumatic that he swore he would never return to Algeria.

After a stint working in Paris in the late 1960s, my father then heard about a Swiss company called Zuellig looking to hire a sales director for their Asia operation based in the Philippines.

They needed someone to run their shipping and forwarding business. He applied and got the job, then moved across the world to Manila in 1970. Soon after he arrived, he met my beautiful mother—and the rest, as they say, is history.

A few years after they married, I was born, at the tail end of one of the Philippines' most violent and destructive super-typhoons, Typhoon Rita, known locally as Typhoon Gloring. This was a scary time for my parents as they awaited the birth of their first-born child. They were terrified that the roof of their house would blow off and that the power would be lost for days, as was often the case in such circumstances. The typhoon lasted twenty-two days, traversing the basin along an erratic path, spreading across Japan, South Korea, Vietnam and the Philippines. Manila was the hardest hit with 90 per cent of the area underwater. Schools and businesses were shut down for two consecutive days and the Red Cross estimated that more than 500,000 people were rendered homeless.

On the eve of my birth, the streets of Manila were still flooded and as Mum went into labour, my father hurriedly drove her to the hospital. The streets were submerged in muddy, murky waters, so much so, that he lost control of the car and the vehicle started floating down the road. It was a heart-wrenching moment. 'Christine, I thought you were going to be born in our car!', my father would say as he recounted the night of my birth. Luckily, he managed to regain control of the vehicle and they made it to the hospital just past midnight, in time to welcome their first-born into the world.

My early years in Manila were simply the happiest and most precious moments of my life. I was doted on and showered with love and attention. My little sister, Nathalie, arrived less than two years after my birth, so I had the benefit of a little playmate early on. My parents were full of joy. I felt our house was bright and cheerful especially now that I had a little sister and knowing my mum's large Filipino family was close at hand, added a layer of comfort and warmth to our family life.

My father was 'Le Chef' of our home and enjoyed cooking for friends and family. My parents hosted many dinner parties at home and that is how one evening, when I was just a few years old, I came to sit on the lap of a famous French mountaineer, Maurice Herzog. He had been invited over to sample one of my father's culinary specialties after my parents had met him at a French embassy party. I like to think of this moment as a sign of things to come, perhaps even the beginning of my love affair with adventure and the mountains.

Maurice was in Manila promoting his bestselling book, *Annapurna*, which was an account of his historic June 1950 climb of the Himalayan mountain by that name, the tenth-highest mountain in the world. As a result of this feat, he had become the first climber in modern history to reach a peak over 8,000 metres. The ascent was all the more remarkable because the peak was explored, reconnoitred and climbed all within one season; and he scaled it without the use of supplemental oxygen. It is also the only 8,000-metre summit that was conquered at the first attempt. Maurice was awarded the 1950 Gold Medal from La Société de Géographie, the world's oldest geographical society, which was founded in 1821. Meeting him at such a tender and impressionable age meant I saw him almost as one of my superheroes. In those days, I used to dress up as Davy Crockett, a freedom fighter known as the 'King of the Wild Frontier' or as Batman, who dedicated his life to an endless crusade, a war on all criminals. In truth, I longed to be just like them. I looked up to heroes almost as magical beings who had the power to make everything right in the world. Perhaps that desire to be courageous in the face of adversity for the greater good of humanity has stayed with me all these years and driven me to find my own unique way of contributing.

Between Two Worlds

One of the most precious advantages my parents gave us children early on, was the 'gift of tongues', or the ability to pick up and speak multiple languages easily. It certainly resulted in my choosing an international career later in life and gave me a deeper appreciation for different cultures from a young age. The fact that I was brought

up as a bilingual child meant that, from the age of two or three,
I could rattle off in French with my parents, then, within seconds and
without a moment's hesitation, switch to English when addressing
our relatives or friends around us. This always seemed to enthral
and impress some people. It was at times annoying though, because
occasionally, my mother's friends, who found it irresistibly cute that
I could speak French, would squeeze my cheeks in delight and beg
me to say something in French—anything! Even if they couldn't
understand a word I said.

People would frequently make a fuss, but despite the unwanted
attention, I knew that not everyone around me could speak two
such languages fluently and this made me feel a tad bit more unique.
Nevertheless, during the early years of my childhood, being bilingual
felt more like I had a cool party trick up my sleeve, rather than a
useful and advantageous skill. It was only years later, as I started
growing up, that I realized what a wonderful gift my parents had
given me by striving to bring me up as a bilingual, and eventually
multilingual, child.

There is no doubt that this skill facilitated a natural flexibility and
adaptability, and boosted my self-esteem and self-confidence, while
increasing my appreciation and acceptance of cultural differences.
In addition to French and English, I also learnt Tagalog, and later
on, in high school, I found it quite easy to pick up Spanish as an
additional subject because of its similarities to French and Tagalog.
Japanese and Portuguese came later as I moved around the world
for my university studies and career. To this day, I credit my parents'
foresight and efforts in giving me this priceless gift of languages
and it has granted me countless opportunities in my personal and
professional life thus far.

In addition to the many languages we spoke growing up, our
home was a wonderful blend of East and West, which was reflected
in the decor, the food, the traditions we celebrated, the books we
read and the topics we debated and discussed at the dinner table.
The guests who came over to attend my parents' dinner parties were

of all nationalities, creeds and backgrounds. Apart from Maurice Herzog, I also recall meeting an ex-KGB spy, many ambassadors, navy commanders, artists and painters, priests and teachers. During dinner parties, we children were expected to troupe down in our pyjamas and greet the guests politely, every time. We learnt early on the art of making meaningful small talk, maintaining eye contact and asking questions, while remaining diplomatic. These social skills as a child were good training for my life and career working with diverse teams across many borders.

In the realm of our household, my parents, despite their differences, found a way to balance their distinctive parenting styles, which was a mix of Asian strictness and filial piety, and western indulgence and openness. The result was a well-balanced authoritative-type parenting style, which encouraged independence and helped my siblings and me develop autonomy, while still imposing behavioural limits and controls. My parents were nurturing, supportive and in tune with our needs. They guided us through open and honest discussions to teach values and reasoning. While they had high expectations of us children, they also gave us the resources and support we needed to succeed academically, in sports, in the arts and socially. I credit them fully for the fact that I grew up self-confident about my abilities to learn new things, that I was able to develop good social skills and that I felt capable of accomplishing things on my own, which fostered in me a healthy self-esteem—qualities that, without a doubt, set me up for success later in life.

Papa would chuckle, 'I am bringing you up with a hand of steel in a velvet glove!' His bon-vivant, good-naturedness used to make him encourage us to enjoy a drink or two with him, much earlier than perhaps my mother was ready to permit. Yet he was scandalized when she allowed my sister and me to wear make-up and high heels at parties quite early in our teenage years, as was the custom in 'Latinized' Philippines. There certainly were many cultural variations we children had to navigate around carefully as we grew up. What was allowed and encouraged in one culture was sometimes frowned upon in the other and vice versa. However, all in all, this made for colourful family conversations and debates, and generally my parents found creative ways to compromise on their parenting styles. This fostered in us a deep respect for cultural norms and differences and made us more open-minded while it helped us realize that, ultimately, we would each pick from a menu of our own cultural heritage and background, to eventually come up with our own unique set of values and preferences—a blend of both worlds.

Although I grew up mostly in the Philippines, which had the greatest influence in shaping the person I am today, I also spent five formative years in France, which had a significant impact on my sense of self and confidence. When I was five years old, the family moved from tropical and warm Manila to a cold and rather austere French country town, thirty kilometres north of Paris called Saint-Witz, located near Roissy Charles de Gaulle airport. At the time, my father had decided to pursue a business opportunity with one of his uncles in France, and as a result, he uprooted the whole family, and took us all to live in his home country for a few years.

All I had known until then had been a beautifully warm and sunny country, with cheerful, smiley people and a happy, somewhat-privileged lifestyle, filled with birthday parties and outings at the country club or weekends away at resorts on the Philippines' sandy beaches. For me, moving to France was akin to a one-eighty in lifestyle. In fact, it was my very first experience with culture shock. France seemed so much harsher and challenging at first. We didn't have family living nearby, as we did in Manila; everyone seemed so much more serious and a bit gloomy. It was a sobering experience and such a contrast to our laid-back lifestyle in the Philippines. While curious about our new adventure as a family, I also worried about making new friends and fitting in.

Soon after we arrived, I started my schooling at a local public school. The French education system seemed strict and more punitive than what I had known in my American-style kindergarten in Manila. I had to adjust to studying exclusively in French, and the first year I struggled, and didn't get the marks I was used to. I remember shutting myself in the school bathroom and crying from frustration after getting a poor grade. I vowed I would try harder. This only pushed me to excel as I wanted to keep making my parents and myself proud. From being at the bottom of the class, I eventually made it to the top five in a class of forty students, and this gave me such a sense of fulfilment and confidence. I will never forget the day our teacher announced that someone in the class had gotten a perfect score in the problem-solving part of our mathematics test. She said she would announce the name of the person first and then this person could come forward and collect their paper at her desk. We all looked around the classroom, wondering who this could be. When she announced my name, I was so shocked that I almost fell off my chair when I tried to stand up. I was eight years old and I will never forget how it felt walking up to get my test paper to the applause of my classmates, with my teacher looking at me with quiet pride. I tried not to tear up from the emotion and sat dazed and starry-eyed in my chair for the rest of the lesson, holding my test paper as if it was made of gold leaves. These early years in France, despite being challenging for me at first, only showed me that if I worked hard and applied myself, with focus and determination, I could find a way to be successful in any system. These life lessons stayed with me throughout my life and gave me the courage to dig deep whenever I found myself in a new and daunting situation.

Despite the beauty of the short European summer months, the cold and dark winters also took some getting used to. We lived in a big house on the edge of a dark forest and occasionally I felt a little isolated. Furthermore, I could sense my mother's longing for the support of her family and friends back in the Philippines, but it also didn't help that my father was often away on long business trips abroad.

During these years in France, we spent quite a lot of time with my paternal grandparents who were now living between Switzerland and France. One of my most vivid memories of time at home, was of my father and grandfather in a cloud of cigar smoke, drinking well-aged cognacs after dinner by the fireplace, discussing the latest book about Winston Churchill, a fixation in our family. They would debate and discuss for hours on end the politics of this legendary leader and politician. To this day, I am fascinated by Churchill's life and inspired by his courage, eloquence and perseverance in the face of unrelenting horror and tyranny. His fearless and valiant leadership is a deep source of inspiration to me.

A big ray of sunshine came to brighten our time in France. My little brother, Guillaume, was born there on 23 April 1980, in a nearby medieval town called Senlis. After two girls, the arrival of a bouncing baby boy made my parents extremely happy. Guillaume had two doting big sisters helping Mum at home and, despite the initial challenges we had faced with the move to Europe, we all gradually adjusted to our new life, and enjoyed our time in France. Eventually, we made the most of our five years there, before moving back to live in the Philippines once again.

This first decade of my life, living between France and the Philippines, contributed to the foundation of the person I am today. My sense of self, my belief in my capabilities, the early experiences, both challenges and highs, all of that, helped me shape my own values, sense of direction and identity. Thanks to our rich family lore, I take great pride in my origins and multiracial roots. I understand that I carry the blood and heritage of a cultural tapestry of ancestors, grandparents and parents in my blood and in my soul. In turn, this has helped me understand and define my own legacy.

When I returned to Manila after five years away, just shy of my tenth birthday, I felt happy to be back in my warm tropical home, but immediately became aware of the extreme poverty and inequality surrounding me. Once again, it was a huge contrast to our life in France, a sort of reversed culture shock. I remember vividly, as we drove from Manila International Airport, through the city and to my aunt's house, staring in disbelief at the rows upon rows of slums and shanty houses on either side of the highway, where children my age or younger were playing surrounded by garbage. I had a big lump in my throat as I watched through the tinted car window and felt a deep sense of injustice. 'Why them and not me?' I wanted to help these children, but I didn't know how or where to start. In the years to come, whenever she could, Mum involved us in charitable activities in the community, donating to orphanages, giving food to families in need, visiting the poor and the sick, and as a result, she taught my siblings and me that privilege comes with great responsibility—her values have stayed with me and I strive to live by them and pass them on to my own four children today.

Despite the noticeable inequality and brewing political discontent that was slowly emerging in the early 1980s, life for our family in the Philippines was still enjoyable and certainly never boring. We settled into a beautiful new home not far from my school, and during the next five years, from 1982–87, I grew to become a conscientious adolescent, devoted to sports and to my studies. I also had the opportunity to discover more remote and untouched parts of the Philippines and reconnect with its thriving tropical flora and fauna.

During school breaks, we holidayed as a family at Palawan and Bohol, two of the most picturesque areas of the Philippine archipelago. My parents also bought a little beach house two hours south of Manila in the province of Batangas, where we spent countless weekends relaxing and island-hopping around the area. One summer, we ventured to visit an untouched 'new' island, called Boracay. No one from our circle of friends in Manila had heard about it. It seemed that the only tourists who ventured to this part of the country were intrepid European backpackers. One of our French friends had heard it was absolutely beautiful, with no electricity or running water, and that you could pay just a few pesos a night for rudimentary but charming nipa-hut-type accommodations. So, my family and I boarded an overnight, rickety and crowded public cruise liner from Manila and after about ten hours at sea, travelling through the night, we docked at Caticlan port, and then transferred to a small *banca* boat, which eventually took us to the pristine shores of this beautiful untouched island. And it didn't disappoint, it was breathtaking, with sand as white as sugar and crystal-clear, turquoise waters lapping at its waterfront. At night the stars were glorious, and I even caught my first firefly there. I remember holding it in my cupped hands, while gazing mesmerized at its glowing abdomen. As I looked up, I realized that hundreds more of these beautiful, incandescent insects were surrounding me, zigzagging happily through the lush foliage just a few metres from the island's powdery shores. I never forgot that exciting feeling of being like Robinson Crusoe on a deserted island. No wonder I kept looking for that pioneering feeling in my travels later on.

Back in Manila, political unrests were starting to brew. In 1983, following the assassination of the foremost critic of the Marcos dictatorship—the man who was among those first arrested in the declaration of martial law—the nation revived out of inaction. Fifteen minutes after Ninoy Aquino returned to the country after three years of exile in the United States, he was dead on the tarmac of the Manila International Airport.

People Power Revolution

The assassination of Ninoy Aquino showed the increasing incapacity of the Marcos regime to deal with opposition. Ferdinand Marcos was mortally ill when the crime was committed, while his cronies and his wife, Imelda, mismanaged the country in his absence. The event was the linchpin that transformed the opposition to the Marcos regime from a small, isolated movement into a nationwide crusade.

I will never forget how, in 1986, a million and a half Filipinos took to the streets to overthrow the corrupt and brutal regime of President Ferdinand Marcos. It was called the People Power Revolution. President Marcos and his wife, Imelda, had ruled the Philippines for twenty years. Following the murder of Ninoy Aquino, a huge opposition movement rallied around his widow, Cory Aquino. She stood against Marcos in a snap presidential election in 1986, but when Marcos was declared the winner amid massive electoral fraud, huge protests began. The protestors were supported by the Catholic Church under the guidance of Cardinal Jaime Sin. Eventually, senior members of the army rebelled against Marcos.

I was fourteen at the time and could not believe this was happening so close to us. Schools were shut for a couple of weeks and, at first, we were thrilled to be at home for this enforced holiday; that is until the fighting began in the streets of our neighbourhood in Makati, near the central business district of Manila, where we lived within a gated community of residences. We could hear gun shots close by and were told to remain in the ground floor of our home, as a safety precaution. I felt anxious because my father was away on a business trip in Tokyo at the time and was unable to return home to us because Manila International Airport was shut. The phone lines were down, the roads were blocked and all supply chains were affected.

When the bullets started flying more intensely nearby, Mum decided to drive out of our home in a convoy with a few other families, to go and stay at the house of a friend, whose home was not in such a perilous zone. TV stations had been shut down and we were getting our news via the radio. I realized that we were living through a truly historical event—the people had spoken, they had had enough of Marcos and his corrupt regime.

Filipinos poured on to the streets to protect the rebel army officers. Loyal troops refused to fire on the crowds. The protests, fuelled by the resistance and opposition to years of oppression by President Marcos and his cronies, culminated with the absolute ruler and his family fleeing Malacañang Palace to exile in Hawaii. Ninoy Aquino's widow, Corazon Aquino was immediately installed as the eleventh president as a result of the revolution . . . and the world was given a new word for engaged, active nonviolence: people power. I remember feeling overwhelmed with joy and emotion. We had won. The dictator had fled. Good had prevailed, and there was a renewed sense of hope coursing through the country as Corazon Aquino took up the reins of power.

My later notions of leadership were profoundly influenced by her. As I saw it, Corazon Aquino operated not with force but with love. She didn't polarize, she integrated. She maintained the people's respect not with a grand lifestyle, but with integrity. She met with rebels, tribal people, farmers and police, not to pontificate, but to listen and she made her ministers listen.

After Corazon Aquino became president, things settled down for a while, but there were many other occurrences that kept life in the Philippines unpredictable and kept us at the edge of our seat. If it wasn't a coup d'état or a revolution, the disruptions came from earthquakes, typhoons, floods, landslides, volcanic eruptions. What about blackouts, or brownouts? For those of you not familiar with the difference, a brownout is a partial, temporary reduction in total system capacity, while a blackout is a complete interruption in power. Same-same, but different, if you will.

Things didn't always work in the Philippines, but life was fun, colourful, often unfair and sometimes a bit dangerous too. But what inspired me the most was the talent, grit and honesty that I had the opportunity to witness among so many of my Filipino compatriots. The Philippines is such a unique cultural melting pot of a nation. It has had many upheavals and growing pains. No wonder they say the Philippines has had 'three hundred years in a convent and fifty years in Hollywood'—this roughly sums up our colonial history and explains why we are so unique. The Philippines has some of the poorest but also happiest people on earth. It is a beautiful country which really tugs at my heartstrings because of the kindness, hospitality and generosity of the Filipino people.

Today, I have had the chance to live and work in four continents and many cities, and all through the years, I have carried deep within my core the values instilled in me by my home country and by my parents. And as I progressed through life, in my twenties and thirties, these values were my north star. They were part of who I was, who I became. Every step of the way, for me to be in harmony, I had to align my career and my life choices with my values and not the other way around. Steve Jobs once said:

> Have the courage to follow your heart and intuition. They somehow already know what you truly want to become. Everything else is secondary.

Indeed, I have taken these words to heart and have tried to live my life this way, at every stage.

Sports as a Passion

Throughout the trials and tribulations, during the more tumultuous times of my life, while the troubles of the world and the nation swirled around me, sports were my safe haven. When my godfather passed way from cancer when I was eleven years old, or when my father suffered his first heart attack at our beach house when I was just seventeen years old, sports were my refuge in the midst of life's storm, something to take my mind off my worries. It was a sanctuary into which I could escape.

Indeed, sports has always been a big part of my life. I was very athletic and competitive growing up and had a strong sense of adventure. As a child I played football, basketball, tennis and touch rugby. I loved biking and swimming, enjoyed running and especially sprinting. Physical education at school was one of my favourite subjects—I couldn't wait for it to be time for the sports period!

In high school I fell in love with 'the beautiful game', football, and played it competitively, regionally and on occasion for one of the local universities, De La Salle College of Manila. My teammates became my second family. Football is more than just a game; it taught me valuable lessons long after I hung up my cleats: teamwork, discipline, perseverance, goal setting, handling success and failure, time management and keeping fit. Belonging to a team taught me when to lead and when to follow, how to take criticism and the power and satisfaction of achieving common goals. Sports in general also gave me much confidence as a young woman, and I believe deeply in the power of sports to bring people together and to help us find physical, mental and emotional balance.

One particular trip abroad left a lasting impression on me. In fact, it ended up shaping my future quite significantly. This is when my love affair with Singapore began. The first time I landed in the Lion City, I was fifteen years old, and my teammates and I were getting ready to play against one of the local international schools in a regional tournament. Arriving from bustling and congested Manila, I never forgot the impression that modern and immaculate Singapore had on me, with its beautiful and pristine architecture and magnificent bougainvillea-lined highways. Everything felt so safe and orderly, things worked, the people were disciplined, it had none of the chaos and corruption I had experienced in Manila, and it made me feel like anything was possible. Singapore looked like the city of the future and I was immediately drawn to it. I vowed there and then that I would find a way to live and work here one day.

And, as if fated by the gods of football, many years later, when I finally moved to Singapore in 2005, I had the wonderful opportunity to meet one of football's greatest legends there—the one and only, Pelé. He was visiting the island state for a conference at the time, and I got to speak with him and even take a picture with him. Pelé has this amazing ability to connect with people from diverse backgrounds; maybe it is his optimism and good-natured spirit, or maybe it is the fact that he understands the hardships that so many people in this world endure.

When I spoke with him, he was warm and friendly, and as charming as you could imagine him to be. Growing up, I idolized him—his style of play and his flair. He has become an icon for people all over the world. His three-time World Cup-winning feat, from four World Cup appearances, is unlikely to be matched. Pelé scored a Guinness World Record—1,279 goals in 1,363 games—and also collected the following personal records along the way: Youngest winner of a World Cup—aged 17, top scorer of Brazil National Football Team and one of only 3 people to have scored in 4 World Cup events. Unbeknownst to many of his fans, Pelé helped save the lives and improve the health of millions of children in Brazil. He also helped promote such worthy global causes as ecology and environment, sports and development and peaceful resolution of conflicts as goodwill ambassador for the UN, UNESCO and UNICEF. Because he is such an inspiration to me, meeting him will count, without a doubt, as one of the highlights of my life.

As I finished high school in Manila and graduated with my International Baccalaureate diploma, I dreamt of working in the sports industry someday. I wanted to be part of a fast-paced and exciting industry that celebrated athletes and inspired everyone to play more sports. I hoped for a career that would be exhilarating and competitive. Sport has a symbolic significance in relation to performance outcomes, success and celebrating achievement that does not seem to occur in other areas of economic and social activity. From when I was thirteen years old, I had been wearing Nike running shoes, my brand of choice. I never forgot the joy I felt when I got my very first pair of Nikes. I was so excited that I slept with them on my feet that night—a sign of things to come. It took several years and several career shifts for this dream to become a reality—but that is a story you will read more about in the succeeding chapters.

CHAPTER 2

Spreading my Wings

In the Land of the Rising Sun

Before I could pursue my dream career in sports, I knew I had to continue my studies. I was hoping to return to France for that part of my life, but my parents had other ideas and wanted me to have a completely different and novel experience. So, two months after my eighteenth birthday, I relocated from Manila to Tokyo to attend university. Prior to that moment, I had never set foot in Japan and did not even know much about this country's great history and culture. Of my 200 classmates at the international school in Manila, I was the only one who ended up going to Tokyo for university. The majority of my friends went on to study in Europe or in the United States. Going to Japan was entirely my parents' enlightened decision. They believed that I would benefit from this unique life experience and from the added bonus of learning the Japanese language—my fifth language. While I was curious about Japan, I really didn't know what to expect, and was a little apprehensive about what I would find once I arrived in the land of the rising sun. One of my favourite novels growing up was *Shogun* by James Clavell. Set in medieval Japan, it tells the epic story of a bold English captain, who had undertaken to break the Portuguese monopoly on Japanese trade by leading five Dutch ships there, and finds himself blown ashore and alone in this alien land. As a result, I had this slightly romanticized vision of

Japan in my head. Yet, I also knew Japan was a first world country and that it had a temperate climate, lots of earthquakes and was the eleventh-most populous nation in the world, as well as one of the most urbanized. Tokyo was a megacity with about 18 million people but had a reputation for being one of the safest cities in the world. In truth, I was ready to leave home, spread my wings and start my own adult life. I had an open mind about Japan, love it or hate it, I just knew I was ready for a new life.

So, off I went on a fresh new adventure. I could never have foreseen the kind of massive culture shock I was about to experience. Here I was, thinking I knew Asia for having lived a total of thirteen years in the Philippines, but soon realizing that Japanese culture and norms were completely different from my own. For starters, to my surprise, people in Japan seemed to be following ALL the rules. Moving from Manila, where traffic lights were a mere suggestion, to Tokyo, where the only people who dared to jaywalk were from the local mafia called Yakuza, was a very strange and novel experience to say the least.

During my freshman year at university, I lived in a strict, all-girls dormitory run by stern Japanese nuns. All activities were severely regimented and everyone had to be up and dressed, ready to clean the dormitory communal areas, such as toilets and showers, every morning at 8 a.m. sharp. Having grown-up with a somewhat privileged lifestyle in Manila, with maids and drivers at my beck and call, this change in my life took some serious adjustment. Sister Takagi, who was the headmistress of our dormitory, reprimanded me often about the quality of my cleaning, which, to be fair, was probably not up to scratch because I invariably rushed through it sleepily and without much focus. As a result, she took a special interest in me and monitored me closely.

Additionally, I often felt frustrated because, despite studying the language for hours on end every single day, I was unable to communicate in Japanese until about six months into my stay. It was only after I spent two weeks working on a Japanese farm in the southern island of Kyushu, where I was forced to speak the language constantly and without any other foreigner in sight, that I finally made a breakthrough with the language. Working on the farm was exhausting. It was a small potato farm, so the harvesting was done manually. We started work at 5.30 a.m. and worked up to about 4 p.m., with a short break for lunch. The local farmers had, for the majority, never met a foreigner, so they bombarded me with questions throughout the day, about my background: where did I grow up? What was university life like in Tokyo? I was forced to dig out my mini dictionary constantly, to search for the right words. The farmers were friendly and genuinely curious; I soon became a local celebrity and people would come from other parts of the neighbourhood, some even took pictures with me as a souvenir. I enjoyed my time working there; at the end of the day I was physically and mentally exhausted and drained, but I felt proud of my supercharged progress with the language. I came back to Tokyo dreaming in Japanese. And based on this particular case, I can confirm that total language immersion really does work!

Upon graduating cum laude from Sofia University in Tokyo with a bachelor's degree in international business and economics and a minor in the Japanese language, I stood at the threshold of new beginnings, about to venture into a new life. I felt a deep sense of anticipation and excitement. Which direction should I go? What career path should I embark on? I felt the world was my oyster.

I knew I needed to find a job quickly if I wanted to stay in Japan because a student visa without a confirmed job offer meant you had to exit the country. I was anxious to stay and put my Japanese to good use, it had been hard enough to learn it. Now, I had to find a great job and prove to myself that I was capable of standing on my own two feet. Thus, six months before graduation, I sent out sixty copies of my curriculum vitae, even hand-delivered several of them, and this while still attending classes at the university, and working two part-time jobs. Thankfully, within a few months, I was gratified to find that I had four serious job offers from well-established companies. In the end, I picked the job that didn't necessarily pay the most but it was the role that offered the greatest opportunity to learn and to use my Japanese, plus exposure to many industries—it was the job that interested me the most.

Hence, I started working in a very exciting industry, advertising—for an agency called McCann-Erickson, Japan's largest foreign advertising agency. I was their first non-Japanese employee to be recruited via their university-hire programme and went through rigorous training during the first few months along with twenty other new graduates, before being assigned to a department within the company. I was proud of myself for having come this far and for joining such a successful agency. I was also relieved that I was finally financially independent and didn't need my parents' support. After my father's first heart attack, a few years ago, I worried about his health and the stress of providing for us all. I knew he still had my two young siblings to look after and put through university, so I was certain Mum and he would be happy that I was now earning my own keep.

My new role was extremely interesting as well. McCann-Erickson had a roster of blue-chip clients that any new graduate would feel lucky to work on. I was thrilled to be working in Japan and on such exciting new initiatives. My hours were long and the work day in Tokyo was also quite stressful. Generally, it started for me with an early morning ride through the world's busiest subway system as about 20 million people took the train in Japan's capital every day. On the platform, everyone shuffled into tight formations beside the train doors to avoid obstructing disembarking passengers, then rushed in, albeit in crowd-enforced slow motion. We would then squeeze on board and movement was near impossible; my feet sometimes didn't touch the ground. And yet, even in these packed trains, resigned silence reigned supreme.

Calm and orderly behaviour tended to be characteristic of even the biggest crowds in Japan, such a contrast to what I had known in the Philippines. This, I soon discovered, is the art of *gaman*, which means persevering in tough times, often stoically. Simply put, gaman is the idea that individuals should show patience when facing unexpected or difficult situations, and by doing so, maintain harmonious social ties. The concept implies a degree of self-restraint: you put the brakes on your feelings, it is a sign of maturity.

Nowhere was this more apparent than when I visited one of my clients, Nestlé, at their headquarters in Kobe after the devastating 1995 earthquake. The city had been at the epicentre of the quake and 4,600 lives had been lost. The damage was widespread and severe. Structures irreparably damaged by the quake included nearly 400,000 buildings, numerous elevated road and rail bridges and around 300 fires, which had been triggered, raged over large portions of the city, disrupting water, electricity and gas supplies. About 22 per cent of the offices in Kobe's central business district were rendered unusable and over half of the houses in that area were deemed unfit to live in. People were wandering in the streets in an orderly way, stoic, evidently trying to grapple with the destruction of their city, yet with dignity and calm, looking ahead at how they would begin to rebuild their shattered lives.

The art of gaman was one of the most significant lessons I learnt from my time in Japan, and I developed a deep admiration for the Japanese people's ability to persevere and tolerate things that are unexpected or difficult, in silence. Gaman, I learnt, originated in Buddhist teachings about bettering oneself. It was honed during Japan's post-war economic boom when work took on the status of nation-building—meaning sacrificing time with family for hours in the office. I certainly developed more resilience during my time in Japan, as I worked long hours in the office, speaking in Japanese throughout the day, which was not an easy task for me. I would come home to my little flat in the evenings, exhausted, with my head pounding from having to concentrate so hard in a foreign tongue during the day. Being a junior account coordinator in an advertising agency also meant I had to learn honorific Japanese or *keigo*, which I was expected to use with clients to show respect.

As the youngest in my team, I also needed to adhere to a mantra called *horenso*, which means always keeping superiors informed about what I was doing. Every decision, no matter how small, needed to go through the chain of command and get the stamp of approval from the boss. Additionally, group consensus was a key part of life in corporate Japan. This activity was called *nemawashi* and was used to build support for a project or decision through discussions with various groups within the company. It was a very time-consuming process, but very effective in getting everyone on board and in sync with a common vision—a method I still use today with some of my teams.

In the end, my time in Japan turned out to be a genuinely humbling but incredibly rich and formative experience for me. All in all, I lived in Tokyo for almost six years, and although I did eventually get used to my new life and succeeded in speaking the language with fluency, I truly believe that up until the very last few months of my stay there, I was in many ways, still adjusting.

A Corporate Career on Multiple Continents

During my time in Japan, I was able to continue playing football at my university, but only sporadically, and only with the men's team, as there was no ladies' football team at the time. At least this kept me connected to my favourite sport, and as fate would have it, after a couple of years working in advertising, this passion for sports led me to find an international marketing job at Nike's world headquarters in the United States. By chance, McCann-Erickson began to handle Nike's advertising work in Japan, in partnership with another agency called Wieden+Kennedy, and hearing about this, I started making inquiries. After much patience and perseverance, through our agency connection, I was able to get an interview with the president of Nike, Japan. It went very well. He saw my drive and passion for sports and facilitated other interviews for me in the United States. This is how I landed my dream job at their world headquarters in Beaverton, Oregon. Nike was growing exponentially in Japan at the time and was keen to hire people who had experience in that market. I was one of the lucky ones and, thankfully for me, one of the reasons

I got the job was because I spoke Japanese. One of my interviews was actually conducted in Japanese over a beer at the Nike sports bar on the main Nike campus. My time in Japan had paid off, making my application stand out.

I bought a one-way ticket out of Tokyo and travelled for a few months across the world, from Fiji, the Philippines, the Caribbean to Europe and finally to the United States to start my new life in Oregon. When I arrived in United States, I felt exactly as if I was on a honeymoon. I had been imagining what it would be like to be living and working there. Everything was different and exciting to me. Things were so much cheaper and more affordable than in Tokyo, and I felt spoiled for choice in local department stores and supermarkets.

In fact, my new life was much easier to get used to than it had been for me moving to Japan. Language was not an issue. Culturally, it was quite similar to the Philippines, which was once an American colony. And except for a few local customs that were new to me—such as hugging people, even new acquaintances, speaking quite loudly in public places, the huge food portions at restaurants, and being carded at the supermarket even if it was just to buy a six-pack of beer—settling in was not too difficult, and much easier once I developed a routine.

While working at Nike, I would pinch myself every morning, not believing my luck, as I drove my red Suzuki jeep into the parking lot, which was hidden behind the green berm surrounding the Nike offices. Then, I would walk into the John McEnroe building— each building was named after a famous Nike athlete—which also happened to be where the founder of the company, Phil Knight's office was—just a few floors above mine.

I used to have posters of McEnroe on my wall as a child, so working in a building named after him was such a wonderful coincidence. Walking around campus to go to meetings, you could see giant banners with photographs of athletes: running, dunking, hitting, jumping, stroking, serving, reaching, blocking, shooting and yes, celebrating. My lunch times were spent either working out at the gym on campus or playing football—or soccer, as they called it in the United States—with a group of female employees. It was such an inspiring place to work at.

Being in the marketing department of a company like Nike was also a thrilling experience, and I found that Americans had a straightforward and practical work ethic that was easy to adapt to. People valued go-getters and hard-workers and it wasn't about spending long hours at the office like in Japan or in France, but rather about being as productive as possible within your time there. Furthermore, in contrast to Japan, where group consensus was often given consideration, I quickly learnt that at Nike, if you didn't speak-up in meetings, it was akin to having no opinion. As a result, I became more assertive and straightforward in my communication style. I would get to the point more quickly and focus on being efficient instead of making small talk or idle conversation.

I enjoyed working with the Americans and living in the United States. In fact, this made me reflect on the relationship between my country of birth and my new home. Indeed, the Philippines used to be an American colony. After winning the Spanish-American War in 1898, the United States paid Spain roughly US$20 million to acquire it. Shortly after, the Americans arrived on the islands in droves, like secular missionaries bringing with them their own kind of institutional gospel: democracy, prosperity and free trade. This colonial relationship lasted almost fifty years and concluded when the United States granted the Philippines independence soon after the end of World War II on 4 July 1946.

Understanding the history between the United States and the Philippines helped me situate myself in my new home and I would take any opportunity to share this historical background with my American friends and remind them that the Philippines was the only true colony they ever had, so our connection was even closer than they realized.

From working at the Nike headquarters in the US where I was their youngest regional PR manager at age twenty-three, to travelling all over Latin America for the company, spending time in Brazil in particular and picking up my sixth language, Portuguese, to getting transferred internationally for Nike to Europe and then later to Singapore—the experience was incredibly enriching and only strengthened my love and passion for sports. I worked on numerous, exciting and aspirational marketing campaigns, coordinated projects with people on multiple continents and of all nationalities and backgrounds. I was constantly learning, growing and discovering new things. I used my languages constantly and honed my multitasking and management skills and capabilities. My colleagues and I were on a mission to make more people embrace sports and the athletic lifestyle. The job was everything I hoped it would be and more.

I joined Nike at a very special time in its history, in the mid-90s as the company was thriving and investing heavily in football—my sport! During the first few years of my career there, I was based in the United States but travelled extensively across the American continent. The company expanded rapidly into Latin America and even though I initially was hired to work on marketing initiatives focused on Japan, I was soon asked to become part of the growing regional Americas team, which included Canada and all of Latin America. In those days, the company already had an office in Canada, but only a few offices in the Latin American region, mainly in Chile, Mexico and Argentina, and distributors in other key markets including Brazil—the largest regional market.

In the space of a few years, Nike signed-up a series of football clubs and national teams around the world. In 1996, the company partnered with the Brazilian National Football Federation—the Confederação Brasileira de Futebol or the CBF—to supply the kit and co-sponsor the squad for $160 million over ten years. This was the largest deal ever involving a national side at the time. I became part of the global marketing team launching this partnership and worked on multiple events around the world to showcase our shiny new asset. In Rio, we hosted 600 international journalists on the iconic *Pão de Açúcar*, or Sugarloaf Mountain, a 396-metre peak at the mouth of the Guanabara Bay, with magnificent views of the city and beyond.

My work in public relations and events management revolved mainly around football and as a result I had to be at most major international tournaments such as the World Cup, Copa America, the Olympics and exhibition matches involving our sponsored teams. These were unforgettable years and a time of massive personal growth and learning. As a regional public relations manager, I learnt to work within the complex matrix organization structure, with reporting relationships set up as a grid rather than in the traditional hierarchy. In other words, I had dual reporting, to both a functional manager and a regional manager, but also managed my functional direct reports within the region. I matured and developed as a manager and learnt to work well across multiple cultures, using multiple languages and on a large scale, on complex projects and events. I grew in confidence and experience and I was enjoying myself so much. This wasn't work for me, it was more of a calling. I was in the zone, thriving and putting all my gifts and talents to good use.

Some of my earliest leadership training came from the management style I experienced at Nike. One of my first bosses in particular, inspired me with his easy-going yet result-orientated approach to managing our regional team. I felt I could be myself even if the expectations and pressure to do well were very high. Nike was still run by founder Phil Knight at the time I was working there. Phil, an ex-accountant by trade, used to set key financial milestones each year for the company, which were widely communicated not just to shareholders but to employees as well. We all knew what that number was and what target we, as a company, needed to hit.

Nike had a powerful cult-like company culture and used to emphasize employee loyalty and the power of the brand at its massive sales meetings and corporate events. Some found this culture overwhelming, but I didn't, I soaked it all up and felt I belonged. The worship of the swoosh—the Nike logo—was so entrenched, that some employees tattooed the symbol on their ankle. The organization's culture centred on creativity and innovation with its main vision being 'to bring inspiration and innovation to every athlete in the world.'

Nike's ethos was set by the vision of bringing out the best in athletes and any other person through its sports gear and apparel. Co-founder Bowerman famously said:

> If you have a body, you are an athlete.

The company endeavoured to give confidence and bring out the boldness in athletes, thus the motto 'Just Do It'. In many ways, the brand message was aspirational and as a result, I thrived in this competitive sports-orientated environment. It not only appealed to my personality and made me want to work even harder, but I also lived through one of its toughest crises as a company, and that experience made my years there even more interesting.

Since the 1970s, Nike had been accused of using sweatshops to produce its footwear and apparel. The company had vehemently denied the allegations in the past, suggesting it had little control over sub-contracted factories. This criticism intensified in the mid-90s when I was there and finally, Nike realized it has no choice but to audit its factories for occupational health and safety. The findings of factory investigations showed that the supervisors often overstepped their duties. The laws protecting the workers were being ignored in favour of cutting costs and lowering health standards. Women in those factories represented a large proportion of factory employees, approximately 75 to 80 per cent, and a majority of those were in their teens or early twenties. When I first heard about this, I was appalled. How could Nike, the brand I looked up to so much, let this happen, and especially to the women who worked for them? But I quickly realized that this was also a blessing in disguise, and that uncovering such an injustice was a step towards making things right. I knew from the internal information I was hearing and the programmes we were implementing that the company was genuinely committed to fixing this urgently.

Nike soon installed a code of conduct for its factories to monitor working conditions there. Part of my role in public relations was to communicate these plans and efforts. In 1998, we also introduced a programme to replace our petroleum-based solvents with less dangerous, water-based solvents. And a year later, we substituted less harmful chemicals in our production, installing local exhaust ventilation systems and trained key personnel on occupational health and safety issues. Following this, the company monitored the factories over the next few years, but soon realized that this didn't work either because factories would improve conditions for the monitoring and then regress afterwards. Nike then persuaded its contract manufacturers that better labour practices and sustainability improved productivity with lower worker turnover and reduced costs. The move became part of a company-wide focus on using its prowess as an innovator to drive sustainability. This was finally a solution that proved to have traction and I was relieved that this was the direction we were going in. Nike also did not hesitate to put its contract manufacturers on notice: basically, they had to adhere to new labour and sustainability standards or risk losing Nike's business. I saw first-hand how this was handled in markets like Vietnam, when I was working for Nike based in Asia. The brand has since earned plaudits far and wide for its efforts, becoming a recognized sustainability leader and one of the most sustainable apparel and footwear companies in the world for environmental and social performance, including labour record.

Even though I left Nike in 2008, I remain a staunch supporter of the brand and still follow its evolution from the side lines with great interest. Clearly, the company left a strong impression on me. No wonder I find it difficult to wear any other sporting brand to date. Perhaps it is because the swoosh still has a powerful hold on me. The brand's strength is partially due to the fact it continuously innovates and delivers state-of-the-art products to a range of consumer demographics. But for me it is a deeper emotional connection. The Nike swoosh stands for athleticism, power, fitness, motivation and the will to succeed—values I still identify with and place front and centre of my life, even today.

It Takes a Village

In parallel with my professional life, much was happening in my personal life. At twenty-two, I got engaged and married my first husband, Mike, a Scotsman from Glasgow, whose surname was Amour, which means love in French, whom I met in Japan and who swept me off my feet. After a whirlwind romance, twelve weeks after we started dating, he proposed. We flew home to my parents, who were living in London at the time, and Mike asked my father for my hand in marriage. My father, whom I had never seen shed a tear in my life, cried, overwhelmed with emotion, while popping the champagne to congratulate us.

Mike then took me to Old Bond Street, in the heart of historic Mayfair in London's popular West End, into the Cartier jewellery store and asked me to pick any ring I wanted. I felt like a princess in a real life fairy-tale. A few months later we had a beautiful wedding on the outskirts of London in a stately home called Danesfield House on the banks of the river Thames. I was so happy on my wedding day that my cheeks hurt by the end of the day from smiling the entire time.

Mike wore a kilt as did all his male Scottish relatives, who came down from 'north of the border' to England, as they say there, to take part in the celebrations with us. We had a Scottish bagpiper and Mum surprised me by booking a troupe of Filipino cultural dancers, who happened to be touring in Europe at the time, to come and perform the *tinikling*, a traditional Philippine folk dance that involves two people beating, tapping, and sliding bamboo poles on the ground and against each other in coordination with one or more dancers who step over and in between the poles in a dance in time with the music. The British guests had never seen such a performance and were enthralled. And I loved the contrast of this quintessential Filipino traditional dance with the elegant and sophisticated English architecture and decor of our wedding venue.

We were married ten happy years and had two children, Yasmine, born in New York and Malcolm, born in Paris. But our international careers and age gap, Mike was almost twelve years older than me, took a toll on our relationship, and sadly, we started to drift apart.

We wanted different things in life, our priorities and focus changed gradually. This eventually led to our separation and soon after we moved to Singapore, we decided to divorce. This was one of the lowest points in my life and it was at that moment that I turned to the mountains for strength and comfort.

I started going on treks and climbing expeditions on my own, a couple of weeks at a time, leaving the children with Mike, as we took turns to alternate our holidays with them. I would spend a week or two in the Alps or in Nepal, climbing in the Annapurna range, imagining Maurice Herzog walking on some of these same trails half a century ago. The time on my own was precious to me. I pondered about my life thus far and wondered what would come next. I asked the mountains to infuse me with their superpower, to help me heal and be strong for Yasmine and Malcolm and the path ahead.

I felt such a deep sense of failure and I was heartbroken. I couldn't help thinking that we had let our children down by not finding a way to make it work. Throughout this painful time in our lives, back in Singapore, Mike and I were both profoundly concerned about their well-being. After consulting with a child psychologist, we decided to live in the same building but on different floors so that it would be less traumatic for the children. We felt that this would give them some form of stability knowing that, although they now lived primarily with their mother, their father was very close and accessible at any time. Adjusting to this new living arrangement was not easy but, thankfully, we survived the experience and found a way to thrive and nurture our relationship as friends and as parents to the children.

A few years later, I met my second husband, Steve, an Australian of Croatian descent, and with a French surname once again, Levar. He was single, never married and out on the town for a good time. On our first meeting, little did he know that I had a six-year-old daughter and four-year-old son waiting for me at home—and an ex-husband living in the same building albeit in a separate flat. Steve was later delighted to find out that I already had two children of my own, and, just ten weeks after our first date, on a safari in South Africa, he asked me to marry him.

From the outset, I felt Steve and I had so much in common. We were both interested in sports, had very similar energy levels and were both extremely sociable. We were the same age, he was just three months older than me, thus part of the same generation. I found him kind, loving and extremely generous, and he had a natural way with Yasmine and Malcolm. I knew from the start, that we could make it work as a new blended family.

Indeed, instead of moving us away from my living arrangements, Steve moved right in with me and my two children, with Mike still living a few floors above us. It worked quite well because even though we were in the same building, we used different main entrance lifts, so we didn't bump into each other often. We also made a conscious effort not to socialize too much with our condo neighbours, so as to safeguard our privacy. We didn't want to take part in condo gossip and so we generally kept a low profile. We lived very close to each other but rarely saw each other, which made it less awkward.

Soon enough, Steve and I had two children together, and during this time, we all continued to live in the same flat. I was delighted and grateful that we had all been able to create this convenient setup for our children. Yasmine and Malcolm simply viewed their father's flat as the upstairs part of our home and would zoom up the service lift several times a day to see him when he was in town. My two younger children, Louis and Angeline, often accompanied the older two to visit their 'uncle' in his flat upstairs. In their innocent eyes, Mike was an important member of our family.

But it was the sight of my ex-mother-in-law and my mother-in-law cheerfully chatting together at one of the children's birthday parties that I still find incredible. My mother-in-law, Steve's mum, a phenomenal cook, would even sometimes invite my ex-husband Mike over for dinner with her and the children when she was in Singapore to babysit, while Steve and I were away on holiday abroad. Most people looked askance at this setup and thought, 'How bizarre! Why would anyone want to live this way, in such close proximity with an ex-husband—or an ex-wife, for that matter?'

The answer is simple: 'It takes a village to raise a child.'

There is much wisdom in this old African proverb. The proverb is from the Igbo and Yoruba regions of Nigeria where it is believed that raising a child is a communal effort. The responsibility lies not only with the parents, but also with the extended family, and in some cases, the community. And this is a proverb that my ex-husband, my husband and I have taken to heart, especially during the formative years of our children's upbringing. In addition to the parents, and in some cases, the stepparents raising the children, every other family member and close friend has a role to play. The larger the community, the better for the child. Every member of this extended family can impart wisdom and tradition that children are extremely receptive to. Rich human interactions make up the fabric of their childhood memories, culture, morals, sense of right and wrong and responsibility, which they will take with them on the road to becoming young adults. As I had experienced growing up in my own multiracial and multicultural village, with many relatives and extended family members close at hand, I recognized the value of building this community around my own children. And I saw how it allowed our family to transcend the stigma and pain of divorce, while giving my children the security, love and comfort they so needed to grow into confident, well-adjusted and happy individuals.

Of course, as one reflects on this unconventional and modern living arrangement, it is obvious that it requires a certain type of individual who can look beyond the petty differences of opinions, the bruised egos and the emotional volatility that inevitably come with any divorce. It helps if the second husband, as it was in my case, was not responsible for the breakup of the first marriage; nevertheless, ultimately, it is about putting the children first, and our feelings a distant second. Beyond the sense of failure, frustration and self-pity that may dominate the emotions of the adults after a divorce, it is the children's fragile feelings and nascent self-confidence that really need to be placed at the centre of this complex situation.

When my oldest son, Malcolm, was eight-years-old he once declared, 'When I grow up and become a famous professional football player, I will buy a big house where all of us can live together!' When probed, he told me what 'all of us' meant: his father, his stepfather, his mother, brother, sisters and all grandparents, including step-grandparents and nannies! In his young mind, there should be no impediment for this situation to one day become a happy reality.

It was not an uncommon sight to see my husband and ex-husband chatting by the condo pool while the children happily paddled and splashed about them. It was a scene that took some adjusting to for a few of our neighbours at first when they learnt of how our unconventional family unit worked.

We all lived this way for six years, and then, as the children grew up, my ex-husband moved to a flat that was just a few minutes' walk away. Today, even if we are not living in the same building any more, we still feel part of the same big, beautiful village. And when I think back on some of these heart-warming moments of my children's upbringing, I thank my lucky stars that I have had two admirable and unique men in my life to have children with. Both men have been able to put egos aside for the love, happiness and well-being of the children. This is what is at the heart of our family's genuine partnership, and at the core of our big, beautiful village.

What this experience has taught me is that failure is not the opposite of success, it is part of success. From failure and pain, you can find success and hope. If you are determined to find a way to make things work, you will find a solution to make the best of any situation, and ultimately, you will be able to nurture it into something positive and beautiful. The learnings from this personal challenge have also helped me in my career and in my life. The experience has made me much more optimistic as a person and has taught me that tough times and obstacles teach us to trust ourselves more, because ultimately, we are more resilient and more capable than we think we are. These lessons served me well as I entered the next chapter of my life. Little did I know that I was about to transition into a life of meaning, purpose and adventure! I was moving towards my tipping point.

WOMEN ON A MISSION

I often wonder why some people are lucky enough to be born into a loving and safe home, just like I was; why some have the same opportunities that I enjoyed growing up and a chance at a really good head start in life and why others don't. Mum would quote the oft-used phrase 'the haves and the have-nots' to describe the two groups into which the world is divided. Our parents and time and place of birth is not for us to choose. It is Nature's, or perhaps destiny's, random process. And it is undeniable that some are luckier than others when it comes to the circumstances of their birth. I often ponder how, across the world, there are probably other women just like me, with similar hopes and dreams, wanting the best for their husband and children, who would most likely be more successful than me if given just half the chance. Only they were born poor, given no education and very few opportunities. They are preoccupied not with how they will advance their careers, but by how they will survive the next day and be able to feed themselves and their families, or whether they will be safe from violence or other dangers. It is so hard for me to understand why this is my life and why that is theirs; why is it that where we are born often defines much of our path in life? It seems so unfair. And yet I realize that all we can do is be grateful for what we have and try to help in the best way we know how.

CHAPTER 3

Women on a Mission to Reach Higher Ground—Everest Base Camp, Nepal, 2012

The Choices that Define Your Destiny

I believe that life is a succession of circumstances, coincidences and opportunities. These choices define your destiny. They manifest themselves in many different ways, through situations, places, people who inspire us or causes that touch us deeply and move us to action.

Once upon a time, in early 2012, I had a chance encounter with an incredible woman called Valerie Boffy. This meeting changed the course of my life.

Valerie started out as just an acquaintance of mine. I would bump into her at the French lycée of Singapore when it was time to pick up the children. She was athletic and walked with confidence and purpose. I was drawn to her energy but didn't know much about her, apart from the fact that she was French. One day, we got chatting and she told me she was going to be away for seven weeks.

'Seven weeks! How nice, is this a holiday? Will you be going to the south of France?' I asked her. She chuckled and said she was going to attempt to climb to the summit of Everest. That response floored me. The hair on my arms stood on end.

Being a mountain lover, I had read many books about Everest, including Jon Krakauer's *Into Thin Air* about three times, which recounts the story of the 1996 Mount Everest disaster, in which eight climbers were killed and several others were stranded by a storm. I knew how dangerous Valerie's climb would be, and I was fascinated by her courage and determination. It's not every day that you meet a woman who is about to climb to the summit of the world, and I felt inspired and excited for her.

I followed her climb very closely, on Facebook and also getting news from her husband who was in touch with her via satellite phone for most of her seven weeks there. She succeeded on the first try and on the summit of the world's tallest mountain, she unfolded a banner that said, 'Bearing the Flag for Women Everywhere' in support of a charity called Women for Women International that champions women survivors of war. Her act of courage hit me in the gut. To this day, when I think about it, I get emotional. To see someone, do something so brave, in support of other women in need—women who have gone through trauma and so much suffering in countries that are ripped apart by the horrors of war—her defiance and courage really impacted me deeply. It was like a wakeup call.

It made me realize how lucky I had been in my life thus far. As you have read, I grew up in a loving home, was lucky enough to receive a good education. I have had so many opportunities in my life and in my career. At the time, I had just given birth to my fourth child. I felt I had innumerable blessings in my life. This realization was an epiphany. I experienced an overpowering sensation. Like a veil had finally been lifted from my eyes. I could now see with a new sense of clarity and purpose, almost as if I had been waiting all my life to be figuratively tapped on the shoulder and offered the chance to do something very unique and meaningful, and tailor-made to my talents. Suddenly, I knew it was time for me to use my skills and experience to give back, to do more—indeed this was my tipping point.

When Valerie returned to Singapore, we met up right away at her home, and she shared with me her incredible experience on Everest. She talked about her highs and lows, her self-doubt and how she found the courage to continue. She told me how much strength and encouragement my little messages of support along the way had given her. She recounted how after summiting, on the way down, she almost couldn't muster the energy to keep descending and that her Sherpa had had to scream at her to jolt her to realize that if she didn't move, she would die on the mountain. I asked about Women for Women International and the banner she had brought with her. And she told me about its founder, Zainab Salbi, whom she had met when volunteering for the charity in London a few years ago.

Zainab's life story is truly inspiring. She was born in Baghdad, Iraq, in 1969, and her life was impacted by her first-hand experience of war as she lived in Baghdad during the Iran–Iraq war. She grew up in fear of the dictatorship of Saddam Hussein, who was very close to her family. Her father was the personal pilot of the Iraqi dictator as well as the head of the Iraqi civil aviation. Experiencing psychological abuse from Saddam Hussein, Zainab's family managed to send her out of the country when she was nineteen, by arranging a marriage for her to an older Iraqi-American living in the United States. The marriage turned out to be an abusive one and although she managed to escape his clutches three short months after her wedding, she never got back to Iraq with the break out of the First Gulf War in August 1990.

Valerie explained to me that Zainab's experience with war sensitized her to the plight of women in war-torn regions. When she learnt of the war in Bosnia and Herzegovina in 1993, and seeing the inaction of the international community, she decided to do something about it by founding Women for Women International and dedicate her life to serving women survivors of wars. Zainab was only twenty-three years old at the time and she started by assisting thirty-three Croatian and Bosnian women. I found it remarkable that she had decided on this path at such a young age, and it made me realize that I had no more time to waste to do my part to support women in need.

Today, Women for Women International has become a charity that provides women survivors of war and conflict with the tools and resources to move from crisis and poverty to stability and self-sufficiency. They support women who live in some of the world's most dangerous places. Women enrol in the charity's year-long training programme, where they learn how to earn and save money, improve their family's health and make their voices heard at home and in their community. Since 1993, the charity has helped more than 500,000 marginalized women survivors of war in Afghanistan, Bosnia and Herzegovina, the Democratic Republic of Congo, Kosovo, the Kurdistan Region of Iraq, Nigeria, Rwanda and South Sudan.

The story of Zainab's life and of her charity touched me profoundly, and I knew I needed to get involved. This was exactly the kind of initiative into which I had to put all my energy and drive to support. Hence, soon after, Valerie and I, plus another friend, Karine Moge, decided to recruit a group of adventurous women from Singapore and beyond, to embark on a two-week trek to Everest Base Camp, Nepal, in the Himalayas in an effort to raise awareness and funds for women survivors of war. The climb turned out to be the journey of a lifetime and a truly transformative experience for us all.

Stepping out of my Comfort Zone

I had hiked in Nepal before but had never attempted anything as gruelling as the Everest Base Camp trek. When I first told my husband, Steve, about my desire to go on this expedition to raise 100,000 dollars for women survivors of war, he said my voice shook and I had stars in my eyes. And despite his worries about any risks such a trek entailed, he could see that he simply had to let me go and give me his full support. I am so grateful, that he did.

The Base Camp of Everest, from which countless attempts to the summit of the goddess of all mountains have been made and continue to be made every year, commands nothing but respect and humility. At an altitude of 5,364 metres or 17,598 feet, the camp is higher in altitude than any mountain in the Alps or any mountain I had ever attempted before. I had heard this trek was considered one of the most worthwhile on the planet because of the region's spectacular mountain peaks, the hard days of hiking required to reach it and the kindness and rich culture of the local people in this part of the world; and I was beyond excited to start planning this incredible journey.

In Sanskrit, the word *Himalaya* means 'abode of snow', and this truly characterizes the vast permanent snowfields above the snow line that we could see as we made our way up to Base Camp. Watching the Himalayan mountain range—immense, lofty and majestic—was a breathtaking and deeply spiritual experience for me. No wonder they say the Himalayas have captured people's imagination for centuries.

The journey to Base Camp can take anywhere from ten days to three weeks, depending on how many days of acclimatization you allow. This trek is classified as moderate to difficult, but it is not the terrain or hours on the trail—between five to seven hours on average per day depending on the itinerary—that are the real difficulty; it is the altitude itself. We set off from the village of Lukla, perched at 2,800 metres above sea level, just a short scenic flight from Kathmandu, where we had landed at Tenzing-Hillary Airport, incidentally considered one of the most dangerous airports in the world. On one side of the single runway, which has a 12 per cent gradient, we could see the mountains, and on the other, sheer nothingness—a complete drop. Thus, it is no surprise that when our team landed there in October 2012, we held our collective breaths and hung on tightly to our seats as the pilot came in for the precarious final approach. I can still remember how excited we all were, even if a bit nervous to embark on such a challenging trek.

While many of the routes through the mountains were arduous, we found ample places to rest and enjoy a meal along the way. Furthermore, it was almost impossible to get lost—all we had to do was ask a local the way to the next village on your route and he, or she, would direct us. From Lukla, we made our way to Monjo, then on to the Sherpa capital of Namche Bazaar, which is 3,440 metres above sea level. A couple of my teammates developed headaches from the altitude and I was worried this would only get worse as we continued our ascent. Even the fittest people can be prone to altitude sickness, and warnings about this were plastered all along the way into Namche. Acute mountain sickness or AMS is no joking matter in the Khumbu Valley; and Monjo to Namche is about five kilometres, four of which are almost all uphill.

In Namche we spent two nights to allow for acclimatization and hiked up to the Everest View Hotel at 3,750 metres. Namche Monastery was also worth a stop to meet the local lama and we received his blessing for the journey ahead. As we continued our trek, we passed through the beautiful village of Tangboche at 3,870 metres, which is claimed to be the highest monastery in the world. The air started to feel thin at that level as we stopped for a quick lunch on our way to Pangboche nestled at 3,930 metres, where we slept another two nights. As we got closer to Base Camp, my excitement kept increasing, but I knew we still had a long way to go and the altitude was starting to have an effect on some of us. I noticed my body respond to less oxygen in each breath and attempt to increase oxygen intake by breathing more often.

The next day was an important acclimatization stage, with a five-hour hike to Amadablam Base Camp situated at 4,460 metres, and back to Pangboche. Massive glaciers are draped beneath the cliffs that soar up above the camp, and I looked up in awe at the dramatic scenery around Amadablam. There, we had lunch with the climbers and Sherpas camping at the Amadablam Base Camp. We spoke with them about their plans and preparation for their final assault on the summit. The air was fraught with tension and anticipation, and this encounter gave us a real sense of how a fully active expedition camp operates.

The next stop was Dingboche, an eight-hour walk from Pangboche, followed by Dzongla the next day, taking us above the treeline to the Cholatse Pass. The terrain started to appear moon-like at this level, with spectacular views of a turquoise lake and stunning peaks with narrow snow and ice ridges. I felt in awe as I took in the magnificent view unfolding before my eyes. How privileged I was to be able to take part in this journey knowing that I had a loving family waiting for me at home! In this moment, I reflected that many women around the world were not as lucky as me, especially women survivors of war, for whom this trek was in support. It felt so right to be doing this for the charity, Women for Women International, and this made me all the more determined to continue—as we were getting closer to Everest Base Camp.

Finally, on the ninth day, we made it to Gorak Shep at 5,140 metres, where we spent one night. The non-stop trekking, and the altitude in particular, had begun to take a toll on us. I had lost my appetite and was not sleeping well, but I was faring reasonably well. Three members of our all-female team were on antibiotics, fighting flu and a hacking cough. Two other teammates had to be put on oxygen. They had been suffering from pounding headaches for the last three days, even after being dosed with paracetamol. They were weak, very pale and their lips were bluish—clear symptoms of the onset of altitude sickness, an ailment not to be taken lightly. Just that morning, a French climber had to be airlifted from Gorak Shep because of this very condition.

Yet, we were not far now, despite the fact many of us started to show real signs of fatigue as the thin air and low oxygen levels began taking its toll on our bodies. The next morning, at 4 a.m., a handful of us set out in complete darkness to climb *Kala Patthar* or 'Black Stone' mountain peak at 5,545 metres. I had to really force myself to drag my dog-tired body out of my snug sleeping bag and layer up before stepping out into the frigid night. This was the only way to get a clear view of Mount Everest, which is not actually visible from Base Camp, hence the added motivation to put myself through this additional climb. A couple of hours later, on the summit of Kala Patthar, we were rewarded with an awe-inspiring and unobstructed view of Mount Everest at sunrise, as well as the other Himalayan giants like Pumori, Nuptse, Changtse and the summit of Lhotse.

Despite the exhaustion and the numbing cold that morning, which had frozen my extremities and turned my already chapped lips blue, this was truly one of the most brilliant panoramas that I have ever experienced. It was worth all the effort and I teared up from the raw emotion and fatigue.

We descended back to Gorak Shep and checked on some of our sick teammates. Thankfully, after a night's rest and receiving oxygen at the camp, they felt marginally better and having come this far, we decided to set off and accomplish our mission together. The added motivation, of course, was the fact that we had committed to taking on this challenge to support such a worthy cause. Thinking about the destitute women around the world, who had suffered greatly and had lost everything because of war and conflict, helped us focus on the task at hand and steel our resolve. Thus, after lunch that same day, our team continued its progress and finally arrived at Everest Base Camp.

Our persistence had paid off, and on a windy autumn afternoon, we finally clambered up the last few metres of uneven ground on to the shifting moraine leading to the Base Camp of Everest. As we arrived, a surge of elation filled my racing heart. I just couldn't believe that we had succeeded in accomplishing our goal as a team, it seemed like such a monumental task when we first decided to organize this, and now we were here, mission accomplished! After embracing and congratulating one another with moist eyes and throats tight with emotion, we began taking in the incredible view from this symbolic place.

Surrounded by majestic snowy peaks, a little breathless from both the excitement and the 50 per cent oxygen level in the air, we could imagine some of the legendary climbers who had stood very close to where we were. Sir Edmund Hillary and Tenzing Norgay were the first to conquer Mount Everest in 1953, using the South Col route, forging a path through the treacherous Khumbu icefall at our very feet. My teammates and I had been dreaming of this very moment for many months while training hard to be in the best

physical and mental shape possible for this demanding trek. Despite
the sun shining brightly in the cloudless azure sky, it was a chilly
−5° Celsius at this altitude. Soon, the sun would move behind the
mountains and the temperatures would plummet to −20° Celsius.
So, it was with haste that we unfurled our various banners to take
the pictures we had planned to capture as souvenirs to cherish for
a lifetime.

Owing to our expedition guides' licenses and connections, our
team had been granted the very special permission of sleeping at
Base Camp that evening. This privilege is usually only accorded to
teams attempting to summit Everest itself. So as night fell, we quickly
set up our tents and prepared for a bitterly cold and windy night. The
icy wind howled most of the night, but bundled up in my tent, my
heart was full of pride and joy. I was elated by our achievement as a
team, and our growth and resilience from this incredible adventure.
I knew my friends and I had forged an unbreakable bond of
sisterhood through this journey. Indeed, every challenge we face and
navigate strengthens our will, confidence and our ability to conquer
future obstacles. Despite the wind lashing at our tent, I fell into a
deep and peaceful sleep.

The next morning at 6 a.m., we packed up our tents and began
our descent from Base Camp back to Lukla airport, where we were
scheduled to take our plane to Kathmandu. The descent took about
three days and despite the sudden drop in altitude and the welcome
increase in oxygen levels in the air, those days felt interminably long
and tiring. We were clocking in about thirty kilometres a day and
despite the fact we were walking downhill, everyone was bone-tired
and weary. By then, all of us were simply ready to come home.

In truth, these voyages combine so many complex dimensions
that are core to our being—overcoming personal physical and
mental challenges, feeling free and empowered to make a difference
in the lives of destitute women, discovering new moon-like grounds,
pushing our fears and limits, leaving our families behind for two
weeks. The experience itself was a transformation. No wonder

many believe the Himalayas retain a small part of your soul, forever captured and resting peacefully awaiting your return. It feels good to know, deep inside, that we do not realize what we can achieve until and unless we try. We just have to dare to dream and leap a little further sometimes.

Looking back and reminiscing, the trek to Everest Base Camp was one of the most meaningful, challenging and magical experiences of my life. It was not only an adventure I will always treasure, but it was also the moment Women on a Mission (WOAM) was born.

Finding a Higher Purpose

There is a Chinese saying, 'If you want happiness for an hour, take a nap. If you want happiness for a day, go fishing. If you want happiness for a year, inherit a fortune. If you want happiness for a lifetime, help somebody.' For centuries, the greatest thinkers around the world from Leo Tolstoy, the Dalai Lama, Muhammad Yunus and even Winston Churchill, have suggested the same thing: happiness is found in helping others.

It has been a decade since WOAM was founded and it has become an organization that combines challenging expeditions to majestic locations around the world, with inspirational events and workshops in Singapore and abroad. Violence against women and girls is one of the most widespread, persistent and devastating human rights violations in our world today and it remains largely unreported due to the impunity, silence, stigma and shame surrounding it. WOAM's core objective is to support and empower women affected by such violence via our advocacy work and fundraising. It has given me the higher purpose I always craved and by redirecting my focus and energy on helping others, a new path in life.

We are a volunteer-based organization. None of us gets paid to do the work we do. Teammates who come on our expeditions fund their own travel costs and are also asked to fundraise for our charity partners. The money goes directly to the charities we support, who then redistribute the donations to the women and girls in their programmes.

WOAM raises awareness and funds for women survivors of war and supports and empowers women who have been subjected to violence and abuse. We partner with existing well-established non-profit institutions that already have programmes and structures in place dedicated to serving the underprivileged, with a particular focus on women's issues. I have forged very close ties with most of these organizations, not just as a fundraiser, a board member or an advisor, but also as a friend to their founders and managers. I have a deep admiration for the work they do, and their commitment to push for female empowerment and economic prosperity.

Over the last few years at our fundraising events, we have hosted artists, adventurers, authors, musicians and even astronauts. These events have forced me to be creative and to become a better multitasker, host and public speaker. As a result of the generous support of our friends, family, partners and the community we have grown and nurtured, I take much pride in the fact that WOAM has managed to raise well over a million US dollars for organizations that advance the position of women around the world.

In addition to women survivors of war, whom we champion via Women for Women International, which operates in eight war-torn regions around the world, we also support and raise funds for AWARE Singapore, a well-known, gender-equality, advocacy group, for United Women Singapore, a non-profit organization that promotes women's empowerment and gender equality, for the International Justice Mission, a charity that protects those living in poverty throughout the developing world by combatting violent forms of oppression, including sex trafficking, and for Pertapis, a Singapore NGO that provides residential care for women and girls who come from dysfunctional families and who are in need of shelter, care and protection. Working closely with these admirable organizations has been an incredible learning journey for me. It has helped me get a deeper understanding of the complexity of the issues that women face around the world. My eyes have been opened to the fact that tackling inequality will help us unlock the power and potential of women and girls—and this is what our world urgently needs most. Inequality has become one of the leading challenges of our time—and pervasive gender inequality is what is primarily responsible for the fact that women continue to be disproportionately affected by armed conflict, sexual violence and economic crisis.

My partners and I are deeply passionate about gender equality and female empowerment, and we believe corporations, governments and society all have a role to play in helping improve that parity. Today, women represent half of the world's population and every day we are growing in economic power and influence yet continue to be underrepresented in leadership roles. WOAM's advocacy work centres primarily on awareness building and helping women understand their rights, while supporting them to build stronger livelihoods. Indeed, it is difficult to combat oppressive inequality if one cannot identify what one is entitled to. This is why WOAM partners with organizations, in Singapore and abroad, focused on providing entrepreneurial and life-skills training for underprivileged women living in conflict and war-prone areas.

In Singapore, we have collaborated with local law firms to provide free workshops for expatriate women to help them better understand their rights and the immigration laws of this country, especially in case of a separation or divorce. I have heard, first-hand, heart-wrenching stories of women left to fend for their children and themselves when marriages end badly, and the law does not protect them. Within the community in Singapore, some women may be endangered financially or psychologically if a divorce occurs. This happens often because they are not aware of their rights, so they cannot be properly protected. Inequality affects women everywhere, not just in poor countries but in first world countries too.

Moreover, over the years, WOAM has also raised funds and awareness for AWARE Singapore's Sexual Assault Care Centre, which provides a vital helpline for abused women in the community.

Their inspiring Leader and Executive Director, Corinna Lim, is a dear friend and has even come on one of my WOAM expeditions in the past. Statistics show that domestic violence in particular is the most widespread, but among the least-reported, human-rights abuse in the world. Indeed, COVID-19 has blurred the lines between work and home life. One consequence of the pandemic is a global increase in domestic violence, including intimate partner violence. In fact, the UN has described the worldwide increase in domestic abuse as a 'shadow pandemic' alongside COVID-19. It is believed that cases increased by 20 per cent during the lockdowns, as many people were trapped at home with their abusers, and although restrictions on movement have been lifted in most regions, unfortunately, the pandemic and its effects still rage on today. It has fuelled in me an urgency to continue supporting vulnerable women whenever I can.

Over the last decade our funds have enabled hundreds of women in war-torn countries, mainly in Afghanistan, Iraq, Rwanda, Syria and Sudan, to participate in Women for Women International's year-long training programme, giving them the knowledge and skills to rebuild their shattered lives. Our expeditions have also raised valuable funds for charities supporting hundreds of women in the countries we have visited, notably Bhutan, Iran, Mongolia, Nepal and Cambodia. And I will be sharing more stories about our expeditions there in the subsequent chapters.

Since 2015, WOAM's big sister programme with Pertapis Centre for Women and Girls in Singapore has brought close to fifty big sisters as mentors for their little sisters at the shelter. Our big sisters aim to support the social workers in their mission with their young wards, by providing further guidance and encouragement. Via this grassroots programme, we hope to help our young mentees to regain confidence, hope and a purpose in life. Getting to know the social workers and little sisters from Pertapis home has given me a different perspective of life in Singapore, which can sometimes feel superficial and gilded, and I am grateful for this added layer of understanding of the complexity of society, and the awareness of who sometimes gets left behind.

WOAM's big sister programme also has an arts-therapy initiative, which works in parallel with our mentoring programme. Over the years, we have funded this programme in partnership with the Red Pencil Foundation, an organization that brings the power of creative-arts therapy to children and families who have been through traumatic life circumstances. Their Founder, Laurence Vandenborre, is an inspiring woman and friend, who after witnessing the distress of victims, both children and adults, of the 2004 tsunami that hit the Indian Ocean coastlines, set up the Red Pencil Foundation as her way of contributing.

As a result of all these efforts, WOAM has directly impacted the lives of hundreds of women and girls and indirectly impacted thousands more. What is wonderful for me to realize is that, because I took a chance and did something outside of my comfort zone through WOAM, it has enriched my existence in countless ways. Indeed, growth and success come by taking risks, versus avoiding them, by speaking out and by taking on difficult challenges. Transformation requires change, change is disruptive and inconvenient, often frightening—even for those who are not faint of heart.

Through these expeditions, my teammates and I have been blessed to experience countless incredibly touching moments with groups of women from around the world. Indeed, the opportunity to change lives is a privilege and taking this mission to heart has made me grow and has expanded my vision of the world in countless ways. By combining my passion for adventure, I found my purpose—helping others—and it has brought me a level of fulfilment and happiness that I didn't even know was possible.

Ultimately, WOAM's objective is to inspire women to want to leave their comfort zone, their families and homes for a certain period of time, while pushing their limits in an effort to rally support for a worthy cause. Our team seeks to travel, to explore the world, and as a result, make new discoveries and flourish as individuals; but most importantly, we want to give back to society.

Violence against women and girls continues to be an obstacle to achieving equality, development and peace as well as the fulfilment of universal human rights. All in all, the promise of the Sustainable Development Goals—to leave no one behind—cannot be fulfiled without putting an end to violence against women and girls. I am deeply committed to doing my part to stop this grave human injustice. Violence against women is simply unacceptable and has no place in our international society today.

This first expedition to Everest Base Camp, which was so transformative and formative for me, and triggered the founding of WOAM, as well as my advocacy journey for women, was just the beginning of many other life-changing adventures, which I will be sharing in the succeeding chapters. This first trek had sparked in me the desire for more growth, meaningful contribution and exploration. I felt reborn and ready for the exciting new journey ahead. We had set out to raise 100,000 dollars for women survivors of war, but succeeded in raising 150,000 dollars, with the expedition and two fundraising events. Our community was growing around us, women were contacting us to join our next expedition. Where should we go next? We started planning for the next adventure and chose a very different environment for our second WOAM challenge—the Jordanian Desert.

CHAPTER 4

Footprints on the Sands of Time, Wadi Rum, Jordan—2013

One of my favourite films of all time is the 1962 sweeping historical drama, *Lawrence of Arabia*, where the young British diplomat-adventurer T.E. Lawrence—played unforgettably by Peter O'Toole—leads a band of Bedouin warriors during World War II to mount a surprise attack on the Ottoman Empire, from whom they seek independence. As Lawrence leads the warriors across the desert in the blistering heat, braving swirling sandstorms, one of the Arab soldiers, Gasim, succumbs to fatigue and falls off his camel unnoticed during the night. When Lawrence discovers him missing, he instantly decides that he must turn around and retrieve the lost man. Sherif Ali, the chief Arab leader, played in the movie by the dashing Omar Sharif, objects. One of his aides tells Lawrence, 'Gasim's time has come. It is written.'

Lawrence snaps back, 'Nothing is written!' Then he turns around in the gale force winds of the sirocco to look for Gasim amid the sand dunes and eventually finds him, staggering about, barely alive. Lawrence brings him back to the camp to a hero's welcome. When Sherif Ali offers him water, Lawrence looks at him, and before quenching his thirst calmly repeats, 'Nothing is written.'

Part of my enduring fascination with Lawrence's tale, is the poignancy of his journey. A man trapped by divided loyalties, torn between serving the empire whose uniform he wears and being true and compassionate to those fighting and dying alongside him, who are facing staggering odds. Indeed, nothing is ever written. We can all shape our own future. The new and meaningful career path I was tracing for myself with WOAM was proof of this. And these thoughts weighed heavily on my mind as I made my way across the desert and mountains of Wadi Rum, retracing Lawrence's trail, with my all-female team in November 2013.

Across the Valley of the Moon

The first recorded successful ascent of the mountains of Wadi Rum was accomplished by women in November 1952. According to original documents from the times, two intrepid British female mountaineers summitted Jebel Rum and other peaks in the area, guided by Sheikh Hamdan Amad, as they journeyed across the region. These adventurers were Charmian Longstaff and her stepdaughter Sylvia Branford, on a quest to retrace part of the route taken by *Lawrence of Arabia*. Six decades later, during the exact same month, as if drawn by distant sisterly voices, our WOAM team of twelve determined women was making its way to this very site in Jordan, on a challenging mission once again, to raise awareness and funds for women survivors of war, via our charity partner, Women for Women International.

During this arduous and majestic journey, my teammates and I trekked in a maze of monumental moonscapes, which rose up from the desert floor to heights of 1,750 metres, creating a natural challenge for serious mountaineers and passionate rock climbers. We enjoyed the serenity of the boundless empty spaces and explored the canyons, rock arches and many other remarkable treasures this vast wasteland had to offer. All of us had been dreaming and training for this expedition for many months, while doing our utmost to be in the best physical and mental shape possible for this demanding voyage.

Shortly after arriving in the Hashemite Kingdom's capital, Amman, we entered its celebrated desert of Wadi Rum, the soul of Jordan, also known as the Valley of the Moon, a desert expanse of amber-coloured sands and high sandstone cliffs that is the traditional Bedouin homeland. Drinking in this vast, silent expanse of ancient riverbeds and sandy deserts, the spectacular landscape unfolding before our eyes held us captivated. With its spectacular rock formations known as jebels, Wadi Rum possesses one of the most stunning geographies on the planet. Split by networks of canyons, spanned by naturally formed rock bridges and watered by hidden springs, we knew this desert would offer a fantastic opportunity to rock climb, which we hungered for and wanted to incorporate as an added dimension to our expedition.

On the first day of our journey, our local guides—themselves Bedouins from the area—opened up their homes, shared their food and introduced us to their families. Their simplicity, boundless hospitality and generosity touched me profoundly. Hospitality matters because it feeds the most basic human need that we all have, to feel loved and accepted. It reminded me of the warmth and kindness in the Philippines. There is a measure of beauty in providing space for others to feel important, cared for and genuinely loved. Bedouins are considered the guardians of Arab virtues as well as the caretakers of the land's historic memory. For centuries, when the weather changed, or foraging became difficult, they simply moved with their herds to find new lands. However, various forces, from the evolution of international borders to the vagaries of the modern global economy, have started to alter this. I asked Abdulla, our guide, if he felt that the Bedouin's rural way of life was being threatened.

'To me, being a Bedouin isn't just about your herd or your tribe,' he replied. 'It's about freedom to choose how and where you want to live your life.' His words resonated with me completely. Indeed, what could be more important than the freedom to choose how and where you want to live your life? I took inspiration from his words as I contemplated the choices I had made thus far in my personal and professional life and how those decisions had shaped the path I was on.

Although both neighbouring Iraq and Saudi Arabia are oil-rich, Jordan's most valuable resource is its five million people, half of whom are under the age of 25. The archaeological records of the area date back millions of years, but the nation itself is young, only a little more than half a century old. Transjordan, as it used to be named, was part of British territory that was carved out of the former Ottoman Empire after World War I; it only won full independence from Britain in 1946. Thus, as we began our journey, and set a determined foot on the warm sands of the desert, it was impossible not to be keenly aware of the historic significance of this site, where so much of the politics of the Middle East had played out.

Abdulla shared his concerns with us about the future of Jordan. Despite being one of the United States' closest allies in this part of the world, the country could easily be swept up in events along its borders, such as the conflicts taking place in neighbouring Syria. Jordan is led by a royal family that traces its roots to the origins of Islam, and which has over the past half century, played a pivotal role in the struggle for power in the Middle East. I had read, with much interest, the story of King Hussein, who governed Jordan from 1952–99, and of his beautiful American wife, Queen Noor, who is the global president of my children's school in Singapore, the United World College of South East Asia. King Hussein, having survived dozens of assassination attempts and plots to overthrow him, was the region's longest-reigning leader and was succeeded, when he died in 1999, by his eldest son, Abdullah II, the current king.

Jordan was always of great significance to our campaign supporting women survivors of violence. Not only is it strategically located at the crossroads of what Christians, Jews and Muslims call the Holy Land, extending into the historic region of Palestine, but it has also played a strategic part in brokering peace between governments at war in this volatile powder keg of a region.

From the start of our journey, the excitement in the air was palpable, as we entered the Rakabat Canyon, which is in the south-eastern part of Wadi Rum Desert. Massive, wide open and without a soul in sight, I felt as if we were stepping back in time, in a place virtually untouched by humanity and its destructive powers.

I was quickly drawn into the desert's warm embrace. I could see how the weather and winds had carved out these towering rock formations, like skyscrapers around us—a rock climber's fantasy come true! As I evaluated the imposing silhouettes of the Jebels in the distance, I knew that each of my teammate's endurance, balance, skill and mental preparation, would inevitably be put to the test. Despite the countless hours of training we had put in on Southeast Asia's tallest, free-standing, synthetic, rock-climbing wall in Singapore, I instinctively felt that scaling natural rock façades, such as the ones standing magnificently before us, would surely be a very different challenge altogether.

Our desert expedition included an average of seven to eight hours of hard hiking per day, during which we carried heavy packs laden with supplies and precious water. We trekked under blistering heat and across a vast multitude of terrains, across an expanse of over 100 kilometres. The team scaled numerous vertiginous rockscapes and as we manoeuvred our way around difficult ascents and negotiated passages along exposed ledges, we bruised, scraped and cut our hands and knees on a daily basis. It was tiring work, but I was so proud of my team, everyone was in great spirits and doing well. I enjoyed the long days of climbing; it was deeply satisfying.

Our group tackled mainly grades three and four ascents, and on occasions some grade five climbs through the wide-open passages. Using the French rating system, which is slowly becoming the international standard in rock climbing, grades start at 1 to 2 (easy), 3 to 4 (hard), 5 to 6 (severe) and can go as high as 8 or 9 for elite climbers. Around Jebel Khash, to the far southern side of Wadi Rum, we managed to complete two first-time ascents—a grade four and a grade five—which, because they had never been climbed by anyone before, we were then privileged to christen: 'Women Rising' and 'Sisterhood'—such appropriate names for women on a mission!

As we scrambled upwards, we quickly learnt to determine what kind of rock to rely on. The traditional problem for climbers in Wadi Rum has been the quality of the rock, which is very porous and tends to crack at the least friction. Undoubtedly this can be tricky especially when you are using bolts or rope already in place. I soon realized that the darker the rock, the firmer it was, and that the lighter-coloured rocks were more likely to give us problems. Furthermore, I was so glad that our team had three fantastic rock-climbing guides with us, experts Dave and Rebecca, plus Abdulla our local guide. All three were highly experienced climbers, who put safety first at every step.

Finally, after a few days of training and familiarizing ourselves with the geography of the area, we set out to climb to the top of Jebel Burdah's famed Stone Bridge, a natural arch high up on the mountain, which took us several taxing hours to reach. After traversing various unprotected sections, my teammates and I finally hoisted ourselves on to the very top of its spectacular stone bridge, where we were able to take in the dazzling 360°-view of the Wadis below. Standing on the Stone Bridge and drinking in the magnificent view, I felt an incredible sense of freedom. The beauty of Nature has such a profound impact on our brains and our behaviour. While there, I could feel my anxiety and stress from the climb ebbing away, and a warm calmness enveloped me.

A couple of days later was when we tackled our most challenging ascent yet. In true WOAM fashion, we had set ourselves the task of scaling the dizzying heights of Jebel Khazali, the most dramatic, and serious—in terms of difficulty—of the Wadi Rum mountains. This full-day climb required us to depart from the camp at six in the morning, in total darkness, using our head torches, commencing our ascent in the filtering light of dawn, as the sun started to edge above the horizon, so that we could return before nightfall the same day. I was excited but had butterflies in my stomach. It was an ambitious challenge that would require us to work very closely together if we were to stay on schedule.

Thankfully, the team summitted Jebel Khazali after only four hours of fast-paced grade three, four and five scrambling. We were working like a well-oiled machine—the training had obviously paid off! Without stopping for lunch, after a short triumphant moment on the mountain peak, where we took in the stunning views of the valley below, we continued across the plateau to find our route back down.

My teammates and I could feel the intense mounting pressure to keep the pace. We absolutely had to complete the descent before nightfall, since we needed to see where to put our hands and feet on the uneven rockscapes. No daylight would mean a much more dangerous descent—we wanted to avoid this at all costs. Finally, eleven hours of scrambling and five challenging abseils later, shattered and exhausted, our team walked into camp just as daylight began to fade. My heart was full of pride. For months we had been visualizing this challenge, most of us had never rock climbed before and some of my teammates even had to overcome their paralysing fear of heights. But we had worked so well together, putting our trust and faith in each other. That night saw us celebrating by the light of our campfire, and as I stared up into the brilliant starlit night sky, I felt grateful to be a part of this extraordinary adventure.

Along the way, during the journey, I will never forget witnessing scenes of remarkable beauty: the crimson sunsets, as they cast their burning light on to the rocks at the end of each long day; the night-time sky, so dark and vast it was almost too easy to spot shooting stars—I caught several and made many wishes. At dinner time, our camp consisted of Bedouin mats and blankets, laid out on the ground, wedged up against the stone façades, while a large fire gave us light and warmth. I felt such a strong bond of friendship with my teammates. Exploring this beautiful part of the world together and tasting new flavours and experiencing a different sunset every night was simply magical.

Our guides would invite us to imbibe sage tea, while they prepared a simple yet delectable dinner, which consisted of tasty local fares. We discovered how unbelievably mouth-watering the cuisine of Jordan could be. We feasted on fresh-baked bread, cooked in a natural sand-oven under the campfire embers, barbecued fish from Aqaba's Red Sea, creamy hummus, multicoloured olives, roasted aubergines, baba ghanoush stew and tabbouleh. Finally, on one of the last nights, our guides slaughtered a young goat in the traditional Bedouin way, and then roasted it for us on the open fire. I don't think I ever tasted food as delicious in my life. Could it be that food tastes better when you are happy? Or more delicious because the journey had so much meaning? I'm sure it had something to do with the positive energy in our group.

When water was available, we were able to enjoy a glorious cold shower in the most beautiful outdoor stone bathroom you could ever imagine. Our guides would wedge a bag of water with cords, via grooves in the stonewalls, around the corner from our campsite, to allow us to quickly wash off the dust and fatigue of the day. We would go in pairs, so that one could stand guard while the other washed quickly. I had never done anything like this before, standing stark naked with a bit of shampoo in my hair, and looking at the miles of wide-open expanse of desert unfolding before me—it was glorious and surreal. And because we were fully exposed while showering, I am certain this outdoor contraption earned us the title of 'the-fastest-shower-ever-taken-by-twelve-women-in-a-row-anywhere-in-the-world!'

On occasion during the trip, we encountered scorpions and I came across a couple of snake tracks myself. We all slept in individual tents that we would assemble every night as soon as we got to camp, and disassemble at first light before we set off in the morning. Moreover, on certain evenings, some of us would brave the creepy crawlies, and simply opt to sleep under the brilliant, starry sky.

At the end of our journey, before flying home, we made our way north from Wadi Rum to the ancient city of Petra, for some rest and relaxation. I had heard about the magical quality of the city, but nothing prepared me for the euphoria that flooded my senses when I laid eyes on this red-rose-coloured city, carved out of pink sandstone rock. I learnt from our guide that the city had lain hidden for centuries until it was discovered by a Swiss explorer and, as one of the oldest cities in the world, today it is also a UNESCO World Heritage Site.

After Petra, we drove to Jordan's famed Dead Sea, which is actually not a sea at all, but a lake that's made up of about thirty-four per cent salt. It is bordered by Jordan to the east and Israel and the West Bank to the west. The lake's surface is 430.5 metres below sea level, making its shores the lowest land-based elevation on Earth. And because of its high salt concentration, which is much denser than the salt content in the human body, when I got in and immersed myself in its waters I discovered you can't submerge at all, you simply float! I enjoyed this relaxing break with my team, we chatted for hours about our journey in Wadi Rum and how much it meant to us that we were doing this for a good cause. We now looked forward to going home and reuniting with our families.

The Importance of Psychological Safety in Teams

One of the most valuable lessons from this experience for me was the importance of cultivating a shared purpose and building a safe atmosphere within the team. High-performing teams have this in common, the absolute conviction that you won't be punished or ridiculed if you make a mistake, require more help or encouragement in the face of a challenge. This allows teammates to take risks, speak their mind, be more creative and often results in breakthroughs and better solutions.

Months prior to my expeditions, I make sure that my teammates join numerous group activities, for those of them based in Singapore, and connect the whole team on various communication platforms such as WhatsApp or email. This allows us all to slowly get to know each other, build trust and openness. I set the tone from the start, keeping the exchanges light and friendly, but always with an eye on the greater mission. I want my teammates to feel they can ask me anything and at any time because, ultimately, feeling safe and free to be open and vulnerable in front of others is essential for teams to be at ease and comfortable together. It can't be rushed or forced but is necessary to build psychological safety within the team prior to our expedition. This close communication is particularly important when teams are coming together from different parts of the world, and in some cases meeting each other for the first time on DAY 1 of the expedition. As I discovered on this expedition and in future expeditions as well, creating an open and safe atmosphere within the team is one of the highest guarantees of success on any mission, especially in environments that are uncertain and unfamiliar. The opposite is also true. When a leader is provocative, or allows aggression and disrespect between teammates, this creates an atmosphere of threat and triggers fight-or-flight instincts and alarm bells that stop the brain from thinking clearly and constructively.

This is why a big priority for me is to ensure that my teammates feel safe in our group, so that everyone is relaxed and can be themselves. This sense of inclusion increases humour, creativity and allows for different ideas to flow more freely. Oxytocin levels in our brain rise and this overall feeling of well-being encourages risk and the courage to be vulnerable among peers. Ultimately, this ensures that everyone is in the best state of mind as we come together and set off on our adventure.

Rock Climbing and Trust

Words like 'belay' and 'bouldering' are examples of what you might learn when you begin rock climbing. Which handholds you prefer and how far you can reach are things you might discover on the wall. But technical lingo and physical strategies aren't all you learn. Rock climbing also, fundamentally, taught me about trust.

While we were training for this expedition on the rock-climbing wall, on many occasions one person would climb while the other would stand at the bottom, keeping the rope taut and using a system called a belay to keep the climber safe. The belay is designed so that if the climber falls, as long as the belayer is holding the rope correctly, they'll stay suspended rather than plummet to the ground.

Trusting others is difficult for many adults. So, the fact that when you rock climb, the rope you are attached to is literally tied to the waist of another person and that is the only thing keeping you from smashing into the mountain, or worse, freefalling fifty metres, is many people's worst nightmare. As we were rock climbing on the synthetic wall and later in the mountains of Wadi Rum, my team and I were literally putting our life in the hands of another person—the person holding on to our rope. Furthermore, part of becoming an approved belayer is demonstrating proficiency with a falling climber. What this means is that, as a climber, you're asked to fall unexpectedly so that the belayer can show you that they're able to operate the ropes in such a way that keeps you safe. And this is what happens, once you know your belayer has 'got you', as it did on many instances on the rock façades of the mountains, because we trusted each other, we took greater risks; we would dare to rest our foot on tiny rocks without worrying about our safety if we slipped, or grabbed for a handhold that looked out of reach. We knew our belayer would be there for us. We learnt that the more we tested the waters and learnt that we had a safety net, the more willing we were to dare greatly. I do believe this is human nature and it holds many parallels with life. The wonderful lesson that rock climbing imparted to me is that, ultimately, it's the person who can find that trust in their teammates, who ends up building their skill set, getting stronger, trying more difficult terrains, and as a result, ends up growing as a climber, and as a person.

The Gift of Wadi Rum

During our expedition to Jordan, there was much laughter, great camaraderie but also tears, both of triumph and frustration. But what we discovered at the end of it all was something far more rewarding. We came to know a people who cherished their liberties enough to want the country to stay out of conflicts and instead chart their own path. We witnessed the immeasurable beauty of the Valley of the Moon and the ephemeral nature of those moments suspended in time is something I want to hold on to for a lifetime.

Deep inside, I knew that what had driven us to push ourselves further every step of the way during this voyage had been the reason we had committed to this campaign in the first place. We had embarked on this journey to support women and return to them their right to live in peace; women who had lost everything to war and conflict, women who had been humiliated and robbed of their dignity, whose bodies had been violated, whose self-esteem and freedom had been taken from them.

Every cut, every bruise, every nauseating instance as we stared at the vertiginous drops below us, every gut-churning moment on the exposed mountain ledges, every cold-sweat and hair-raising situation, as we tilted backwards into the abyss before abseiling down, every time we pushed our limits—and for some of us—every time we conquered our paralysing fear of heights, the sum of these experiences made us feel more alive and resilient than ever before.

Our expedition was dedicated to these women: mothers, daughters, sisters who have lost so much to war and conflict; women who needed our help and encouragement, who craved our support and who we had to empower at all costs, so that they could climb out of their misery, lay down their shame and sorrow and, in the end, conquer their own personal summit.

Undoubtedly the desert of Jordan cast a spell on me. Its beauty is forever imprinted on my soul and as a result, I will always carry this fervent yearning to return. True to our WOAM mission, the creed that I want my team to uphold is simple: Follow your dreams. Live to the fullest. Push your limits. Always challenge yourself. Give back to those who need it most. Celebrate often. Stay humble. Be thankful, always. Travel whenever you can. Write your own rules because footprints on the sands of time are not made by sitting down.

CHAPTER 5

Retracing the Ancient Trade Route to Tibet— Tsum Valley, Nepal—2014

After our second WOAM expedition to the sweltering desert of Wadi Rum the following year, we chose to return to the cool mountain air of Nepal, but this time we picked a very different region . . .

I firmly believe that it's in having adventures and pushing ourselves to our limits that we learn where we truly belong and see with more clarity what we want to strive for in life. Journeys to unknown lands, especially when they are undertaken for a higher purpose, rather than simply for our own personal enjoyment, are a tremendous build of character and spirit. By challenging and immersing us in a whole different environment and rhythm and compelling us to look beyond our own petty needs and desires, these adventures as a team turn into voyages of self-discovery and make us see the world with fresh eyes.

In October 2014, for our third WOAM expedition, I took such a journey with eight courageous and passionate women. The objective of the expedition was, once again, to raise awareness and funds for women survivors of war, but our aim was also to discover an unknown and hidden part of Nepal called the Tsum Valley by retracing the ancient trade route to Tibet. This magical and untouched region of Nepal, one of the most secluded of Himalayan valleys, which only became accessible to tourists in 2008, had a profound influence on me and affected me in ways I took a while to fully comprehend.

Trekking Across Sacred Land

Tsum, also known as a *beyul* or sacred land was once a part of Tibet. The region looks completely different, in terms of the people and its culture, from the other parts of Nepal, and much less populated than the Annapurna and Everest regions that I had travelled to. The people of Tsum are Tibetan in origin with their own ancient dialect, art, culture and religion; and, to my surprise, I learnt that they still practise polyandry in some villages, marrying a girl to all the brothers in a family. Polyandry is believed to be more common in societies with scarce environmental resources. It is believed to limit human population growth and enhance a child's survival. Very few adventure travellers have made it to this mysterious valley, and we rarely came across other trekkers during our sojourn there.

In addition to the spiritual richness of this expedition, our itinerary was challenging and at times even a little perilous. It required us to push our physical and mental limits, conquering fears and dealing with extreme cold and exhaustion, while climbing to increasingly higher altitudes. We gained a total of 4,400 metres over a distance of 150 kilometres in less than seven days. Although shorter in terms of actual days than some of our other treks, this expedition was more intense and physically demanding because the distances and altitudes covered between days were far greater than on our Everest Base Camp trek; it forced us to push our limits a little further every day. I found this trek particularly difficult and exhausting, because food was scarce in this region and our options limited. After a few days on the trail, I found that I had lost my appetite and had to force myself to eat just to ensure I had enough fuel for the long and tiring days of hiking.

We started in Soti Khola, in the lowlands at only 730 metres of altitude, visiting sacred caves, coming across walls of hand-carved Buddhist prayer stones and secluded villages. As we continued to climb higher, we saw the vegetation and landscape change before our eyes, from thick tropical foliage to lush pine trees and autumnal forests. We continued our journey on steep mountainous trails, passing brightly coloured prayer wheels inscribed with mantras and numerous stupas, little Buddhist shrines, which I found enchanting. I would make a wish for each of my children every time I came across one, turning the prayer wheels clockwise, as you are meant to do. The people of Tsum believe that spinning such a wheel is equivalent to reciting scriptures, and it's the best way to repent for one's past transgressions, purify negativities (or bad karma) and accumulate merit (or good karma). The merit of turning the prayer wheel increases with the number of rotations. As I ascended to higher altitudes in the journey, turning the wheels as I went, it became a spiritually uplifting experience. I felt I was increasing my good karma, getting a special blessing from the Tsum gods and sending my children loving thoughts and good wishes.

As we gained altitude, the temperatures plummeted, and as I looked around me, the landscaped turned moon-like, with a thick blanket of powdery snow covering the peaks surrounding us. Every day, on our journey upwards, we came across caravans of mules and yaks laden with supplies on their way to and from Tibet. And on the narrow trails, which often had steep drops, we quickly learnt to give way to them, lest we wanted to risk getting trampled, stepped on or, even worse, pushed off!

From the locals we met along the way, we learnt that the people in this region of Nepal have been trading with their Tibetan neighbours for centuries and continue to do so despite the political vagaries affecting Tibet's status as a nation in relation to the People's Republic of China. To them politics don't matter; they simply want to continue trading peacefully as they have done for so long.

Furthermore, since this part of Nepal had not yet been developed enough to cater to trekkers, our accommodations were quite rudimentary. We were able to take a few cold showers early on during the trek, while still at lower altitudes, but past 3,000 metres, that was no longer a healthy option. I will, however, never forget the unique experience of trying to wash myself using a small basin of water inside one of the tiny outdoor squatting toilet sheds.

Since there was no 'shower room' in that particular lodge, the only place available for such private ablutions was the latrine, and so I literally bathed hunched over a squalid, hole-in-the-ground-type toilet. This certainly made me appreciate the basic comforts which I often take for granted back home, but also made me realize how wonderfully practical we can all become, when we have no choice. Indeed, for me, authentic experiences trump opulence and comfort any day—as I like to say, adventure is the new luxury!

After an intense week of trekking made even more difficult and exhausting because our trail followed the path of a meandering river which meant that to get to the next village on this route, we often had to descend rapidly by hundreds of metres at a time to cross the river on a bridge situated at a lower altitude, just to ascend again by the same distance or even more to continue on our itinerary. There were days when I was so dog-tired and drained from the long days of hiking on this sinuous trail that, upon reaching our shelter for the night, I didn't even have the strength to unzip my bags to put on a dry shirt; and one day, tears just rolled down my cheeks from sheer exhaustion.

Finally, on the seventh day, we reached Mu Gompa (3,700 metres), where we began a three-day retreat in a century-old monastery. Despite our efforts to be discreet, the arrival of our boisterous trekking team in matching, bright-red, fleece jackets caused quite a stir within the monastery. This was the first time the monks had come across such an eclectic group of female mountaineers, with team members from all four corners of the globe. We did our best to respect the monks' rituals and need for silence, while we enjoyed their chanting against the stunning backdrop of the Ganesh Himal mountain range looming over us in the north.

As soon as we settled down, we set aside quiet moments in our day for meditation and reflection as we rested and prepared for our challenging day climb to the Ngula Dhojhyang Pass perched on the Nepalese-Tibetan border at an altitude 5,093 metres. I was happy to recuperate for a couple of days, while I made plans for the journey ahead.

Finally, the time came for us to scale the famed Ngula Dhojhyang Pass. However, because Mu Gompa Monastery is the last available pit stop for trekkers on this route, if we intended to return before dusk, we would have to set out no later than 4 a.m. An intense thirteen to fourteen-hour trek lay ahead of us.

Luckily the weather had been glorious over the past few days. I was conscious that just a few weeks ago, not far from this region, in the Annapurna mountain range, a freak blizzard had hit. This unseasonal storm, arriving in late October, at the peak of the trekking season, had caused the deadliest mountaineering disaster in Nepal's history. At least forty-three people were killed when the blizzard caught them off guard on the trails, while many hikers got buried or trapped by avalanches, suffering from frostbite and other injuries. Of those, twenty-one were foreign nationals, while twenty-two were Nepalese guides, porters and villagers. It was sobering news to hear just before the last leg of our climb.

A few other obstacles lay ahead of us on this attempt to traverse the high pass. For the team to reach that section of the Tibetan border, we had to cross six landslide areas in complete darkness and once again, on our way back, carry out this feat, ideally while there was still some daylight left. Time was certainly of the essence on this next adventure but, after a reconnaissance trip the day before and an intense discussion about the calculated risks of crossing such an exposed and slippery façade, most of us felt confident that we would get across safely. I soon realized that, when walking across the side of a 45° mountain ridge, especially one that is quite slippery, the natural instinct is to lean into the mountain, which actually causes the climber to have less stability, and increases one's chances of slipping down the mountain. I understood that the key to crossing these steep gradients safely was to maintain a low centre of gravity, by remaining as upright as possible and actually leaning away from the mountainside instead of in. The team and I, therefore, practised this a few times in daylight knowing it would be much harder in darkness the next day. After a few dry runs, we all felt fairly comfortable and confident that we could go ahead in the morning.

Our determined team, armed with head torches, left Mu Gompa Monastery at 4 a.m., in below freezing temperatures. I said a silent prayer in my head that we would all get to the pass and back safely. That morning, the cold was so intense that the water in my Camelbak—water pouch—remained frozen until 9 a.m. After crossing the steep gradients without any incidents, despite the added hurdle of suddenly discovering icy patches in precarious places during the crossing, we carried on at a fast pace, only stopping occasionally to catch our breath.

We continued climbing, crossing vast windy plains, traversing numerous icy rivers, scrambling over slippery rocks and small glaciers, and scaling a total of 1,400 metres in one go. The last few 150 metres were the most difficult. I found myself stopping to catch my breath after ever fifty steps or so as we neared the summit ridge. This was a massive altitude gain for any mountaineer to undertake on a single day's climb. Finally, at noon, exhausted and cold, but euphoric beyond words, we all made it to the Nepalese-Tibetan border at the highest pass on the ancient trade route of Tsum, the most secluded of Himalayan valleys.

At the top we unfurled a banner reaffirming our commitment to empower women around the world. We stayed for about twenty minutes on the windy summit, drinking in the stunning views on both sides, from a distance we could see Chinese soldiers patrolling below, guarding the border, and we were careful not to wave at them. We ate some of the provisions we had brought with us, a few boiled eggs and a piece of cheese, and then headed straight back down to Mu Gompa, racing to return before dark.

Thirteen hours later, just as daylight began to fade, we walked into the monastery's dining hall completely shattered and drained, but standing tall despite the overwhelming fatigue, with a deep sense of achievement and pride in our hearts.

Taking Calculated Risks Takes Courage

As I look back and think about the learnings from this beautiful experience, I am reminded of the hesitation some of the teammates felt when faced with the crossing of these steep gradients on the way to the pass. Ultimately, some decided to stay behind at the monastery that day and go on a separate hike, while others decided to go ahead with me. It was a very personal decision, which depended on how each person assessed the risk involved. I didn't want to force anyone to do something they were not comfortable doing and so another option was provided. However, I knew that for me it was important to reach the pass and I had evaluated the risk along with some of the other teammates and my co-founder Valerie, and we had decided it was a risk we felt comfortable taking.

What I realized at that moment was how vital it was to trust my gut instincts and to have the courage of my convictions. When leaders take a decision, they need to stick to it, not in an immovable way, but with faith that the judgement is sound. Indecisiveness in the planning of the itinerary and fluctuations in the day's agendas can undermine the motivation of the team as a whole and result in inertia. So, what I learnt was that it's good to pick a plan and run with it.

Indeed, one of the most valuable lessons from this expedition was the importance of trusting my gut when taking calculated risks. It made me realize that too many people confuse fear with gut instinct and assume their discomfort means they should not proceed; so, rather than stepping outside of their comfort zone, they avoid risk at all costs and miss out on opportunities to go forward.

Fear causes us to overestimate risk. Our level of fear usually has nothing to do with the actual level of risk we face. The key is to balance emotion with logic because taking the right calculated risks in life could be the difference between living an ordinary life and living an extraordinary life. Over time, I've come to understand that it is good to take calculated risks from time to time, based not on the level of fear but rather on facts, weighing the potential risks versus benefits, looking objectively at the obstacle and planning accordingly to increase the chances of success.

Aristotle said, 'Courage is the first of human qualities because it's the quality which guarantees the others.' In other words, any remarkable trait or skill of a person will always remain in the shadows unless they have the courage to use it. You can't be honest if you don't have the courage to tell the truth. You can't be innovative if you don't have the courage to try something new. Confidence, decisiveness, growth and trust are just a few of the traits that suffer in the absence of courage. I've come to realize that a lot of people believe courage is something you're born with. And while it's true that some people are born braver than others, the majority of us have to learn to become more courageous by pushing ourselves.

Courage shows up for all of us in a number of ways. It takes courage to take initiative and taking initiative involves risks— embarking on a new adventure; trekking in unknown, faraway lands. Speaking up or even taking initiative at work means exposing one's self to risk and potential failure. But taking a risk is essential to creating change and growth. I've seen this time and time again in my life. Courage also means letting go of the need to control outcomes. This is a tough one for me as it is for many people. In leadership, letting go and taking risks means trusting your team or the people around you. In many ways, the Tsum Valley trek taught me that courage is a bit like a muscle, the more you use it and test it, the stronger it gets.

The Gift of Gratitude

Another beautiful gift that resulted from this trek to the Tsum Valley of Nepal was the feeling of overwhelming gratitude that I experienced. There were numerous occasions along the trail when the local people welcomed us, perfect strangers, into their homes. Their hospitality, kindness and generosity touched me deeply. Their simple way of life, the few material possessions they owned, the little food they had, they shared it all with us gladly. It made me all the more grateful for the life I had back home. Indeed, travel teaches us so many things: acceptance, flexibility, awareness, curiosity, a growth mindset. And, if we allow it, gratitude. Gratitude for one another, gratitude for what we have, gratitude for what we don't need, gratitude for new experiences, gratitude for life.

In these remote places, the concerns of the 'real world' fade away as life is enriched with experiences, not possessions. And, without a doubt, it has taught me to be more grateful for what I have in life. I have a roof over my head, a warm place to sleep and plenty to eat. It's the little things in life that should be appreciated. A life of travel has made me realize what truly matters the most to me—my family's health and happiness. Indeed, one of my favourite mottos is a quote by Buddha, 'expect nothing, appreciate everything'—certainly wise words to live by.

Overall, the Tsum Valley trek was a truly unforgettable journey in the land of the clouds. Pushing our limits in this magical and remote land to raise funds for some of the most marginalized women in the world made the journey so much more poignant and meaningful. We knew there was much more work to be done, and another WOAM adventure to plan for the following year. But for now, it was time to say goodbye and come home. From the many multicoloured prayer flags fluttering in the wind high above our paths, to the beautiful *khata*—silk scarves—we received as parting gifts, undoubtedly, the beauty of the Tsum Valley will remain alive, etched in our memories forever.

CHAPTER 6

36°C Below Zero with the Nenets Reindeer Herders of Siberia, Russia—2015

If the Tsum Valley was a place that stirred notions of mysticism, magic and the power of taking risks, then my adventure to Siberia was one of community coming together for survival in the face of extreme weather conditions. This next expedition, while still in support of women survivors of war, opened my eyes to the effects of climate change on indigenous peoples. Because of their deep connection to the land, the increased negative effects of climate change on their lives can be widespread and immediate.

So how did I find myself here in the first place? Our team of women from Singapore, Dubai, London and Kuala Lumpur embarked on this incredible adventure in December 2015 in search of a pioneering challenge. By trekking in such harsh conditions, we hoped to inspire women to push their limits in an effort to rally support for a worthy cause. Even if we could never claim to truly understand the suffering experienced by the survivors of war, by doing something challenging, so alien to our own way of life, and dedicating it to these brave women, we believed we were standing in solidarity with them, and it gave us strength as we faced the howling Arctic winds and debilitating temperatures of Siberia.

The Nenets and their Reindeer

Its head facing east, the animal's eyes bulged out and its tongue hung limply to one side as the rope around its neck, pulled taut by three, broad-shouldered herders squeezed the remaining life out of it. Slowly its resistance weakened, its eyes glazed over and fixed on a point in the Arctic sky above, then suddenly, complete stillness.

For centuries, the Nenets of Siberia have been living off reindeer meat and blood, utilizing every inch of the animal, from hide to heart, to bone and antlers even—nothing is ever wasted. As soon as the animal is dead, the hide is meticulously removed and kept in one piece to be used for clothing. Then the feasting begins, and everyone starts to tear out pieces of kidney, liver, heart, or whatever parts they most enjoy, occasionally dipping and swirling the bits in the open carcass, which still holds the reindeer's warm blood. Usually, a small saucepan containing blood is passed around and each one takes a turn to have a drink. When it was my turn to take a sip, I hesitated for just a moment. I grabbed the dripping saucepan, took a couple of small gulps and swirled the warm blood around my mouth to show that I appreciated the full flavour. It tasted salty and not at all unpleasant. I'm certain my eagerness to try these new-found treats was fuelled by the fact that my WOAM teammates and I felt extremely privileged to accompany these exceptional people during a portion of their epic, yearly, winter migration across the frozen gulf of Ob, in northern Russia.

Danger Sharpens the Senses

It actually took us two days from Moscow to reach the Nenets tribe, flying north to the Siberian town of Salekhard and driving eight hours over the frozen Ob river in an old, Russian, six-wheeled truck—well, not quite frozen enough as it turned out, because three hours into the drive, the ice cracked under the weight of our vehicle and we plunged head first into the dark and icy waters of the river.

In that instant, my heart froze in horror and a paralysing fear invaded my veins. I didn't make a sound, my breath caught in my throat, and I just sat there petrified, in complete shock. The sense of panic that washed over our group was like nothing I had ever experienced before, as if death had arrived at the door, suddenly and without warning. Luggage and backpacks flew into the air inside the vehicle and bodies were hurled forward. The screams of my teammates shook me to the very core.

'Get out!' one person howled in a voice thick with fear, as some women reached for the door handles, elbowing others out of the way. Surprisingly, I stayed very calm and quiet, almost as if I was having an out-of-body experience, watching myself as if in a movie.

And I remember thinking to myself, contemplating this situation, almost puzzled, 'Is this how it all ends? Thousands of miles away from my family, at the bottom of an icy river? This was not part of my life plan!'

Then, just as some were trying to get out of the vehicle through the side doors, above the panicked screams, the voice of the Russian driver, Dimitri, boomed, '*Amfibiya! Amfibiya! Ne prygay!*' He could not speak English, but luckily for us one of our teammates, who was part Russian, understood him perfectly and said, 'I think he means it's amphibious, it can float! Don't jump!'

Indeed, the six wheels of the truck were so huge that they made the vehicle float; so, instead of sinking to the bottom of the Ob river, it tilted at a precarious angle as water started to seep in. Pure relief washed over me . . . The tension in the vehicle diffused in an instant and I heard some of my teammates laugh nervously. I regained control of my movements and stood up on wobbly legs to lean forward and peer out the window. I could see the cracked ice around our tires. I wanted to assess the situation. How bad was it? Were we out of immediate danger? My brain was still in a fog, trying to process what had just happened. I checked in with my teammates to ask if anyone was hurt; thankfully everyone was okay.

I sat down again and reflected on the fact that we were lucky to be alive. What a revelation it had been to witness how a team reacts in the face of imminent danger! And how quickly the fight-or-flight response had kicked in for some. I also realized that my hands were cold and clammy, my neck was icy cold with sweat, and my heart was still racing. I suddenly thought about the water seeping in and decided to reach into my backpack that was lodged between my legs, pulled out my passport and slipped it into my pocket. I thought, 'If I get out of here alive, I will at least have my passport!' Despite the panic, I was relieved to discover that I was always the planner, no matter what. That gave me a bit of comfort and a small sense of control.

The Moldavians

With some difficulty, my teammates and I managed to scramble out through the back door of the truck and stood on the ice as the last few hours of daylight started to fade. Temperatures in winter in Siberia can easily dip to −45 or −50° Celsius, so we knew we were not out of the woods yet. We had narrowly escaped drowning in the Ob river, but the situation was still precarious. Here we were, ten women and one rattled Russian driver who spoke no English, stranded in the middle of nowhere, in plummeting Arctic temperatures, with just a few snack bars in our pockets.

A few hours later, as we were desperately trying to keep our spirits up and staying warm by dancing and huddling together on the ice, we spotted the lights of another truck in the distance, coming towards us. We screamed and hollered with relief, waving out to them. We were going to be rescued! It was about time; our extremities were starting to go numb. As the vehicle approached, and finally came to a halt in front of us, I could see two burly men in the front seats of the truck, staring in disbelief at the strange scene before them.

I thought to myself, 'I hope they're friendly . . . '

The door of the vehicle swung open and out jumped, one, two, three, no ten large men. We stared at them in silence, not sure what to think. Were these our heroes or would they turn out to be trouble? After a few seconds one of them broke into a toothy grin and said, 'Hello ladies, do you need help?' in perfect English. We burst out laughing. Oh, I was so relieved . . . our rescuers had arrived!

It turned out, that they were a group of Moldavian oil and gas men on their way back to Salekhard after a long, hard day's work. They were absolutely delighted to find ten women stranded in the middle of nowhere. They greeted us warmly, smelling of strong vodka and sweat. They were dressed in jeans and leather jackets, barely seeming to feel the cold, with bright red noses and bushy beards—such a contrast to the way we were dressed in all layers of clothing, multicoloured expedition jackets and trousers, which we had dutifully pulled out of our luggage to wear as added protection from the cold. It was quite a comical scene actually and I thought to myself, this is a story I must tell my grandchildren one day.

Thankfully, our jolly Moldavians wasted no time in producing sturdy ropes from their truck and attached our vehicle to theirs to hoist it out of the icy waters. This was followed by a series of obligatory, celebratory vodka shots, a few Moldavian songs of course, and finally, after big bear hugs, we were on our way again, to the town of Yar-Sale, where we were scheduled to rendezvous with our Nenets hosts and join their epic, yearly migration south.

The Migration

We arrived in Yar-Sale in the dead of night, almost five hours after our accident, and were joined by our local guide, Edward, who was British and spoke Russian fluently. Exhausted and sleepy, we couldn't see much of the town, which was poorly lit, except for a few houses covered in snow. Yar-Sale is the capital of the Yamal Peninsula of Siberia or Nenets territory. It counts a few thousand people, mostly Nenets or Russian, or a blend of both as many intermarry. We went straight to sleep in a local inn that night. The next day our Nenets tribe would be picking us up. We had much to look forward to. Despite the fatigue, I was excited. I had read and researched the Nenets extensively and knew that they were among the world's oldest surviving true nomads, guardians of a style of reindeer herding that is the very last of its kind. In their language, *Yamal* means 'the end of the world' and indeed, as I prepared to journey with them in this vast Arctic desert, along with their gigantic reindeer herds, I felt as if my teammates and I were pioneers, standing at the very edge of humanity's first settlement. What were we going to find living and migrating with them? Surely it was going to be an epic adventure.

The next morning, four Nenets men arrived in full regalia on their snowmobiles with wooden box-freight sleds attached to them. This was to serve as transport for us to their camp, which was set up about twenty kilometres away. The Nenets were wearing their traditional coats made of reindeer skins, the fur being closest to the skin on the inside and the leather on the outside. Their coats had an integrated hood and gloves that looked similar to a poncho with no zips or buttons. They also wore hip-high, reindeer-skin boots and apparently, Edward shared, this is the warmest and safest thing you can wear in these Arctic conditions. The Nenets men were friendly but not overly talkative and spoke to our guide in Russian, who then translated for us. We were instructed to climb into the box-freight sleds in groups of twos or threes and hang on tight. We had been given the traditional Nenets outfits by Edward that morning, so the thick and bulky, reindeer coats and boots served as padding in these rudimentary transport vehicles. I felt like a Teletubby as we hoisted our luggage and stuffed ourselves into the sleds. Laughing and chatting, my teammates and I were full of eager anticipation as we tried to get comfortable, sitting on our bags which served as seats. I just couldn't believe we were about to start our journey and meet the rest of the tribe. This was a moment I had been trying to imagine for months now and I was a little nervous too—would they be welcoming? I would soon find out.

After the bumpiest and coldest ride of my life, we finally arrived at the Nenets camp where we were greeted by the rest of the tribe, who seemed as curious to meet us as we were to meet them. I was in awe at how pretty and charming the camp was, surrounded by miles and miles of snow and mused at what a contrast it was to our life in equatorial Singapore. The tribe consisted of about forty-five Nenets, twenty herding Laika dogs and seven chums, or traditional

conical tents made of reindeer hide. I found the rosy-cheeked Nenets
children irresistibly cute, in their little traditional coats; they seemed
happy to have visitors. Nenets are a Samoyedic ethnic group native
to northern arctic Russia and look almost Eurasian, some of them
blue-eyed or green-eyed. They are tall with fair skin but have distinct
Asian features, and I found them very beautiful.

Soon after we arrived and exchanged greetings, the team split up
in groups of threes and twos again, and we were each assigned to live
with a Nenets family in their chum. The whole tribe had been waiting
for us to begin their migration south. We were told that we would be
packing up the camp the next morning and starting the journey along
with the 10,000 reindeer which were grazing not far from the camp.
The migration was beginning, and I pinched myself in disbelief. This
was really happening.

Indeed, the next morning at 4 a.m., and every two or three
days after that, we were up early, helping the women dismantle
camp and load our belongings on the sleighs, while the men went
off to lasso the specially trained transport reindeer from the main
herd. These reindeer are domesticated and fairly friendly, since they
have been reared and hand-fed by the tribe since they were babies.
The males can grow to a height of 135 centimetres, from hooves
to shoulders and around 1.8 to 2.1 metres long with a weight of
up to 240 kilograms. Females are typically 25 per cent smaller. The
reindeer are usually grey white with brown and are covered in fur
from their nose to the bottom of their hooves. The furry hooves
may look funny, but this gives them a good grip when walking on
frozen ground, ice, mud and snow and especially when pulling a
heavy load. As soon as the reindeer were harnessed to each of the
sleighs, the tribe was ready to go. We perched on the sleighs and
began the 20 to 25-kilometre journey to the next encampment,
forming a 2-kilometre-long convoy snaking its way across the
frozen landscape. Some of the younger Nenets men would then
use their snowmobiles and the dogs, to move the reindeer herd and
guide them south along our route.

During these travel days, no one ate or drank, at least until the new camp was set up. It was often dark and overcast, and so dreadfully cold. When the wind picked up and the blizzard set the snow swirling around us, the temperatures would plummet to −30 or −40° Celsius. As we travelled, I sat in silence on my sleigh next to one of the Nenets men, with whom I could only communicate using gestures and reflected on this unique life experience. As of today, just a handful of people had ever experienced travelling in this way with Nenets. We were in fact the largest group they had ever hosted and certainly the first all-female team to journey with them during a migration. The privilege was enormous and I felt grateful to witness this ancient migratory tradition.

As we journeyed with the tribe in the dead of the Siberian winter, I was appreciative of the reindeer fur coats and thigh-high boots Edward had sourced for us. However, in these extreme conditions, despite the many layers I wore, my extremities still felt dangerously numb. The biggest risk, as we spent close to ten hours without shelter on migration days out in the cold, was frostbite and hypothermia. I was well aware that if our body's core temperature dropped by just one or two degrees, hypothermia could set in. Hypothermia was a medical emergency, which happens when the body loses heat faster than it can produce heat to counterbalance the cooling. As the body's temperature drops, the heart, brain and internal organs cannot function, and so the body begins to shut down. Thus, I kept a watchful eye on my teammates, throughout the travel days, for any early warning signs.

Nenets Leadership

When the Nenets found a suitable place to set up camp, usually by a large plateau where the herd could easily be rounded up, Yuri, the chief, would stick his *khorei* (herding stick) into the ground at the place where he wanted the centre of his chum to be. Everyone would then start unloading the sleighs, unharnessing reindeer and setting up their chums, with Yuri's chum always on the far right as viewed from behind and the entrances of all chums facing the same way.

I had been assigned to Yuri's chum, which he shared with his wife, Elena, their children, his parents and nine dogs. Thus, I got a chance to know and observe him quite a bit. Despite the fact he wasn't overly friendly or warm with us, he was always courteous and protective. Luckily, I had one of my half-Russian teammates in my chum, Maysoune, whose mother is from St Petersburg and father, from the Emirates. She served as our interpreter throughout the journey and this is how I came to learn more about why Yuri had been selected as the chief.

Elena explained to us that in a Nenets tribe, the leader is often the most-skilled reindeer herder. The one most capable of ensuring the tribe is fed. 'This leader is a selfless person, who is responsible for the protection and survival of the tribe and serves not just as a role model for others but as a caretaker for the tribe,' she shared. I realized that in some ways the Nenets chief is a type of servant leader, who puts the needs of the tribe and the community above his own. Watching Yuri in action, leading and caring for his tribe crystallized for me that tribal leadership is not simply an act or a series of acts; or directing a process; or playing a role. Tribal leadership is the embodiment of a culture, of traditions, of learnt patterns of thought and behaviours, values and beliefs. It convinced me that culture and stewardship are the foundation of tribal leadership. These essential ingredients shape the purpose, process and ultimately result in the kind of leadership we could all emulate in our communities, especially in times of crises.

One evening in the chum, after a few vodka shots, Yuri opened up and shared with us his concerns about the dramatic changes he was seeing taking place on the Nenets territory, including thawing permafrost which was affecting the reindeer migration.

'With the ice melting earlier in the spring and not freezing until much later in the autumn, we are being forced to change centuries-old migration patterns as the reindeer find it difficult to walk over a snowless tundra. Sadly, the rising temperatures also affect the tundra's vegetation, the only source of food for our reindeer,' he said. Indeed, the next day, Edward confirmed that in November 2013, 61,000 reindeer starved to death in the Yamal Peninsula. It marked the largest 'mortality episode' of reindeer ever recorded in the region. Earlier, in November 2006, 20,000 reindeer had succumbed to the famine. The immediate cause, according to the team of researchers, was an unusual ice barrier that smothered the reindeer pastures. Reindeer can stamp through ice about three-quarters of an inch thick, using their hooves to access the nutritious lichen and plants below. But, in early November 2006 and 2013, the ice was a lot deeper—several inches thick—too tough even for the reindeer's sharp hoofs. The animals died of starvation.

The Laws of the Tribe

The more time I spent with the Nenets, the more I learnt about their values and the traditions they upheld. I found it fascinating to hear about how they viewed the role of women in their society. Some days, when she was not working, over warm tea and a feast of frozen fish and bread in the chum, Elena would take the time to explain, 'In Nenets culture, women not only have mystical powers, we also have many rules and laws to follow. Anything to do with the "birth-giving" area of a woman's body can be harmful and is considered somewhat of a taboo; because of this, we are not allowed to step over men or any of their tools. If a woman comes across one of the men's lassos or tools on the ground, while walking through the camp, she has to walk around it—and never across it—lest she triggers incredibly bad luck for the whole tribe.'

Additionally, we were told women are not allowed to cross or put their hands through the 'invisible line', which goes from the centre of each chum all the way to the back of the tent and extends another 100 metres outside. Toileting activities for women have to be very carefully conducted, out of sight of any of the men, which in itself is a real challenge given the fact that the Nenets men are in constant motion, doing chores related to the herding, and coming in and out of the camp from any side and at any time. Furthermore, the landscape around the camp is for the most part usually completely flat, thus trips to the 'toilet' can turn into real treks of 200 to 300 metres or more, sometimes in knee-deep snow. During our stay, despite carefully planning our toileting expeditions with great precision and strategy, I discovered, to my horror, that the reindeer craved the salt in our urine! Thus, the animals constantly shadowed us like ninjas and pounced on us when we were at our most vulnerable, trousers down, clinging without much success to the very last shreds of our dignity.

Other camp activities included chopping wood, in order to keep the stoves in the chums burning and drawing water through a manmade hole and hauling it back to camp on a sleigh. The work was constant and yet when I looked up on occasion and took in the magnificent scenery around us, I was reminded of the extraordinary journey we were experiencing and drinking in this otherworldly landscape, which kept me quite literally, spellbound.

Living with the Nenets was a truly unprecedented honour. I enjoyed and soaked up every minute. As the days went by, I learnt to appreciate the tranquillity of the boundless empty spaces, while the deafening silence of the frozen tundra kept me suspended in time. The dramatic sunrises and sunsets were unforgettable; even if I often confused the two, given the days were so short.

Despite the harshness of the environment, I felt we adapted surprisingly well to our new way of life, but it was also because the Nenets were so hospitable, treating us like their daughters, making sure we were warm and always well fed. One day, Elena saw that I was about to step out of the chum to go herding with the men, who had made an exception by inviting our team to see how they moved 10,000 reindeer across the tundra. I couldn't find my balaclava, which is an essential item to avoid frostbite when riding on the snowmobiles to reach the herd. Before I ran out, she quickly pulled off her own embroidered scarf and tied it tightly across my face to make sure the skin was protected, whispering words of motherly concern in the Nenets language.

Community and Survival

The Nenets' way of life and how it contrasted with our own comfortable, materialistic lives, could not have been more extreme. Despite the fact that their world now incorporates some modern items such as phones, generators and snowmobiles, it remains untainted by the drudgery, the hustle and bustle of modern-day society and, in many ways, far richer and more meaningful than ours. By sharing the simplicity of their existence, the Nenets reminded me of the importance of community and family for survival. I felt this very strongly when I was living in Yuri's chum with his family, in the way they cared and looked after me with kindness and attention. As human beings, we all need a sense of belonging, and that sense of belonging is what connects us to the many relationships we develop during our lifetime. Community is where we find solace and security in difficult times. Most people in today's world rely on a community for practical purposes. The necessities of life rarely come from one's own hands, but rather from a complicated 'web of mutuality' as Martin Luther King, Jr. once phrased it. And, while most people need to be part of a community for life's essentials, most of us want to be part of a community simply because there is something indescribably reassuring and comforting about belonging to a group of people who share something more substantial than geographical location . . . a common purpose, mission and priorities. Something that, when shared, makes individuals seem less lonely and vulnerable. A community is a safe place that allows us to find peace and some order in the fragmented and chaotic world we live in.

However, quite sadly, as I learnt from Yuri, despite building strong communities, the Nenets' way of life is being threatened by climate change. Melting permafrost has not only affected the reindeer migration and food supply but has also caused some of the tundra's freshwater lakes to drain, leading to a decline in the Nenets' supply of fish. For the Nenets, their lands and reindeer herds remain vitally important to their collective identity and survival. They slaughter reindeer and drink their blood to stay alive in the Arctic tundra. They need unobstructed access to their pastures and an environment untouched by industrial waste. The Nenets have lived on and stewarded the tundra's fragile ecology for hundreds of years and they have succeeded in doing so because they are a close-knit community that looks after each other at every step. Needless to say, this unforgettable and rich, cultural experience, migrating with the reindeer herders of Siberia, is another reminder that it is vitally important that we do more collectively to preserve and protect the simplicity and peace of the Nenets' precious traditions and way of life. Indeed, as humans we have a moral obligation to be more nurturing and protective of nature and our environment, to promote the sustainable development of our planet for future generations.

CHAPTER 7

The Cycle of Life, Biking for a Cause in Cambodia—2016

If Siberia was a lesson on the importance of community for survival in the face of adversity, then my next adventure to Cambodia, opened my eyes to the fact that education can change the course of a life for the better by being part of the solution to tackle human trafficking. Thus, in line with WOAM's objective of championing the cause of underprivileged and abused women and girls, I wanted to shine a light on the tireless work of Sala Baï, a hotel and restaurant school that was launched in 2002 by the French NGO, Agir pour le Cambodge, to fight poverty and human trafficking in Cambodia through social and professional training of young underprivileged Cambodians. And so, in March 2016, I took a team of fourteen women to Siem Reap, Cambodia, to see what we could do to help.

About a Girl

The young woman sat at the edge of the wooden porch of her house in Mechrey, a floating village in the northern reaches of the Tonle Sap, west of Siem Reap. She stared dreamily at the riverbank, gently paddling her feet in the murky waters below. This was the house of her parents, the house in which she, Ratha, was born. Her father had been a fisherman for as long as she could remember, and her mother,

despite her poor health, tended the house and took care of Ratha and
her six younger siblings.

Ratha felt happy to be home for a few days to see her family and
had that warm fuzzy feeling inside her. Soon she would head back
to work at the luxurious and glitzy five-star hotel in central Siem
Reap, wearing her elegant, silk uniform and welcoming international
guests from all over the world. As she thought about her life and how
lucky she was, a smile lit up her face. 'I'll never forget the day father
agreed to let me go to study at Sala Baï . . . Mama was so sad to see
me go, but both she and Papa knew in their hearts that it was a once
in a lifetime opportunity and a dream come true for our family,' she
reminisced.

Prevention is better than the Cure

Ratha was just one of the young women that my teammates and
I met on our bicycle tour of Cambodia. She was one of the lucky
students to graduate from Sala Baï. The idea for the trip to Siem
Reap had come up when I was introduced to the school via an
American friend of mine called Sam McGoun, who had established
a fundraising arm for them in Singapore. Being an avid biker, Sam
suggested I organize a bike tour with WOAM to support the school
and I jumped at the chance.

Learning about the school, I was impressed by the work they had
done over the years. Since its launch, Sala Baï has seen more than
2,000 students graduate and each student has been employed within
four weeks of graduation. During their free eleven-month course,
the students study English, French, labour laws and technical skills
in their chosen speciality. They can learn about catering, tourism,
front-of-house and even beauty therapy. With their new skill sets,
each student is then able to earn around three or four times their
average household monthly income, which means the lives of these
young adults and their families are changed forever. I felt this was a
beautiful cause to get behind and I was eager to learn more about
how this opportunity impacted the students in the long term.

Ratha is now able to help pay for her little siblings to go to school as well as buy her mother's precious medicine. Like Ratha's journey, the stories of other Sala Baï students are heart-warming but also often gut-wrenching. They remind us that education can change lives and give young people from underprivileged backgrounds a brighter future. In a country like Cambodia, where primary-school dropout rate is close to 40 per cent, Sala Baï is impacting the local community and making a difference.

While the future for the students of Sala Baï is bright, the future of these school dropouts isn't always as rosy because Cambodia is a hunting ground for human traffickers. The traffickers are reportedly organized crime syndicates, parents, relatives, friends, intimate partners and neighbours. While researching this issue, I was horrified to find out that a large number of children in Cambodia are trafficked for sexual exploitation and forced into organized begging rings or factories. A UNICEF survey found that 35 per cent of Cambodia's 15,000 prostitutes are children under the age of sixteen.

Discovering Siem Reap

During our trip there, we visited Sala Baï during its annual alumni festival and met the students, graduates, teachers and managers of the school. Because a few of my teammates worked in the hospitality industry in Singapore, I organized interactive leadership development workshops with them as teachers, so as to share best practices with the students. It was rewarding to see the Sala Baï students excited about these workshops, raising their hands to ask questions and even volunteering to take part in the role-playing which was part of the programme.

We also took an arduous 55-kilometre bicycle ride, in blistering heat, in and around Siem Reap's UNESCO World Heritage sites and I fell in love with the country's magnificent temples of Angkor, built by the Khmer Empire at the apogee of its power. Our journey then led us out to the floating village of Mechrey, where many of Sala Baï's students grew up. It was our chance to see first-hand how this innovative project is changing communities. It was there that we met Ratha and she was able to show us just how valuable the work of this NGO has been to her village. She welcomed us warmly into her home and introduced us to her family. I could tell how proud she was to show us how her job had helped pay for the extension and renovation of their little house. As we chatted, she looked dotingly at her younger siblings who were playing nearby, telling us how well they were doing at school—once again something her role at the hotel was facilitating. Ratha had an air of quiet confidence, and it was clear she had become the role model in her community. Other little girls looked up to her, and it made me realize just how important it was to support such positive and constructive initiatives.

Cambodian history is fascinating even if marred by terrible violence and bloodshed. When King Sihanouk was overthrown in 1970 and Cambodia was renamed the Khmer Republic, Cambodia entered its darkest period ever. We learnt from our guide that the Khmer Rouge killed as many as three million Cambodians between 1975 and 1979, spreading their brand of terror like a virus from the jungles until they controlled the entire country, only to systematically dismantle and destroy it in the name of a communist agrarian ideal.

Today, more than thirty-five years after Vietnamese soldiers removed the Khmer Rouge from power, the genocide trials still continue—a bittersweet note of progress in an impoverished nation still struggling to rehabilitate its crippled economic and human resources. As we cycled through the countryside, I saw the scars from its war years, including the Killing Fields, where the Khmer Rouge had slaughtered millions of Cambodians. It sent a shiver down my spine and made me feel empty and sad. How could human beings do this to each other?

Despite the fact that Cambodia has faced such horrors and is still a poor country, there is every reason to be optimistic about its future. In the early years of the twenty-first century, the Cambodian economy grew rapidly. As of today, the textile industry in Cambodia is booming and, in 2005, oil was discovered in the sea off Cambodia.

But, if one had any concerns about the future of the country, the Sala Baï scheme would instantly placate these. No longer do the young women of Cambodia see only one way out. Education has proven to be one of the most efficient ways to prevent human trafficking before it starts. As they say, if you educate a woman you educate a nation . . . or in this case, save a community.

Education and Female Empowerment

The tour of Sala Baï and our meeting with Ratha, especially, opened my eyes to the fact that education is one of the most critical and vital pillars of empowerment for women. It helped me understand that it is also an area that offers some of the most blatant examples of discrimination against women and girls. Today, around the world, among children not attending school, there are twice as many girls as boys, and among illiterate adults, there are twice as many women as men.

My journey with WOAM has allowed me to dive deeper into this important issue and has made me understand that providing basic education to girls around the world is one sure way to give them more opportunities in life—enabling them to make real choices regarding the kinds of lives they want to lead. It is not a luxury. The United Nations Convention on the Rights of Children and Convention on the Elimination of All Forms of Discrimination against Women establish it as a basic human right.

As I have seen with the female graduates of Sala Baï, an educated woman is more likely to marry at a later age and have fewer children. The children she does have will tend to have a greater chance of survival, be healthier and better educated. Studies show that an extra year of schooling for girls reduces fertility rates by 5 to 10 per cent. In Cambodia, the infant mortality rate of babies whose mothers have received primary education is half that of children whose mothers are illiterate. An educated woman will also be more productive at work— and better paid. Indeed, the dividend for educational investment is often higher for women than men. I've spent some time trying to understand what it would take to improve girls' access to education. Experience in scores of countries, including Cambodia, shows the importance, among other things, of an extra year of schooling to increase a woman's future earnings by about 15 per cent, compared with 11 per cent for a man. Women earn less than men and if a woman is uneducated, the chance of getting a job or one that pays reasonably is slimmer. Education has more impact for women than for men and this is why there is the 4 per cent difference in earnings. And also, this is what empirical data seems to be showing.

Astrid's Story

Without a doubt, it is through education that young women come to realize their full potential. To illustrate this point further, I would like to share with you the story of a very dear Filipina friend of mine called Astrid Tuminez, because her life is a testament to just how profoundly education can impact and change lives.

Astrid grew up in the slums of Iloilo, in the Philippines, as one of seven children. Her family had so little money that she only had one pair of socks that she washed once a week. She had to plug the holes in her shoes with lollipop wrappers when it rained. The arc of her life changed when she was five years old, as Catholic nuns invited her and her sisters to join one of the best convent schools in Iloilo. Astrid excelled at school and didn't stop there. Thanks to the scholarships she received, she went on to study at Harvard and MIT, finishing up with a PhD in political science. Astrid assisted in peace negotiations between the United States, the Philippine government and the Moro Islamic Liberation Front in Mindanao, Philippines, during her time at the US Institute of Peace, and later became the vice-dean of the Lee Kwan Yew School of Public Policy in Singapore. Today, she is the seventh—and first female—president of Utah Valley University in the United States which has close to 40,000 students. It all started because she was given a chance at scholarships and a good education. Astrid's story inspires me often, and more than a friend, she is a role model to me.

Indeed, the biggest lesson from my time in Cambodia and from Astrid's story is that through education we can truly shape the world for the better. And when it comes to human trafficking, as I learnt from Sala Baï, prevention is absolutely better than the cure. I firmly believe that proactive early encounters and intervention, not just rescuing and rehabilitating, are key to curbing this crisis. And as Desmond Tutu wisely said,

> There comes a point where we need to stop just pulling people out of the river. We need to go upstream and find out why they're falling in.

The journey to Siem Reap and the people we met along the way, especially Ratha and the other young women we met at Sala Baï, drove home an important lesson. The future is in the hands of the young and education provides women with the knowledge, skills and the self-confidence they need to seek out economic opportunities. I left Cambodia inspired and even more determined to continue my mission of empowering women and providing them with the opportunities and tools they need to lead, successful, healthy and happy lives.

CHAPTER 8

Into the Eye of the Lut Desert of Iran—2016

A few months after our bicycle trip to Cambodia, in November of the same year, we set out on a very different kind of challenge. Once again, we chose a desert, but this time one of the hottest in the world, the *Dasht-e Lut* of Iran—also known simply as the Lut desert. This pioneering expedition was nothing short of surreal. In truth, it was breathtaking, marked by some unexpected challenges . . . and ultimately, transformational. Our WOAM group became the first all-female team in history to cross the Lut desert on foot.

Into the Vast Emptiness

Visibility was almost nil. The howling sandstorm rendered walking along the narrow ridge almost impossible, engulfing us in a dense cloud of golden sand particles which felt razor-sharp on exposed skin. The gale-force winds roared furiously from all sides, ramming into us, imperiously demanding we get off this 600-metre mega-dune at once. Ignoring the angry storm and balancing precariously on the spine of this gigantic, shifting monster, our team of twelve women carried on resolutely, carefully putting one foot in front of the other. As we advanced in close formation, trying in vain to use the person in front of us as a human shield, I realized we had no choice but to keep moving forward. If we turned back, we would simply find ourselves in the same impossible predicament. Squinting through my goggles while battling with the straps of my backpack, which were flapping wildly in the wind and whipping my face, I said a silent prayer that the next gust of wind wouldn't hurl us off this sandy mountain.

In 1271, the legendary Marco Polo journeyed through the Lut, as did British explorer, Wilfred Thesiger, in 1964—but both used camels. Our team covered more than 200 kilometres in seven days, across a magnificent and varied landscape, which boasts wildly contrasting temperatures and climates. The Lut is truly exceptional and full of contradictions. From the sweltering heat of the mega-dunes to the icy cold nights in the valley of the *Kaluts*—with sandcastle-like rock formations—from the salt plains, cracked by the fierce sun, to the sand storms blasting through the meteorite craters, the desert kept me captivated during this epic crossing by its raw beauty and versatility.

In Persian, *Lut* means 'emptiness'. This immense expanse of sand is home to the hottest recorded temperatures on Earth. Global satellite surveys once registered ground temperatures of 70.7° Celsius. 'NASA scientists say it's the closest thing we have to the planet Mars,' declared Mehrdad, our Iranian guide, as we strode across the Eye of the Lut. The Eye is a massive crater believed to have been formed when a large meteorite struck the earth. Mehrdad proceeded to point out the similarities between the Lut and Mars; the scorching temperatures, unyielding aridity and the sheer force of the winds, which converge from all four directions at once, causing the formation of massive, star-shaped, sand dunes, which radiate across the desert plains.

During our voyage, despite the long and tiring days of trekking, the team stayed positive, motivated and fiercely determined. Our head guide, Dave, was an ex-British military officer, who had extensive experience leading expeditions in these parts. He came across as warm and efficient, didn't make small talk, and had come highly recommended by our tour operator in London. I had complete confidence in him and my teammates liked him. Dave was assisted by five local Iranian guides, three of whom were brothers and expert desert trackers. They had a carpet business in Teheran, which they ran together, but on the side, they had a successful travel company and specialized in off-the-beaten-track experiences in Iran. They were the boys the police called to assist them if anyone went missing in the desert. I knew we were in very good hands.

On most days, we were up at 4.30 a.m. and on our way by 6 a.m. Majestic and imposing, the dunes led us up their sinuous paths, charming us at every turn with promises of vistas more awe-inspiring than the last. Every day, we hiked till sunset, averaging a distance of thirty kilometres a day, made all the more tiring because of the uneven sandy terrain. A steady rhythm was maintained, alternating fifty minutes of fast-paced walking with a ten-minute break and so on. This gave us a good cadence throughout the journey, with a short stop for lunch, usually around noon. Then onwards again, charging ahead all afternoon, lured by the serpentine curves of the Lut's hypnotic landscapes. Walking, walking and more walking . . . The days seemed endless. During those hours and long days of walking, if I was not chatting with one of my teammates, my mind would go quiet naturally and I would slip into a meditative mindset, using the rhythm of the walk—left foot, right foot, left foot, right foot— as my point of gentle focus. By doing this, I could bring my mind to a place of rest where I could fully engage with the environment and the present moment. My mind would then wander and think about the women we were supporting via this special expedition. Had some of them crossed wide expanses like this, not by choice but to escape dangerous situations? It was a sobering thought and made me appreciate the opportunity I had to make a small difference in their lives.

Towards the end of the day, as the last thin rays of sunlight glimmered and our shadows lengthened against the amber-coloured sand dunes, we knew our daylight hours were running out. We resisted the temptation to stop for more pictures and picked up the pace in order to reach camp before nightfall. Upon arrival, our individual tents would still need to be set up, and our preference was not to do this exercise in total darkness. As soon as the tents were up, those who still had some energy would do their best to 'de-sand' and treat blisters and other sores. Since showers were not an option, we freshened up by using wet wipes in the privacy of our tents. By day two, I had given up trying to brush the sand out of my hair, which had turned into a matted, straw-like mass. But it didn't matter, I was loving every minute of this beautiful and unique experience with my team.

As soon as everyone had settled into camp, our guides would then serve tea and prepare a hearty dinner, which usually consisted of a bean and vegetable stew served with white rice. By 7.30 p.m., eyelids would begin to droop as we stared at the spectacular, starry galaxies above. I would sometimes try to put off my bedtime hour by drinking more tea and chatting around the campfire. Looking up at the stars, I would send out a special thought of love and gratitude to my children and husband back home. In truth, my teammates and I were all exhausted from the day's exertion. Thus, after a quick visit to the loos, which were usually downwind and not too far from our camp, we'd drift off, one by one, and retire to our tents. By 8.30 p.m. most of us were either sound asleep or at least tossing and turning in our sleeping bags, trying desperately to ignore the aches and pains in our muscles and bones and praying that the gods of sleep would soon arrive.

The next day, it would start all over again. A cacophony of different alarm clocks would go off at around 4.30 a.m. Torches would be strapped on to the sleepy, dishevelled heads, lighting up our green tents one by one like a cluster of glowing caterpillars. Next, as we struggled to get out of our sleeping bags and tents, the sounds of shuffling, packing, zipping and unzipping resonated across the camp, as if suddenly a flurry of gigantic plastic bags had descended on us.

As the campsite gradually emerged from its torpor, the sound of women chattering and giggling would inevitably ensue. Despite temperatures being close to zero degrees at this ungodly hour of the morning, the noises of a waking-up camp were strangely comforting.

While people continued to move around drowsily, packing up things and sorting out backpacks, the deep voice of Mohammad, our guide— aka the-best-breakfast-chef-in-the-world—would bellow, 'Ladies, your eggs are ready!'—and that never failed to put a smile on my face.

Soon my fellow explorers and I were off again, fresh and ready to tackle another long day of hiking in the sand. Our group was eager to see what new sights and creatures we would encounter. We happened across a few lizards and dead birds along the way and, one morning, a slithering, sand-coloured snake zigzagged across our path. We were told that, over the past few years, drug smugglers from the nearby Afghan and Pakistani borders had used the southern part of the Lut as a travel route. Luckily, apart from a few wolf, fox and camel tracks, we encountered no other signs of life.

The Unexpected Twist and Caring for your Team

One day, when we were about halfway through our journey, an incident occurred, that I will never be able to forget. As we finished breakfast and were getting ready to set off, we realized that Dave was missing and nowhere to be found. Normally, he was up before everyone else making sure our tents were packed, our backpacks ready and water bottles refilled, so that we could be on the road by 6 a.m. That morning, he was absent, and no one had seen him leave the camp.

We walked around the campsite calling out for him, but there was no sign of Dave. We peered into his tent and discovered that his GPS equipment, water bottle and boots were all still in place. When he still did not appear about an hour later, we found it strange. This was not like him at all. At first I wondered whether he had simply gone for a stroll and had gotten lost. When he didn't show up for quite some time, I started to worry in earnest: 'This is not good. We depend on this person to get across this vast desert.'

In the desert, survival time without fluids is measured in days. Dave had neither water nor shoes nor food—I feared the worst.

Luckily for us, our local guides led by Mehrdad and his brothers Babak and Mehdi, along with their friends Ali and Mohammad, knew the Lut inside out. Their presence and cool heads gave me a sense of security and deep in my gut I knew we would get through this somehow.

Using their support vehicles, our guides tracked Dave and found him a few hours later, wandering around, barefoot, severely dehydrated, shirt unbuttoned, sun burned and disoriented with pupils dilated to the size of saucers. He was mumbling apologies incoherently, but otherwise he was unharmed. I was so relieved in the moment, but then pondered what to do. Often on expeditions, you try to plan for the unexpected—weather inclemencies, adjustments to the itinerary or emergency rescues in case of injury. Never could I have predicted that something like this would happen. Our head guide, our leader, was basically out of action. I felt responsible for the safety of my team; but now, also for him. We needed to get him the medical attention and help he needed, but I also needed to ensure the team was safe and would get across this desert unharmed.

First, clearly, Dave needed help. We were unsure if he had accidentally ingested a hallucinogen or was experiencing some sort of a mental breakdown. We could find no logical explanation for the state he was in. How could he have had such a dramatic change of personality? From the logical, coherent Dave, to the erratic and unstable Dave who was now before us. We knew we could not split up the team at this point in our journey. The unwritten rule in such situations is that you never separate from the group in the desert. You keep supplies, water and vehicles together until you exit the desert as a unit. We were halfway through the Lut and had another four days to go before we got to our destination. We decided to continue and complete our journey together, while caring for Dave. Over the next few days, our local guides took turns to watch Dave during the night as he was not sleeping at all. He was a strong man, but was behaving very strangely—sometimes crawling around on the sand, at other times stripping naked. One day, he started playing with a knife; on another day, he scaled one of the kaluts and teetered at the edge of a steep cliff, almost as if he were contemplating jumping off. He remained in this fugue state for several days as we continued our journey across the Lut.

The tense situation took a toll on my team. In addition to the fatigue caused by the punishing pace of our trek, we went through a range of emotions. I was deeply concerned about the mental state of my team. Some of the women became very quiet and kept to themselves, saving their energies to focus on the long days of walking, while others attempted to talk to Dave and keep him company. A few made the best of the situation and would sing and dance at breakfast time in an attempt to lighten the mood, while others slept poorly because of nightmares and worries about Dave's condition. It was a strange and uncomfortable situation because Dave's reactions were so unpredictable and wide ranging. I felt responsible for the women under my care. I had invited them to join me on this expedition and had organized it with Valerie, but here we were with a guide who could not function, whom we had to care for now, who could potentially harm himself or even worse, harm one of us. I thought about the families of my teammates who had entrusted me with their care. I simply wanted to ensure that we could all get across the Lut, and eventually get back home safely to our families.

I made a conscious effort at that point to communicate clearly with my team, letting them know that we had a plan to get across and get Dave the care he needed. I stayed calm and worked with the other guides to ensure we got through this tricky situation. My co-founder, Valerie, and I were on the satellite phone every day with the UK headquarters of our tour-operating company. We arranged an immediate evacuation for Dave under medical conditions upon our arrival in the oasis of Kerman at the edge of the desert. We had found nothing suspicious in Dave's tent that would suggest he had taken drugs or alcohol, but we still could not explain his strange and erratic behaviour. We certainly did not want to flag up what had happened to the local authorities. We were in Iran after all, where alcohol and drugs are strictly prohibited. Any suspicion of usage of such substances would be immediately investigated by the police. The hardest thing for me was the fact that we didn't know what was wrong with poor Dave. Nothing in his behaviour when we met him, or from the information we received from the people who had recommended him, suggested that something like this might happen; in any case, we didn't want to take any chances because, as we had been warned, Iran had extremely strict laws. Anyone found being in possession of, using or trafficking illegal drugs could expect a long jail sentence, heavy fines and even the death penalty.

Mission Accomplished

After a few tense days, we finally arrived in Kerman and Dave was met by a medical team and safely flown home to England. Then, suddenly, the success of our expedition dawned on us. We had been so focused on getting Dave to safety that we had almost forgotten what a monumental task we had just completed. We had succeeded in our mission of crossing the Lut as the first, all-female team—200 kilometres in seven days, and as a result we had raised over $100,000 for women survivors of war. Despite the mixed emotions and our concern for Dave, we felt a huge sense of fulfilment and elation at our pioneering achievement.

It was wonderful to finally be able to celebrate this epic milestone as a team. My heart was full of gratitude because I felt extremely privileged to have been able to undertake such a journey by choice. Indeed, sometimes during the journey, I thought of women fleeing their country because of war or unrest, escaping with just the clothes on their back, crossing vast expanses on foot, uncertain of their future. It felt good that we had rallied our strength in support for these women survivors of war and other hostilities.

There is no doubt that this experience in the Lut bonded us as a team. As we pushed our physical, mental and emotional limits across the desert, the intimacy of our sisterhood became rock solid.

It also made me see, very clearly, the importance of empathy and compassion in times of crisis. I came to realize that these are perhaps two of the most important and vital leadership super-skills needed to harness and develop the power and resilience of any team. And although the two qualities are closely related, they are distinctly different—even if equally important.

While empathy refers more generally to our ability to take the perspective of and feel the emotions of another person, compassion is when those feelings and thoughts include the desire to help and alleviate another's pain and suffering and leads us to take action. I came to understand that, when combined, these qualities are powerful human skills that allow us to connect at a deeper level because they involve more than our minds, but also engage our heart, values and body.

As Theodore Roosevelt once said,

> . . . nobody cares how much you know, until they know how much your care.

This experience in the Lut made me realize that an empathetic leader is able to establish a connection with her teammates, encourage collaboration and influence the team in the right direction. Empathy and listening go hand in hand. Why? Because listening shows you care. You can't show empathy if you do not listen. The quality of our listening determines the quality of our influence because listening transmits that kind of respect and builds trust. Listening to your teammates fears and worries, talking through their emotions with genuine care and empathy is vital. This applies as much on expeditions as it does in a work setting.

I aspire, every day, to be a more compassionate leader, one who has the ability to help others grow and overcome tough situations via encouragement and empowerment. I've come to realize that when you treat people with compassion, they never forget it. You cultivate people who want to work for you, or join your mission, not because of what you do, but because of who you are and the values you represent. Compassion stirs leaders to use their position, or personal influence, to direct resources that alleviate suffering.

Finally, in hindsight, if we had based our travel plans on what some of our friends and family had said about Iran, we probably would never have made it to the Lut. For decades, the county has been cast as the bogeyman of the Middle East by many in the West, for various reasons; one being Iran's dire human rights record. Nevertheless, during our travels there, and especially during our time in Teheran and in the towns of Birjand, Keshit and Kerman, I found the people to be incredibly kind, spontaneous and generous, with hearts of pure gold. Indeed, our own logistical 'dream team' in the desert, as we liked to call our local guides, looked after us with every care and attention and brought Dave safely across the Lut too. The local guides had treated us like little sisters, and today, Mehrdad and his team have become dear friends for life.

I felt incredibly safe and warmly welcomed in the Islamic Republic of Iran. Its proud civilization and rich cultural heritage are remarkable. Walking around the sublime, turquoise-tiled domes and minarets of the cities, the atmospheric teahouses, bustling bazaars and, of course, witnessing the sheer force and beauty of the Lut desert, contributed to weaving for us a rich tapestry of colours and experiences of magnificent proportions.

On our last day in Teheran, the team spent a day at the OMID foundation in Teheran to better understand some of the issues faced by underprivileged women in Iran. The foundation, which was set up in 2004, helps young women who are victims of sexual, physical or mental abuse, and houses many of them who have been displaced or seeking refuge from oppression, systematic abuse, institutional and domestic violence. The bonding with the women from this foundation added an even more meaningful dimension to our trip and, as soon as we returned to Singapore, we organized an Iran-themed event to raise funds to support them.

Undoubtedly, we left behind a piece of our soul in Teheran and in the vast emptiness of the Lut desert, with the people whom we came to know during our journey in this astonishing country. Our ordeal in the desert had bonded us so strongly together it made us see, with absolute clarity, that a team that collaborates and works efficiently together, looking out for each other with genuine kindness and compassion, can accomplish and overcome just about anything. In the end, our time in Iran surpassed all our expectations and gave us memories and life lessons to treasure for a lifetime.

CHAPTER 9

Turning the Tide in the Land of the Thunder Dragon, Bhutan—2017

After the pioneering crossing of the Lut desert in Iran, where we had pushed our limits crossing giant sand dunes, I was looking for a very different kind of experience. I wanted to organize an expedition that would put my team and me in the water, which is not my comfort zone. Despite growing up swimming often, in the Philippines, I am not the most confident of swimmers. It is not my preferred environment, and I knew this would be a good area for me to explore my comfort level and push myself. This is why, in early 2017, at a party in Singapore, when I met a lady called Celine Hivet, who told me she was a SUP or Stand-Up Paddle Board instructor, I perked up and asked her a ton of questions. I told her that I was looking for a pioneering challenge and wanted to do it, ideally somewhere remote, culturally interesting and very beautiful. She suggested Bhutan in the Himalayas, a place I had always wanted to visit, as she knew SUP had not yet started there, only kayaking had. Within a few weeks, I had recruited a team, selected a worthy and highly recommended charity in Bhutan to support, and Celine became our SUP instructor and WOAM teammate.

The Land of the Thunder Dragon

As eleven of us advanced resolutely into the flowing, glacial river, a rush of excitement gripped me. Admittedly, we were all a little nervous; feeling apprehensive because the currents below were strong. After months of training in the warm, tropical, coastal waters of Singapore, and for a couple of my teammates out of Dubai, I could hardly believe we were finally in Bhutan, ready to begin the challenge we had set ourselves a few months ago. The pristine, gushing rivers of this hidden Himalayan kingdom was a brand-new environment for us to paddle in. In truth, the moment was made even more exceptional because, ultimately, we knew we were here to support women impacted by domestic abuse, a cause in line with WOAM's mission, and also because the adventure itself was pioneering. Indeed, we were the first team to ever Stand-Up Paddle Board in the Kingdom of Bhutan and attempt the descent of two of its rivers.

In Bhutanese the country is called 'Druk Yul', which means the Land of the Thunder Dragon. Today, as the kingdom manoeuvres through the process of development, the royal government of Bhutan has committed to achieving gender equality for the Bhutanese people. Furthermore, through its Gross National Happiness Commission, Bhutan prioritises the happiness of its citizens; and this is part of the reason why I chose to lead an expedition there. The other was because I was fascinated by the fact Bhutan is the first country in the world to be carbon-negative, with more than 70 per cent of its land covered in trees. This has allowed Bhutan to become a carbon sink—meaning that it absorbs more carbon dioxide than it produces. Bhutan also exports most of the renewable hydro-electric power that it generates from its rivers. And I was curious to discover those rivers via our SUP challenge. Interestingly, by 2030, Bhutan plans to reach zero net greenhouse gas emissions and to produce zero waste. The Bhutanese people believe that conservation of the environment is a way of life and children are taught environment protection and basic agriculture techniques. I felt there was so much we could all learn from Bhutan.

Our team's added objective was to raise awareness and funds for RENEW, a charity founded by one of the Queen Mothers of Bhutan, which is dedicated to the empowerment of women and children, with specific attention to survivors of domestic violence. I had been in contact with RENEW for months now, introduced to them by the directors of Druk Air in Singapore, Bhutan's national carrier, who serve as the de facto representatives of Bhutan's government in Singapore, given there is no Bhutanese consulate. I learnt that the charity offers survivors shelter and care to help them heal from their physical and emotional wounds, while also providing them with life-skills training to allow them to eventually become financially independent.

Navigating the Rapids

A few days earlier, when we landed in Bhutan, after a hair-raising albeit breathtaking final approach, we felt ecstatic that we had finally arrived. Paro International Airport is known as one of the most dangerous airports in the world. Its tiny airstrip is 2,200 metres above sea level and surrounded by jagged, mountainous peaks. Pilots have to manoeuvre past dozens of houses scattered across the ridges, while often battling strong winds that whip through the valley, resulting in severe turbulence. So treacherous is the airport that 'only about twelve or thirteen pilots in the world are qualified to land here,' confirmed our charming and ever-smiling Druk Air steward as we made our way towards the rear of the plane to disembark.

From the moment I stepped off the aircraft, and breathed in the fresh mountain air, I was captivated. Paro is situated in a deep valley on the banks of a river, with the surrounding peaks as high as 5,500 metres; the view is simply stunning. I was thrilled to be back in the Himalayas, one of my favourite places in the world. Indeed, the last time I was here was four years earlier for our Tsum Valley trek in Nepal.

Soon after, we meet our local guide, Karma, a man bubbling with enthusiasm, who, we later learnt, was somewhat of a local celebrity, having starred in a documentary called *Power of the River*, an adventure documentary which explored the rivers of Bhutan—clearly, the perfect guide for us. As we drove out of the airport, he told us about his country: 'Bhutan is situated on the ancient Silk Road between Tibet, India and South East Asia. Today it is in the midst of reconciling century-old cultures with rising modernity; in fact, it was isolated from the outside world for centuries and only began to open up to foreigners in the 1970s.'

During the first couple of days of our journey, our group travelled from Paro to the capital, Thimphu, and after a visit to Buddha Dordenma, a gigantic Shakyamuni Buddha statue, and a blessing at Thimphu Dzong, we swapped the expedition bus for bicycles to descend from the high Dochula Pass at 3,200 metres to the Punakha valley, where we based ourselves over the next few days for our challenge, the first ever SUP descent on two of its icy rivers, Mo Chhu and Pho Chhu, in the valley of Punakha. This would be followed by some river rafting on the surrounding rivers and a hike to the iconic Tiger's Nest, at 3,200 metres, to visit the Taktsang Monastery, perched on the very edge of the mountainside.

There was an incident early on in the trip. One of our teammates had a bad fall while on the bike descent. She swerved to avoid some rocks on the road and crashed violently to the ground. As a result, she cut open her chin and fractured four of her teeth. Because of the shock, she nearly fainted. We tried to keep her alert and conscious and carried her on to the team bus, which was following us, to take her to the closest hospital. She was my youngest teammate so I felt particularly protective of her. At twenty-two, this was the first time she had done anything as adventurous as this in her life. She was shaken but undeterred; after a few stitches and despite being bandaged up, she resolved to join us the next day as we SUPed down the rivers.

Over a period of four days, we paddled down the confluence of the Mo Chhu and Pho Chhu Rivers with the backdrop of the stunning Punakha Dzong and the multicoloured prayer flags fluttering high above the suspension bridges. The locals had never seen anyone on

SUP boards before. The equipment had been shipped into Bhutan especially for our expedition and we became quite a sensation along the riverbanks; the King, apparently, even drove by while we were SUPing.

The currents and rapids were more unpredictable than I had expected and very different from what we had experienced at sea. Fortunately, Anthony, our expert SUP guide, gave us a crash course on how rivers flow and the confidence and technique to tackle them safely. Originally from the UK, he had been working in Bhutan for years and knew the country inside and out. In fact, two decades ago, he was asked by the royal family of Bhutan to map out the rivers of their country, and then decided to stay on as a guide.

'Most people assume a river follows the curves of the banks, but in reality, a river flows in a straight line,' he told us, drawing a sketch on the sand, while a local dog looked on intrigued. 'This means that when a paddler approaches a turn in the river, he or she has to be very careful not to drift to the side and crash into the rocky riverbanks. The key is to try to remain in the central part of the river, which is usually the deepest and safest place to be,'— easier said than done.

We learnt the hard way and spent our first day falling off the boards so many times in the churning rapids that we lost count. As a result, when things got choppy, we became very good at dropping from the standing to the kneeling position at lightning speed. Lowering our centre of gravity made us more stable and reduced our chances of falling off. Ultimately, we came to understand that a flowing river's calm surface can be deceptive, and that currents should never be underestimated. Getting back on the board as soon as we fell into the flowing river while avoiding oncoming rocks was probably the most challenging task. Many of us got badly bruised and cut through our wetsuits; but we kept going, without losing momentum. Adrenaline was pumping and despite feeling exhausted, soaked and miserably cold at times, I was proud of the fact we were attempting such a unique and complex challenge.

One afternoon, while we were paddling down the Pho Chhu River, one teammate got stuck in a logjam in swirling rapids. She couldn't tug at her quick-release belt to free her from her board, which caused her to stay submerged, wedged between two rocks, for some time. The water crashed wildly around her and the current was extremely strong. Luckily, Anthony's assistants, our two intrepid safety kayakers, were with her within seconds of her fall, and helped her get untangled. She managed to swim safely down the rest of the rapids and put on a brave smile when she re-joined the team. In the evening we discovered that she had a massive bruise and a cut from a rock that had pierced her wetsuit down the whole length of her leg. Thankfully, she was otherwise okay and keen to continue on the board the next day. This was my second teammate to get hurt and I, as their team leader, was naturally concerned. I was, indeed, responsible for their well-being and safety, but I felt that with Anthony and our two safety kayakers by our side, we were going to be just fine.

On the last day, we set off early in the morning. It was a beautiful sunny day, the sky was blue, the birds were chirping and the sparkling rivers were crystal clear. We were getting more confident on the SUPs and the team was well-coordinated as we navigated the rapids together with ease and completed the last leg of our itinerary successfully. Once again, I was proud of our progress and achievement as a team. Most of us had never SUPed before, and here we were, descending the rapids in Bhutan! And the fact that this had never been done before made the moment and achievement even more special.

RENEW and the Pursuit of Happiness

When it was time to get out of the water at the end of the SUP challenge, we were sad that our journey on the rivers had come to an end, but the women and children at RENEW had prepared a special show for our visit, and we couldn't be late for that.

We arrived just in time. The children in particular had been waiting excitedly all day. They greeted us with huge smiles and shining eyes. To my disbelief I learnt that they were not the children of the women survivors of domestic violence living at the shelter, but survivors themselves, and it broke my heart. Some of them were as young as four or five years old and had been beaten or abused in some way prior to their arrival. RENEW was their shelter and sanctuary. I knew from my research that domestic abuse has devastating effects on a child's sense of self-worth. Older children may begin to play truant or resort to alcohol or drugs or begin to self-harm by taking overdoses or cutting themselves or develop eating disorders. Knowing this and watching the children play happily around us as we arrived, made me feel incredibly sad, my chest felt so constricted that I had trouble breathing.

The children danced beautifully as they had been practising all week and we could see on their little faces that they were eager to do well. We met the women survivors too. There was deep sadness etched on their faces but when we asked them about the weaving which they had learnt at RENEW, their eyes lit up and they showed us their beautiful work with great pride. We were told that the funds we raised for them via this expedition would go towards building more shelters for the survivors; it was a small gesture, yet, after speaking with the dedicated management team at RENEW, I felt confident our efforts would have a lasting impact. As we parted ways, they gifted us with the traditional ceremonial silk scarves, or khata, which symbolize prayer, purity, goodwill, auspiciousness, compassion and sincerity. I still have mine, and treasure it even to this day.

Our trek culminated with a hike up to the iconic Tiger's Nest to visit the Taktsang Monastery, perched on the very edge of the mountainside. This is a famed pilgrimage site for Buddhists from all over the world and Guru Rimpoche, who introduced Buddhism to Bhutan, is said to have reached this place on the back of a flying tigress. The climb and the views from the peak at 3,200 metres was simply awe-inspiring.

Looking back at this expedition and the SUP challenge in particular, I realize that one of the greatest lessons from this experience came from how I grew to view feelings of fear as a positive thing. Fear helps us focus. Fear in the face of churning, freezing rapids in an unknown environment is intimidating, even paralysing at times. The best way to conquer fear, I came to understand, was to recognize when fear was useful and when it was not. Understanding why I was afraid gave me power to act on that knowledge.

Fear can motivate us all to be safe and take challenges rather than stop us from moving forward. The key is to face our fears and interpret them in ways that help us develop and grow stronger. We must learn to turn fear into a productive force. It's true that humans are hard-wired to physically feel fear. Sudden fear can propel us to take action to make us safe. The challenge is to interpret those fearful feelings in ways that are useful and constructive. Honouring the power of fear to keep us away from danger and protect us from reckless behaviour is vital, but it should not control us.

Fear is a powerful trigger and can be repurposed to push us emotionally. Instead of being frightened and paralysed when facing rapids, I learnt that we can gain expertise and knowledge about the best ways to tackle them and as a result, have more control—just as we had learnt from Anthony about how rivers behave and the best ways to navigate them—this gave us much more confidence when the time came to face the rapids.

For our team, this expedition was a journey into a different and unique reality. A rich, learning experience on so many fronts. Navigating rapids, facing our fears, bonding as a team, meeting the women and children of RENEW, discovering the striking natural beauty of Bhutan and its unique architecture and ancient culture. It felt as if we had stepped into an alternative universe and witnessed a whole new way of life that is still desperately trying to shield itself from the shrillness of this planet. The Bhutanese truly live in harmony with Nature. Our bus driver accidently crushed a fly one morning when he was driving, and he was incredibly upset—every living creature matters to them.

A country that opened its doors to the world only in 1974 and the last country in the world to allow satellite television in 1999, Bhutan continues to be an enigma. This Buddhist Himalayan kingdom, landlocked by India in the south and China and Tibet in the north, with a population of less than a million, is a country unlike any I've ever visited and the closest thing to heaven I have ever experienced. No wonder many believe Bhutan to be the last, real-life Shangri-La; most of all because of its unwavering pursuit of one of life's most elusive concepts—national happiness.

CHAPTER 10

Cycling Through the Gates of Hell, Ethiopia—2017

A few months after our return from Bhutan, I set out to plan our next big WOAM challenge. My co-founder, Valerie, had been talking about going to Ethiopia for years, she was drawn to this rare and fascinating destination and curious to explore its topography. While she wasn't always able to join all of our WOAM expeditions, this was one she was keen to take part in, and it turned out to be one of the most incredible terrains we ever trekked across. Mother Nature threw out the rule book when she cooked up this place and this is the reason why . . .

Biking Through the Inferno

Ethiopia's Danakil Depression is an inferno of burning salt, sulphuric acid, lava and volcanic rock—tantamount to 'hell on earth'. Our WOAM team had set itself a bold and pioneering challenge—to cross the Danakil Desert on mountain bikes. No one had ever attempted such a feat before and we soon realized why. With its furnace-like temperatures, bone-drying aridity and noxious chemical composition, the Danakil is an alien-looking desert. Known as the hottest place on earth, with daytime temperatures soaring over

50° Celsius and an average year-round temperature of 35° Celsius, it is considered to be the most inhospitable environment in the world.

Located in the Afar Region of northeast Ethiopia, near the border of Eritrea, the area is part of the East African Rift System, a place where the earth's internal forces are currently tearing apart three continental plates, creating new land. Since the region sits along fault lines, the valley is often disturbed by tumultuous earthquakes and volcanic eruptions. Undeniably, the conditions in the Danakil can only be described as brutal but, against all odds, people do live there. In fact, the Afar people, who are mainly livestock holders, primarily raising camels, but also tending goats, sheep and cattle, call it their home. They have settled in semi-permanent villages throughout this region for generations.

In November 2017, we flew in from Singapore to Addis Ababa, the capital of Ethiopia, which sits in rolling hills at 2,355 metres above sea level with a population of three million people. There, we met up with our guide, Mulugeta Sisay, or Mule for short, a young and very knowledgeable man, in his early thirties, who took us around the capital on a cultural immersion day tour.

From Addis Ababa, the next day, we then flew together to Mek'ele, the capital city of the northern Tigray Region of Ethiopia, perched at an altitude of 2,000 metres, where we met the rest of our convoy and guides who had been handpicked by Mule for this expedition. They were local guys from the region, whom he trusted and had worked with before, consisting of two cooks, five drivers, three guides and two armed guards. The guards had been assigned to us by the local regional police chief because venturing into this abyss can be risky. In truth, the Ethiopian government requires armed militia to escort all tourists who travel through the Danakil. Skirmishes with Eritrean armed forces were common in those days and tourists were sometimes kidnapped and even killed. In 2012, gunmen attacked a group of European tourists, murdering five, injuring two and kidnapping four. After more soldiers were stationed permanently in the area, things slowly improved for a while, until they flared up more recently again in November 2020 with the neighbouring Tigray region at the centre of the crisis. I had some concerns, naturally, given the volatility of the region and had pondered long and hard about the risks involved in taking ten women on such an expedition. What if something were to happen to us? Was I pushing my luck? These were the kinds of questions I would invariably ask myself before almost any expedition; but this one was particularly tricky as we needed an armed escort. The tour-operating company that Valerie and I had chosen, who had provided Mule as our guide, was extremely experienced in this area and had conducted many excursions there, although none as adventurous as ours and certainly none involving biking across the Danakil Depression. Thus, I was reasonably confident, even if a little apprehensive, as we started our journey.

After reassembling our mountain bikes, which we had brought with us from Singapore, we loaded them on to our jeeps with a week's supply of food and water for the five-hour drive east to Hamed Ela, a tiny village located 150 metres below sea level. Finally, in the early evening, after an uneventful drive, we arrived at our first campsite, just outside Hamed Ela.

Jumping out of our airconditioned jeep, it was an initial shock to the system to inhale the sweltering and damp air at 38° Celsius. It was 7 p.m. and it was still that hot. I was not used to these kinds of temperatures in the evening. Singapore, which is on the equator, can get quite hot on a sunny day, but cools quickly after the sun has set. This was also a stark contrast to the breezy 23° Celsius we had experienced in Mek'ele earlier that morning.

We unloaded the equipment and settled into our camp. We hadn't brought tents as they were not suitable for such hot weather, instead, we planned to sleep under the stars on the rudimentary wooden beds already at the camp. After a quick dinner consisting of pasta, a cabbage salad and warm bottled water, we prepared to sleep on our camp beds for our first night under the stars. The heat was oppressive and I found myself dripping with perspiration as I lay motionless on my thin camp mattress. I thought about the day ahead and wondered what it would bring. I tried to feel more excited about discovering the landscapes in daylight and beginning our challenge across the Danakil Depression, but the hot and humid conditions made it difficult to relax and get comfortable, casting a pall over my initial elation at finally being here.

After a restless night, we woke up at 6 a.m., eager to tackle our first day of biking. The plan was to cycle to Dallol, a cinder-cone-shaped volcano, twenty-three kilometres northeast of Hamed Ela. After some delays, because of safety checks on the bikes, we finally left camp at around 8.30 a.m. The cycling across the salt plains was magnificent and the team arrived in high spirits at Dallol at 11 a m. We immediately started hiking up to the luminescent hot springs and realized it was already a blistering 45° Celsius.

Mule shared with us that Dallol was formed in 1926 by a phreatic eruption. This is when groundwater is heated by magma—essentially, a steam eruption without the lava injection. The resulting hydrothermal activity created a series of spectacular, bubbling, sulphuric acid pools that are extremely acidic and salty. Arata, one of our local Afar guides, showed us springs that had not been there just a week ago, explaining to us that Dallol is constantly changing and very unstable. For our safety, he urged us to follow his footsteps with precision, lest we fall through the porous rock into one of the acidic springs. I was absolutely mesmerized. I had never seen anything like this in all my travels. The ground was covered by a crust of salt and solidified black lava with unearthly, luminescent pools of yellow and green, steaming acidic vapour, bubbling up like a cauldron, and just inches below us toxic gases seeped through the ground we were walking on and choked the air with a pungent smell.

After exploring this alien-like environment, we decided to continue hiking to see the salt canyons nearby. Mule shared that, 'salt serves as a potential source of conflict in the region. Dallol's salt is worth a good deal of money, they call it "white gold", and this is why, over the years, various groups in the region have vied for political and territorial control.' It was good to get this perspective and it helped me better understand the complexity of the region.

Boasting some of the most impressive features of the Danakil, the canyons are reddish pillars of salt that rise up sixty metres high. It is truly a sight to behold and despite the oven-like atmosphere, we continued our exploration. By noon, the heat was completely debilitating and coming from every direction. The thermometer read 50° Celsius. The air on my face felt exactly like the blast of heat that hits one when one opens the door of a baking oven. It was the kind of searing heat that the human body isn't built to handle. The unrelenting sun shone down on the rust-coloured, baked earth and we foolishly chose that very moment to cycle back to Hamed Ela.

A Near Miss

After about two hours of biking, we arrived back to Hamed Ela. We tried to cool down but there was barely any shade at the campsite, which was very basic, with no electricity or running water. We splashed water on our heads and those who could eat, had a bite, but most of us had no appetite at all. One of my teammates was bright red and had even started shaking slightly,

'I'm okay . . . just a bit dehydrated,' she shrugged it off, putting on a brave face. I started to feel uneasy myself and my head had started to pound. Most of us were not feeling well at all.

That afternoon, I realized we had made a grave mistake by underestimating the effects of the heat on our bodies. By 4 p.m., while we were visiting the salt lake in the neighbourhood, a place where miners carved out salt slabs for trading, 70 per cent of the team started experiencing mild to very severe symptoms of heatstroke. I suddenly threw up and a teammate had the same symptoms. At that moment, another teammate fainted and had to be carried to one of the jeeps. Three others felt very weak and by nightfall several of us were vomiting violently and burning up with fever. I was scared. What a disaster this day was turning out to be. Heatstroke is a medical emergency, a type of hyperthermia, that can result in unconsciousness, organ failure and even death. I quickly realized the situation was serious—we had no trained medic with us, very limited facilities and the closest hospital was a good five-hour drive away. I thought about the families of my teammates. They had entrusted their wives/mothers/daughters to me, and so I started to pray that we could all pull through without losing anyone.

We decide to wait it out and throughout the night, the women who felt well enough took turns, every hour, to check on the unwell, putting cold compresses on them, reminding them to take sips of water and soothing them with reassuring words. I, too, wasn't well enough to help out and felt all the more frustrated because of this. Thankfully by dawn the fevers had broken, and although still weak, we all felt much better. For the rest of the journey, we adjusted the schedule to depart earlier every morning so as to not have to bike at the peak of the day's heat—a much smarter decision. At that moment, I promised myself that I would reflect, at a later time, on what had just happened. This miscalculation of the effect of the heat on us could have had some very serious consequences and I vowed to learn from this set back and take full responsibility. But for now, the rest of the expedition awaited, and we had to get back on the road.

Fortunately, the next three days after this incident unfolded smoothly. We recalibrated our schedule and adapted to the new situation. From then on, we woke at 4 a.m. every day, were on the road by 5 a.m. and tried to cover our target distances by noon. By the third day. the team was a well-oiled machine, leaving promptly and always on time. We had learnt to use this crisis to pivot towards better efficiency and were even more determined to succeed in our mission.

The afternoons were spent resting under whatever shade we could find, counting the hours in the sweltering heat. Those moments were true mental challenges for most of us, even drinking water or doing anything else seemed like a chore. The air was stifling, our drinking water was tepid and the heat enveloped us completely, hanging like a heavy veil around us, suffocating us both physically and mentally.

During these moments of inactivity, we had a few precious distractions. One of them was when our guide, Mule, would share stories of how Ethiopia is home to a truly diverse landscape and peoples, with a very rich and colourful history. Thanks to him I gained a new perspective of the country and began to learn more about the Afar people, who are Muslim and believed to be the descendants of Arabs, presumably from Yemen. In this way, they are very unique to the rest of the country, which is Christian—with the majority belonging to the Ethiopian Orthodox Church. In fact, Ethiopia is considered to be the second oldest Christian nation in the world after Armenia and remains the only country in Africa that has never been colonized. Mule also entertained us with an amusing account of the way courtship is conducted in some parts of Ethiopia: 'A man drops a lemon at the feet of the woman he wishes to date hoping that she will accept his suit by picking it up.' He was speaking from personal experience here, and we enjoyed teasing him about it.

On another occasion, the team visited the village of Waideddo, where the local Afar chief and his family received us. We spoke to him about their customs and the future of the region. I asked him what he thought about educating the young.

'We don't need our children to go away and get an education. We are very happy here the way we are and do not want to change,' he declared defiantly. The Afar people are proud of their origins and very protective of their land. They are not particularly fond of tourists, or friendly to strangers, and often refuse to have their photo taken. This was a good reminder that sometimes, indigenous people do not want help or interference from outsiders. Despite the fact the chief had agreed to speak with us, I could feel his resentment of our presence.

Mule explained to me that it was because, 'For the Afar, more people on their territory means less water for everyone in this blistering hot area. Also, Afar men invariably carry a spear or a broad-blade knife as they traditionally divide their time between herding and fighting, either with each other or with neighbouring tribes.' This made me understand and appreciate the chief's firmness and his desire to put some boundaries between his tribe and visitors such as us. Indeed, even if we don't always agree with local customs or cultural norms, respect should be our guiding principle.

Erta Ale Volcano

One of the highlights of the trip was our visit to Erta Ale, which was situated a little over the halfway mark on our itinerary. I had been looking forward to discovering this famed volcano, also known by the Afar as the 'smoking mountain'. Erta Ale is a 600-metre-high volcano that is one of only a handful of continuously active volcanos in the world, and a member of an even more exclusive group: volcanos with lava lakes. While there are only five known volcanos with lava lakes globally, Erta Ale often has two active ones—making it an extremely unique site.

On day four of our trip, we made our way to the volcano by biking up to the small settlement of Askoma, navigating the jagged, volcanic rocks leading up to the village. As we laboured uphill on our bikes, the occasional convoy of tourists—mostly French scientists and photographers—driving to visit the volcano would cheer us on by shouting encouragements: 'Le Tour du Danakil!—Bravo ladies!' That always made us laugh and we waved back, grateful for the support.

We then forged on to the Erta Ale base camp, at the foot of the volcano, where we prepared to stay for the night. Because of the volcanic rock on the ground, it was impossible to pitch a tent; instead, we used one of the rudimentary stone shelters available at the campsite, which had no electricity or running water, as is the case throughout the Danakil Depression.

Already there was a camel caravan from Eritrea at the base camp. This is the traditional way of exporting goods to Ethiopia considering the arid landscape is landlocked. With not much to do at camp, we entertained ourselves by playing games like charade or just chatting amongst ourselves. I befriended one of the camels that kept staring at us and nicknamed him Jean-Francois, which made my teammates laugh. Mule also taught us a hack to cool the water in our bottles, by soaking toilet paper in water and wrapping it around our bottles, then putting the bottle somewhere where there was a little breeze. It actually works! Indeed, necessity is the mother of all invention, as they say.

The next day we hiked up ten kilometres to the rim of the volcano, with an elevation gain of about 600 metres, which took us two hours and forty minutes. There, in all its glory, was the world's longest-existing lava lake. It was everything I had envisioned: livid, fearsome, incandescent. The lava blistered and exploded, making us yawp in wonder. It was extraordinary, but less explosive than I had anticipated. The lava, which was not concentrated in a single vent, oozed, flowed and erupted across the vast amount of space in the caldera. We spent an hour watching it, filming it, taking pictures of it, committing it to memory. There were no safety railings so we could get as close as we wanted, but the strong toxic gases stung our eyes and made us cough; we had to cover our noses with a cloth.

After an hour, we decided we'd had enough of the toxic gases and descended back to camp. On the way down, we came across several groups of local men who stared in silence at our group of women; for a moment I wondered just how vulnerable we were. The risk of visiting Erta Ale is real and tangible. Indeed, it is an active volcano but what is more troubling is the tension that exists in the area because of the Eritrean-Ethiopian conflict. Despite our armed guards, I felt a bit unsafe. The area has experienced kidnappings and killings of tourists by local rebels, referred to by our guards as 'Eritrean Terrorists', and so I was profoundly relieved when we got back to our campsite safely.

The next two days of biking unfolded without any incidents. We had settled into our routine and arrived on schedule at Afdera, our final stop, where we swam in Lake Afrera, a beautiful hypersaline lake, and took a long-awaited bath in a natural hot spring nearby. It felt divine to just relax and bask in the pleasure of our accomplishment.

Indeed, this was one of our most gruelling expeditions, and the heat had made everything all the more exhausting. After much blood, toil, tears and sweat, our all-female team had successfully completed the first ever crossing of the Danakil Depression of Ethiopia on bicycles and it felt wonderful. 200 kilometres in six days over vastly contrasting terrain, from sand, sulphuric acid and salt, to bush, lava and volcanic rock. It had been one of our most arduous challenges, but we persevered, and every day we pushed on, finding resources we did not know we had.

Having Humility and Taking Responsibility

In retrospect, my only regret was that this expedition had been too close for comfort; the heatstroke we experienced on the first day could have taken a turn for the worse very quickly. The mistakes in logistics made by me and my co-founder, Valerie, the leaders of the pack and main organizers of this particular expedition, were an important lesson in humility. I swore I would never make such a mistake again. One of the most important leadership qualities, in my opinion, is having the courage to show your true self with all your vulnerabilities—not just your strengths. This is not easy to do. Acknowledging that you are not perfect and that you've made mistakes, but also understanding that you have a great capacity to learn from your mistakes and from your team is a vital quality for any leader to grow and improve after setbacks.

Indeed, it takes humility to admit to one's failures and mistakes. And yet, in my opinion, humility is one of the most noble qualities and one that authenticates a person's humanity. Having humility is vital to self-awareness and shows we care to listen and learn from others. Humble leaders understand they are not the smartest person in the room, nor do they need to be. They encourage their teams to have open dialogues and to speak up. They respect different opinions and will highlight good ideas regardless of where they come from. To this day I am thankful that everyone came away from this trip unharmed and well.

Additionally, the setback we experienced early in the trip highlighted to me the fact that the well-being and safety of the team was my absolute responsibility. Part of me felt that I had failed them; but through this experience, thankfully there were three other valuable lessons:

1. Leaders need to take full responsibility when things don't go as planned.
2. How you react to your mistakes is what defines you as a leader.
3. The importance of stepping aside to credit the team when things do go well.

These three points are such vital components of leadership. I now understand that it is about having that strength of character to withstand the blows and punches when things go wrong, as they inevitably sometimes do, while shielding your team, but giving absolute credit to the whole team when things go well. When a mission is successful, it means celebrating the team's accomplishment and shining the spotlight on the ones who deserve it the most, remembering the individuals who contributed to the overall objective, such as the ones who stepped up to help a teammate who was feeling low or sick during a particularly challenging time and the ones who brought everyone's morale up when the pack was going through a really difficult moment. These failures are defining moments for any leader—indeed, often, the biggest test of character and lesson in self-awareness—but also the real opportunity to be generous and elevate other teammates.

Throughout the journey in the Danakil Depression, we were rewarded by breathtaking, surreal landscapes—especially the almost unbelievable spectacle of bubbling molten lava when we hiked up to Erta Ale. Sitting a few feet from the rim of this magnificent active volcano, we felt completely transfixed and overwhelmed by Nature's raw power and might. However, the ultimate satisfaction for me had been how we had pushed ourselves far beyond our comfort zones for a cause that bonded us together: the plight of women survivors of war.

They said biking across the Danakil was impossible, it had never been done. We showed them that 'impossible' was just someone else's opinion. Challenges like these unveil the mysterious roots of perseverance that human beings possess and bring to the fore insights on how to make the best use of the traits we all possess, but rarely use to our fullest potential—grit, resilience, determination, courage and perseverance. Our team of women found resources deep inside us that we didn't even know we possessed, and it made all the difference.

In Mule's words, 'Women are capable of anything if they set their hearts and minds to it.' On the last evening, the whole Ethiopian crew shared in the celebration of our achievement and felt equally proud to have taken part in this extraordinary, pioneering crossing. It was truly a voyage to an otherworldly place, an unforgettable adventure to the most inhospitable place on earth—no wonder they call the Danakil Depression 'the Gateway to Hell'—and yet for me it was also one of the most valuable and humbling learning experiences of my life.

CHAPTER 11

Rwanda: A Success Story of Female Empowerment—2017

One of the most satisfying moments in the last few years was not on a trek or expedition, it was on a visit to Rwanda in Africa, which took place right after our Danakil Depression trip. We had planned it this way, because Ethiopia is right next to Rwanda, where the charity for which we were raising funds, Women for Women International, had a presence. We thought it would be a perfect opportunity to kill two birds with one stone, i.e., go on an expedition and simultaneously visit the programme it was supporting. We had been keen to see for ourselves the work of the charity we had supported for more than five years by then, but because they operate in war-torn regions, visits to their facilities had never been advisable until now.

Indeed, Rwanda is a country that is widely believed to be relatively stable since it has risen from the ashes of a civil war and genocide to become one of the fastest growing economies on the African continent. Two decades after the 1994 genocide that killed an estimated 800,000 people in 100 days, the great untold story of Rwanda's rise is how women rebuilt the nation and I knew from my research that Women for Women International had been a part of that movement, on the ground there, supporting women since 1997. In fact, they helped more than 77,000 Rwandan women move from crisis and poverty to stability and economic self-sufficiency. Thanks to their one-year programme, women progressed from cleaning buildings to reconstructing them. They started businesses throughout the country, creating stability in the aftermath of unspeakable violence.

During our visit to this tiny, 26,338 square kilometres of landlocked country at the heart of Africa, I discovered a nation that was incredibly clean, green and safe; so much so that it had even been dubbed the 'Singapore of Africa'. I learnt that Rwanda had a remarkably corruption-free government, where women hold key leadership roles and whose policies are cited as a model for gender inclusiveness.

After landing at Kigali International Airport, a small but immaculate and efficient facility—incidentally voted one of the best airports in Africa—I got chatting with a businessman in the immigration queue. As it turned out, he was a Singaporean economist collaborating with the government of Rwanda on a development project. At the time, I was working as a consultant with the philanthropic arm of Singapore's Sovereign Wealth Fund, Temasek Trust, and so I shared with him the work we were doing in helping countries build infrastructure and capacity. We found some common ground and he shared with me that since 2008, Singapore and Rwanda had signed a memorandum of understanding to provide a framework for public-sector collaboration. Since then, other partnerships have formed with some of the projects he was working on, and Rwanda also looked at Singapore's housing model for inspiration to develop green buildings and cities. Indeed, it was strangely comforting to discover that Rwanda had such a strong connection to Singapore.

On the drive in from the airport, Rwanda continued to impress me. Not a leaf or flower in the neatly manicured planters was out of place and not a single candy wrapper littered the pavements. The country was sparkling clean—very much like Singapore, if not cleaner!

Our guide, Alain, shared with us that progress had come to Rwanda because of the nature of its leadership. 'Rwanda's president, Paul Kagame, a former guerrilla who led an invading force to suppress the genocide, rules with an iron fist here, and allows little dissent. Seeing his country so devastated and broken because of the genocide, Kagame realized he needed the Rwandan women, who were the majority of survivors of the genocide, to step up and fill the vacuum.'

I couldn't wait to meet the management from Women for Women International the next day to learn more.

Stronger Women Build Stronger Nations

The following day, we met Antoinette Uwimana, country director of Women for Women International Rwanda at her office and she confirmed what Alain had said, 'A new constitution was passed in 2003 decreeing that 30 per cent of parliamentary seats be reserved for women. The government also pledged that girls' education would be encouraged and that women would be given leadership roles in the community and in key institutions. Women soon blew past the 30 per cent quota and today, with 63 per cent of its seats held by women, Rwanda's parliament leads the world in female representation.'

Antoinette and her team operate several women's centres and shelters across the country, and while giving us a tour of their office, she told us more about Rwanda's bloody history: 'After the genocide, Rwanda lay in ruins. Hundreds of thousands of cadavers were piled up on roadsides. Churches and schools were destroyed; offices and businesses plundered. Above all, the nation was traumatized by the horrific crimes that had decimated the population. Because most of those killed were men and because many male perpetrators fled to bordering nations, approximately 70 per cent of Rwanda's post-genocide population was female. Faced with ensuring their families' very survival, necessity bred innovation, women stepped up, and Women for Women International played an important part in the country's reconstruction.'

During our journey across Rwanda, we visited many of the Women for Women International centres where we saw with our own eyes how the programme participants and graduates were thriving as they put their newly acquired practical skills, such as basket-weaving, yogurt-making, beauty-care, jewellery-designing, brick-making, hospitality-management, and so much more, to good use. It was overwhelmingly moving to hear their personal stories of survival and their hopes and dreams for the future. I could see more clearly now how change starts at the heart of it all, with little steps at the grassroots level before it builds into a wave of palpable change.

As one proud graduate told us, 'I am no longer poor. I can now support my family by making bricks and selling them as part of my cooperative. My children go to school and we have enough to eat. I have you to thank for my good fortune.' These women are courageous, determined and hardworking survivors of a decimated generation. They told us their stories through songs and dance, with tears in their eyes. I was deeply moved by these encounters and even today, I often think of them and get emotional. They are a towering beacon of hope and resilience in a world often fraught with violence and hate—and true inspirations to me.

What is wonderful to realize is that life expectancy has doubled in Rwanda in the last twenty years. The country has built a near-universal health care system that covers more than 90 per cent of the population, financed by tax revenue, foreign aid and voluntary premiums scaled by income. Deaths of children under five have been cut in half. A compulsory education programme has put boys and girls in primary and secondary schools in equal numbers. Women can now own and inherit property and are active leaders in all sectors of the nation, including businesses, while national mandates are reducing violence against women. All these factors point to the fact that, despite its past trauma, Rwanda has come out on top.

Clearly, stronger women build stronger nations. And if one looks at the state of the world today, with over twenty brutal armed conflicts taking place at any given time and unprecedented levels of violence against women, there has never been a greater need to support such initiatives that truly change the world through education and economic empowerment.

Changing the World One Woman at a Time

This trip to Rwanda inspired me to deepen my knowledge of women's rights and leadership. Over the years, through my research, I've come to better understand the myriad issues women face around the world. Sadly, even today, in many parts of the world, being born female is dangerous for your health. In fact, for most women living in poor countries today, it is devastating. The danger starts even before birth. Sex-selection abortion is pervasive in many regions because parents decide, for various reasons, that they cannot bring another girl into the world. In China, India and Korea, thousands of girls have been prevented from being born, causing imbalance in the sex ratio. Poor people everywhere are at a disadvantage, but the gender differences are shocking.

The statistics paint a confounding picture:

- 77,000,000 girls worldwide, compared with 65,000,000 boys, do not go to school.
- Some 3,000,000 girls, most of them in Africa, are at risk of being genitally mutilated each year.
- HIV/AIDS is spreading fastest in one segment of the population: adolescent girls and young women.
- More than 350,000 women die each year from almost completely preventable childbirth-related injuries and illnesses.
- One fourth to one half of women worldwide suffer violence at the hands of an intimate partner.
- Three out of four fatalities of war are women and children.

As I've seen time and time again across the world, gender inequality doesn't just affect women, it affects everyone—women, men, trans and gender diverse people, children and families. It impacts people of all ages and backgrounds. This is why I continue to be an advocate of, and push for, more gender equality, so as to prevent violence against women and girls and increase economic prosperity for all.

Societies that value women and men as equal are safer and healthier. Gender equality is a human right after all, which should benefit everyone.

I care deeply about this issue, and I believe corporations, governments and society all have an important role to play in helping improve that parity. Today, women represent half the world's population and every day we are growing in economic power and influence, yet continue to be underrepresented in leadership roles. It is extremely important for women to continue to support and empower each other to push this agenda forward and history has shown us that, when women's voices are heard, the cycle of poverty becomes easier to break, children are healthier, environmental standards improve and socially constructive values are passed on with greater frequency to the young. What we are learning around the world is that, if women are healthier and have access to education their families flourish. And when families flourish, communities and nations thrive.

The trip to Rwanda and our wonderful encounters with the inspiring individuals of Women for Women International made me think a lot about my own growing-up years surrounded by very strong women in the Philippines. Unlike the women of Rwanda prior to the genocide, women in Philippine society have always enjoyed a greater share of equity. In fact, the Philippines is described as a nation of driven women, who directly and indirectly run the family unit, businesses, government agencies and haciendas, or plantation estates. We've had two women presidents thus far and the Philippines has been ranked number one by many surveys for women in business, with the country's female population holding senior positions at a far higher rate than the global average.

Over the past decade, I have also had the opportunity to learn about the challenges facing women in many other parts of the world. I have met working mothers in Greenland who talked about the challenges that climate change has caused in their community. I have spoken with women in Kenya who are taking leadership positions in their local communities to ensure young girls get a chance at a good education. I have met women in Iran who offered guidance and protection to young girls who came from broken homes. I have listened to women in Mongolia who told me how they were working every day to promote literacy and better health care for young girls in their country. Ultimately, I wholeheartedly believe in the potential of women to uplift their families, change a community, a nation and the world—for the better. And all these encounters have only reinforced my determination to push forward and empower and support women whenever I can.

Women's Rights

The great challenge of this age is to give a voice to women everywhere whose sacrifices and suffering go unnoticed, whose pleas go unheard. Women are the primary caregivers for most of the world's children and elderly, yet much of the work we do is undervalued by governments, societies and corporate leaders. Everywhere around the world today, women are giving birth, rearing children, preparing meals, planting crops, running businesses and leading countries. Women are also struggling to feed their children, prevented from getting an education, forced into servitude and prostitution, and in some parts of the world, denied the right to vote and own land.

Those of us who have a voice have a responsibility to speak up for those who cannot. And we must all recognize that women will never attain full freedom and dignity until their human rights are fully upheld. It's so tragic that in the twenty-first century women are still the ones whose human rights are violated, that rape continues to be used as an instrument of armed conflict, that so many women and girls around the world are denied basic rights and still forced into child marriages, forced to have abortions or be sterilized and brutalized by the painful and cruel practice of genital mutilation. Indeed, 'women's rights are human rights and human rights are women's rights' a phrase first used in the 1980s, and again in the mid-1990s by Hillary Rodham Clinton at the United Nations Fourth

World Conference on Women in Beijing, where she expounded on the fact it was time to act on behalf of women everywhere.

I am so grateful for the fact that my chance encounter with Valerie a decade ago changed the course of my life and made me transition into a life of meaning, purpose and adventure. And this in turn opened my eyes to the fact that so many women, even today, have no voice. They are deprived of the most basic freedom, the right to live in peace and happiness with their loved ones, the right to education and self-accomplishment, the right to live with respect and decency, the right to dream—even.

I believe with the strongest certitude that more women need to play a central role in decision-making at all levels of society. Clearly, we need to see more women in positions of power across the world. As witnessed in Rwanda, where women in leadership roles have completely reshaped the country for the better, it makes absolute sense to push the women-empowerment agenda forward. My experience there further invigorated my zeal and passion for gender equality, and this is why today I use my voice to convince as many people as possible that diversity does matter, not just in terms of principle but because it breeds innovation and innovation breeds business success. This topic has been the central theme and focus of my life over the past decade, it is at the very core of who I am today, and it is something I intend to pursue for many more years to come. Simply put, diversity is crucial for any ecosystem to adapt, grow and thrive successfully in the long term. I am convinced that only then will environmental sustainability, gender equality and peace become a true reality.

CHAPTER 12

Fly Like an Eagle Across Mongolia's Altai Mountains—2018

Six months after my return from Ethiopia and Rwanda, I led another WOAM team to Mongolia, and this time, swapped bikes for horses. Mongolia had been on my bucket list for the longest time, and I was thrilled to finally take a team there. Thus, in May 2018, I set out with fourteen women from Singapore and other parts of the world on a magnificent journey to the Altai Mountains, home of the famed Eagle Hunters, close to the border of Russia and Kazakhstan. Once again, in true WOAM tradition, we were set to raise $100,000 dollars for women survivors of war.

With the Eagle Hunters

The lone Kazakh rider galloped majestically towards us with a seven-kilogramme golden eagle perched on his arm, racing across the wide-open steppe on an ebony-coloured, Mongolian stallion. We watched transfixed as he approached, dressed in his traditional fox-fur cloak and hat with richly embroidered trousers, looking just as his ancestors must have looked some 2,000 years ago. He halted in front of us and smiled proudly as he greeted us warmly in the Kazakh language.

It had taken our all-female team two full days of travel to reach this extreme western part of Mongolia from the capital of Ulan

Bator—or UB as it is also known to locals. The Altai Mountains, a UNESCO World Heritage site, is located in the far western region of Mongolia. *Altai* means golden and the range is the largest and highest in the country with towering white mountains, glaciers, deep lush valleys and beautiful lakes. I was intrigued to discover Mongolia because my maiden name 'Huni', which is Swiss from my paternal grandfather's side, means Hun. Huns were warlike Asiatic nomadic people who invaded and ravaged Europe between the fourth and fifth centuries AD and who, originally, it is believed, came from the exact territory of today's Mongolia. So, in some ways, I felt this trip was a return to my roots.

Heavy snow and gale-force winds had resulted in significant delays to our itinerary and thus, when we finally arrived—after many hours of driving off-road, speeding across rocky trails and snow—and saw such an extraordinary rider appear before us, it only contributed to the feeling that this was one of the most remote places on earth.

The Kazakh Eagle Hunters of this region are a nomadic people spread throughout not just Kazakhstan but also in patches of Central Asia. For thousands of years, they have lived a life based around herding five types of animals—goats, yaks, sheep, Bactrian camels and horses—and have hunted with golden eagles. Still untouched by mass tourism and deeply steeped in their cultural roots and traditions, the local people have trained their eagles to hunt for food and fur—an essential part of the nomads' survival. The birds live for twenty-five years or so, and when they are twelve, they are repatriated to the wild, so they are able to breed and thus provide another generation of hunting birds.

For the first few nights of our journey, we were privileged to be hosted in our eagle-hunter's own family home. Bekhbolat, as he was called, lived with his parents, his wife, Mariya, and their three children. Upon entering the nomads' home, I immediately felt welcome in their midst as they shared their way of life and their provisions with us. They treated us like honoured guests. Nurka, our wonderful Kazakh guide, explained that in the past, harsh travelling conditions made nomads rely on each other, 'and this is why the Kazakhs have a strong tradition of being warm-hearted and hospitable,' she added proudly.

During our stay there, our team slept in traditional *ger* houses, which are incredibly comfortable circular tents covered with skins or felt, fabricated with wooden lattices for walls, a door frame and a crown of light wooden poles that join at the top for the roof. Chatting over hot tea, vodka, sweet clotted cheese and hard, dehydrated yoghurt, we learnt a lot about the family's life and their concerns for the future. We discovered that 30 per cent of Mongolians still live a nomadic life, but the number is dropping as the city-dwelling population increases. In truth, these resilient people are the remnants of a disappearing culture that has survived for ages, mostly in harsh, isolated conditions. The Mongolian climate is extreme and often unpredictable, with winter storms, droughts and desertification, all of which threaten the nomads' existence and affect their livelihood. Summer droughts have resulted in animals not gaining sufficient weight to withstand the ferocity of the freezing winters of late. Herding life is tough, and it seems winters have been even more severe than over the last decade.

Nomads of Mongolia

'Mongolian nomads have to adapt or die,' shared Nurka. 'For generations, their lifestyle survived, protected by their isolation. But, with improved transport and modern technology, things are changing very fast for Mongolia's remaining nomads. Their ancient traditional lifestyle has been impacted by technology, from mobile phones, motorcycles to iPads, mostly in a positive way, but sometimes I wonder if it's really for the better.' Nowadays, riding out to herd animals in Mongolia is often done on motorbikes instead of horses. And during our journey across the Tavan Bogd National Park, we came across such herders. Even the renowned shaman, Naraa, whom we consulted at our campsite one day, came riding across the plains on a gigantic motorbike.

Meeting the shaman was certainly one of the highlights of the trip. Naraa was warm and friendly with a wide, toothy smile. She spoke to each of us privately, answering our many questions and clarifying our doubts. She told me that my father, who had passed away twenty years ago, was well and looking down proudly at the woman I had become. This made me happy but also incredibly emotional. It felt good to think about him in this remote and beautiful place. After I spoke to Naraa, I sat quietly on the grass outside her tent to reflect on her words and sent up a silent prayer to Papa. The shaman inspired each one of us in a powerful way, asking us to meet her once again at dawn before we packed up camp, so that we could soak up more strength and energy from the sun's morning rays.

Mongolian shamanism is an animistic and shamanic ethnic religion that has been practised in Mongolia and its surrounding areas since the age of recorded history. When we first landed in UB, our guide there had told us about Mongolia's rich history, explaining that, during the soviet years of the twentieth century, shamanism had been heavily repressed and had since made a comeback. In reality, the nomads had adapted well to all these changes, but the speed of twenty-first-century progress was truly testing their resilience. Although technology could perhaps make their lives easier, such as with solar-powered generators and motorbikes, many nomads have moved into settlements in provincial towns and many more have relocated near the capital, where they have become semi-settled, neither here nor there. Those who move often struggle to make a living, since the towns lack easily available work for those with few skills or experience that don't involve milking or shearing.

After a few days with the Eagle Hunter's family, our team set off deeper into the mountains to discover the region. Western Mongolia is still relatively unexplored and we came across no other tourists during our time there. The journey took us into the vicinity of the 20-kilometre long Potanin glacier, which is the largest and most imposing of the twenty glaciers in the Mongolian Altai range. The views were magnificent, with the snow-covered peaks surrounding the glacier, and I could feel the land's ancient history under my very feet. Indeed, the region has been home to the hunters and herders since the Bronze Age.

We continued on to the Khuitas valley, where we successfully summited two iconic peaks over 3,300 metres in the surrounding area. Soaking in the profound silence, stunning views and vastness of the Altai Mountains from those mystical summits, was all the reward we could have asked for after the long hours of climbing.

Our trekking was punctuated by days of riding on nomadic Mongolian horses across the huge open plains. When not on the trail with us, our horses would roam free. Their normal life throughout the year includes grazing on natural pastures and living within a herd. Facing harsh, cold winters and fending off predators is also a part of their daily lives. Since they were used to moving in herds, as soon as one of us yelled 'Chu! Chu!', all the horses would start trotting and soon break into a gallop, flying across the steppe. The herders would howl with laughter as some of us clung on for dear life.

I will never forget the incredible sense of freedom I felt when riding in the Altai Mountains. It was a heady combination of adventure, exhilaration and deep relaxation. My mind would wander as we explored the steppes. And the wind on my face, as I rode in this magical setting, added to the overwhelming feelings of well-being and happiness inside me. Ultimately, the horseback riding was just phenomenal. Some days we would meander along rocky ridges, passing herders and their flock along the way and on other days we would traverse pristine streams and rivers, taking in the wide, blue skies, open spaces, magnificent snowy mountains and untouched lakes. On occasion, we would come across ancient petroglyph carvings, which illustrated the development of culture in Mongolia over a period of 12,000 years. The earliest images reflected a time when the area was partly forested and the valley provided a habitat for hunters of large game. Later images show the transition to herding and a horse-dependent, nomadic lifestyle as the dominant way of life—a real archaeologist's dream and a fascinating catalogue of the evolution of life in the region.

All in all, over a period of eight days, we traversed 900 kilometres of terrain on foot, on horseback and travelling in incredibly sturdy—and seemingly unbreakable—Russian minivans, dating back to the 1960s. Often, the Mongolian wind would blow unbelievably hard, reaching up to 90 km/h, and almost flattening our tents. The team also experienced hugely varying temperatures, ranging anywhere from bone-chilling −17° Celsius to a glorious 24° Celsius spring day.

During our time in the Altai Mountains, we bonded at a deeper level, sharing a lot of raw emotions and vulnerabilities but also finding solace and comfort in one another. A few of my teammates were going through some big changes in their personal lives. A couple of them were dealing with the pain of separation and divorce, another navigating the emotions of discovering her Mongolian roots for the first time, having grown up in France all her life, and coming to terms with the loss of her twin sister very early in life. As it had been for me after my separation from Mike, the mountains were generous with their healing powers and infused us with their therapeutic magic. Day by day, our sisterhood grew stronger and we felt rejuvenated by Mongolia's magnificent landscapes. I sometimes wonder if it was the encounter with the shaman that brought these feelings to the surface, or perhaps it was the incredible beauty of Mother Nature around us. This expedition was probably one of the most spiritually powerful ones I've ever experienced with a team of women. The exquisite simplicity of getting out into Nature removed the barriers around my ego, allowing me to be much more self-aware and helped me connect with my team at a deeper level. Everything was up close and real. On the last night out in the plains, we shared a celebratory dinner in one of the gers and took turns saying a few words about our time together. Tears of happiness and gratitude flowed freely that night. It was an unforgettable evening, filled with sisterly love and powerful emotions—and best of all, we were truly present in the moment.

The Eagle Huntress

Back in Ulgii, the capital of the Altai region, we met Aisholpan Nurgaiv, the first female eagle huntress of Mongolia who impressed us by her poise and intelligence. She became famous in Mongolia and beyond as the star of the 2016 documentary *The Eagle Huntress*.

The film shows thirteen-year-old Aisholpan, a herder's daughter, succeeding in the male-dominated world of hunting with eagles in the Altai Mountains. But Aisholpan, now seventeen, had done more than help break down gender stereotypes, she also shifted the attitudes of Mongolia's dominant ethnic group toward the country's Kazakh, Muslim minority, of which she was a part. Through her actions, she inspired other young Kazakh women to venture into an arena long dominated by men, not all of whom welcome their new rivals.

From the moment she walked in to meet us at the local tavern where we had arranged to have lunch together, she was warm and friendly. Aisholpan shared that she had been looking forward to meeting us and had read up on WOAM and our expeditions. As we feasted with her on traditional Mongolian meat dishes, serenaded by musicians playing the *dombra*—a long-necked lute with two strings and the oldest Kazakh musical instrument—she told us about her hopes to find a way to improve the condition of the Kazakh people in her community—demonstrating a maturity far beyond her years. She may practise an ancient discipline in a remote part of the world, but I found her to be incredibly modern and aware of the issues which women face around the world. Aisholpan is a young woman with plenty of ambition who knows, without a shadow of doubt that she can be as strong or brave as any man.

As with many of our WOAM trips, we made it a point to connect with women's groups locally to better understand the issues they face in the country we are visiting. And thus, our voyage culminated with a visit to the NCAV, or the Centre Against Violence back in Ulaanbaatar, where we conducted workshops around psychotherapy, social entrepreneurship and shared more about the work we do with the devoted social workers at the centre. The time spent sharing our experiences and connecting with women locally is incredibly uplifting and adds a meaningful dimension to our WOAM treks. It makes my teammates connect at a deeper level and allows them to contribute, not simply by fundraising, but by sharing their own life and career experiences. At the NCAV, we also met the women and children survivors of domestic violence, who were temporarily housed in their shelters. Understandably, they seemed shy and downcast. I could only imagine their trauma and despair at having to find shelter in a home.

We learnt from the social workers at NCAV that over the last seventeen years they had worked incessantly and systematically to develop a system of comprehensive services for victims of domestic and sexual violence and raise public awareness on gender equality and human rights. Although Mongolia has done well on some facets of gender equality, Mongolian women still face problems and the rates of violence and evident power imbalances remain significant challenges.

Furthermore, we were shocked to learn that a recent survey had highlighted that Mongolia had one of the highest rates in Asia of sexual violence at the hands of people who were not the victims' partners. On the other hand, one out of three women there (31.2 per cent) who had ever been in a relationship had experienced physical or sexual violence at the hands of a partner in their lifetime. The most dangerous place is the home, followed by out on the streets. One out of ten women said she was sexually abused before the age of fifteen. We learnt that the two major triggers were jealousy and alcohol consumption by their partners. It was an eye-opening day to say the least and only strengthened our commitment to stay connected with the NCAV once back in Singapore, to continue our support and mentorship.

Indigenous Communities Living in Harmony with Nature

As I look back on this voyage to the Altai Mountains of Mongolia, I can truly say that it was a spiritually enriching experience on many levels. The strong bond of sisterhood I forged with my teammates was deeply meaningful and remains intact to this day. This expedition will always be etched in my heart and in my soul. But the most important gift for me was learning from indigenous communities such as the Kazakh Eagle Hunters, who continue to live in harmony with Nature. I was inspired to learn about how they capture, train and keep eagles in a highly ritualized manner. It takes a dedicated 3 to 4 years to train them and requires constant daily attention. The eagles are tamed by tethering them by their ankles with leather straps to a wooden block on a rawhide line. Every time they try to fly away they flip upside down. After two days or so the eagles are exhausted and tame. Training continues by dragging a fox fur behind a galloping horse. I enjoyed witnessing how the Kazakhs act and speak with a deep respect for the life and health of natural ecosystems and how they understand and recognize that their survival and livelihoods depend on Nature. It highlighted for me the urgent need to preserve and safeguard the knowledge and practices of indigenous people like them, so that we may integrate their indispensable insights into our way of life and conservation efforts.

To many Kazakhs, a mountain is a goddess not just a pile of rocks, a river is a fertile deity to the land it flows through, not merely a source or a tool to be exploited for irrigation. A forest is a sacred area, not just a place to get timber. If we think of the earth as our mother, surely, we would respect her more. For indigenous peoples something that is sacred cannot be bought. Land is not just property to them but a place they can hunt or where their ancestors are buried and where their ceremonies take place. Their land is what gave them life. They are part of it; they understand that it should be shared and thus they honour it as a gift from the gods. Every stone, every tree has a voice, a story to tell. The Kazakh Eagle Hunters listen to the wind; it's a form of enhanced mindfulness and to me there is nothing more precious than regarding Nature this way.

HER Planet Earth

Five years after setting up WOAM, in 2017, I became increasingly frustrated and alarmed by what I was reading in the news; by what I was seeing around me in Nature during some of my expeditions. I was horrified by the destruction of our planet's ecosystems, the pollution of our oceans, the burning of our forests and shocked at the increasing havoc that climate change was wreaking on impoverished and indigenous populations. Climate change is, in fact, the most critical challenge facing humanity today and I was feeling powerless. What could I do to make a difference? So, I decided to inform myself, to better understand this crisis that was gripping our planet. And the more research I did, the more I realized that despite the fact that climate change is a global phenomenon, its effects are felt locally and poor people suffer the most.

The statistics revealed that, of the 1.3 billion poor people around the world, the majority are women. Furthermore, in all the chaos surrounding the news about climate change, I noticed that gender often remains the untold story behind it all. In many countries around the world, women still number amongst those who are most vulnerable to climate change and environmental degradation. They are hit the hardest. Partly because women make up the larger share of the agricultural workforce and tend to have less access to income-earning jobs.

I also realized, through my research and especially through my past expeditions, that women and Nature share an undeniable rapport. In fact, we are completely interlinked, and this relationship is as old as time. Women have a cultural and symbolic connection with Nature through the characterizations of Mother Earth and this connection has been reinforced throughout history via religion, philosophy and other cultural norms.

This is why, in May 2017, I decided to set up my second NGO, HER Planet Earth, because I wanted to support underprivileged women affected by climate change. As I learnt more about the plight of women impacted by climate change, I also realized that, despite the fact that women are the most vulnerable group when it comes to climate, we are also a huge part of the solution. In fact, one of the best ways to mitigate climate change is to empower, educate and invest in women and help them build livelihoods that are compatible and in harmony with Nature.

CHAPTER 13

Surfing in Siargao—Asia's Newest Resort Destination—2017

One of my first trips with HER Planet Earth was to my home country of the Philippines in October 2017. I took twelve women on a surfing experience for four days to the island of Siargao, located 800 kilometres southeast of the Philippine capital, Manila, in the province of Surigao del Norte. There we pushed ourselves to our limits to support a local environmental NGO called Nature Kids of Siargao that promotes and encourages the collection and recycling of plastic from the beaches to convert into reusable items like bean bags or beach bags to be sold at local hotels.

There is no doubt that tourism is a double-edged sword. On the one hand it brings about awareness of a beautiful place, economic development and prosperity for the local population; on the other, the exposure often leads to over pollution, damage of the ecosystem and ultimately, the ruin of the local community. I was overwhelmed with a sense of excitement and dread during my visit to Siargao, the teardrop-shaped island, one of the 7,000-plus islands making up the Philippine archipelago, which, at the time, was standing at the threshold of a massive tourism boom.

The island is known as the surfing capital of the Philippines with its famous break called Cloud 9, a fast and powerful fiend with monumental tubes that sweep in from the Pacific Ocean. Local legend has it that a drug runner-turned-surfer put Cloud 9 on the map—and in the decades since, it has drawn world pros for international tournaments, including the Siargao International Women's Surfing Cup sanctioned by the World Surf League since May 2017.

When I visited Siargao with my HER Planet Earth team, it seemed as if everyone on the island had turned into a real-estate broker. Locals and foreign developers alike were snatching up beachfront property. Big hotel and resort chains had staked their claim on prime, ocean-facing acreages. Foreign chefs and entrepreneurs were moving to Siargao, setting up boutique hotels, restaurants, coffee shops, lounge bars, retails shops and even a casino was in the works.

Yet the island was not well known even to Filipinos until a few years ago. Before the airport opened in 2011, getting to the island meant an overnight ferry ride from Cebu. Today there are many direct flights, which operate daily from Manila and Cebu, with an international airport rumoured to be in the pipeline in the next few years.

I first heard about Siargao, in 2007 from my brother-in-law, Gregoire, who loves to surf. He mentioned the island to me in passing as a dream place to visit one day, but it was not until I set foot there with my teammates that I realized Siargao was so much more than just a surfer's paradise. From the outset, I was enchanted. Surrounded by crystal-clear, turquoise waters, covered in coconut palms and home to some of the most beautiful beaches, I felt I had indeed landed in paradise.

I had heard from a friend who had invested in a property there that the island was at a pivotal time in its development, quickly getting a reputation as Asia's newest heartthrob resort destination. Indeed, it has so much to offer: not just stunning beaches, but also enchanting lagoons, forty-eight islets, coral reefs, unusual rock formations, exotic wildlife—including crocodiles! It boasts endless rice fields, waterfalls, large mangrove forests and of course, world-class surfing—it really has so much at stake. I couldn't help but wonder whether Siargao would be able to escape the fate of islands such as Boracay, Phuket or Bali, which have sadly turned into over-developed, over-crowded and over-polluted resort meccas.

While speaking about this to one of my teammates, Pia de Lima, who is based in Siargao and who runs the Siargao Environmental Awareness (SEA) Movement, which focuses on marine conservation, she shared that she believes this is achievable if we act now. The SEA movement community which she belongs to is made up of surfers, artists, writers, entrepreneurs, journalists and policymakers who want to preserve the natural resources and beauty of the island of Siargao, while developing it in a sustainable way to provide jobs and opportunities for the local community. 'It is crucial that all sectors—government, businesses and NGOs—work together to tackle the risk of environmental degradation. As the influx of tourism keeps intensifying, empowering the local community is vital so that it doesn't remain passive to the changes taking place. For starters, we need a proper waste management system, both solid and sewage. This is by far the biggest challenge facing the island. We also require access to good medical facilities, affordable and quality education, typhoon-proof housing, clean water, a sustainable tourism plan and real jobs with salaries. These things should be prioritized over international airports and massive bridges,' she said.

Ultimately, I chose Siargao because I longed to experience the thrill of surfing in this emerging paradise, but more importantly, because I wanted to support a local NGO that was making waves in conservation and contributing to keeping the island clean while helping the local community. A friend introduced me to the founder of Nature Kids of Siargao, a Swedish lady called Sunny, and I learnt that she had left her native Sweden a few years ago, to create a more meaningful life for herself in Siargao.

I found Sunny's work inspiring and impactful and spoke with her extensively prior to our trip to better understand the programmes she had set up focused on addressing the growing trash problem of Siargao, while educating local children about becoming eco warriors in their communities. I felt her NGO was a perfect partner for our

first HER Planet Earth expedition and we were happy to support her
with our fundraising and awareness raising.

Lesson from Surfing in Siargao

During our few days on the island, the team and I explored the
surrounding white sand islets, enjoyed stand-up paddle boarding in
the turquoise lagoons and surfed to our heart's content at the famed
Cloud 9 beach, which was a remarkable and challenging experience
in itself. For many of us it was our first time surfing and a big push
outside our comfort zone. Cloud 9's thick, hollow tubes make it ideal
for surfing, and the waves had plenty of swell. These extra inches
of water lifted us comfortably above the reef, which otherwise
lurked perilously close to the surface of the water. Cloud 9 also has
a fantastic wooden boardwalk and a three-storey viewing platform at
the very end from where you can look down the coast to the east for
sunrises or to the west for the breathtaking sunset views.

Surfing was not easy and finding the right balance to stay on
the board took time and effort. Indeed, surfing is one of the most
difficult and complex sports in the world with elements such as
wind, time of the day and swells affecting the waves differently.
It was challenging but enjoyable too. The hardest part about surfing,
by far, was paddling out, not surfing in. Carrying the board, getting
back into the water, paddling through the waves, waiting for the
next set. It was exhausting and I realized that surfers expend far
more time and energy doing this exercise than on the surfing itself.
I learnt that to surf you have to have courage because you are
battling an ever-changing environment, and everyone needs to go at
their own pace. Some of my teammates got the hang of it right away,
while others needed several hours, or days even. I managed to get up
after a few hours but never managed to stay on the board for long;
I needed much more practice and through this experience, I gained a
new-found respect for professional surfers.

What was wonderful about the experience was that I quickly
discovered that the sport teaches you some invaluable life lessons

too. Firstly, surfing forces you to pay attention and to recognize a good wave, a great wave and a bad wave. It's often a subtle thing and determining when to make your move takes some practice and experience, but the only wave a surfer ever regrets, is the one they let pass by. Life is very similar. Most people tend to regret the things they didn't do, the chances they didn't take, rather than anything they ever did. Surfing helps you develop good judgement to know when to seize an opportunity, and this sense of decisiveness is an invaluable life skill to hone and develop.

Secondly, finding balance. If there's one thing you have to have to surf, it's balance. The exciting thing, though, is that finding balance when you surf is a constantly changing endeavour. Water can be a little unpredictable, as can the energy flowing through it; so, even if you eventually find the right balance to stand up, you can't rest on your accomplishment. You must continuously seek to retain that balance to see it through to the end. Surfing teaches you that doing the work to maintain your balance is entirely worth it.

Lastly, surfing teaches you to lean into life. Surfing is not like walking, climbing or jumping. Surfing is the pinnacle of understanding your environment, working with it and being attuned to your mind, heart and body. You have to develop trust that you can bend this way or that way to maintain yourself and to keep going forward. You can't just stand there or the power of the wave will knock you right over. Life is like that as well. Once you jump into life, you have to lean into it. You have to lean whichever way you must to keep moving forward, even when logic tells you it doesn't make sense. It's the only way to keep making progress.

The Importance of Sustainable Tourism

As we met more local residents like Sunny and Pia during our idyllic sojourn in Siargao, we discovered a growing community of passionate environmentalists focused on preserving the pristine beauty of the island. So many of their values aligned with HER Planet Earth's: protecting the environment, the natural resources and the wildlife;

providing socio-economic benefits for local communities to live in harmony with Nature; conserving cultural heritage and creating authentic and sustainable opportunities and experiences for tourism that will allow the local ecosystem to thrive. It made me all the more determined to plan my next HER Planet Earth expeditions around supporting solid programmes that impact the local communities positively and support women, especially, so as to strengthen their resilience in the face of climate change.

Thankfully, Siargao is now classified as a conservation area and in the last few years, the Philippine government's department of science and technology announced that it would bring Eco-Sep to Siargao. Eco-Sep is a septic water management system technology, which will stop contamination of wastewater in sewage systems. It's a start, and programmes like these can certainly impact the development of Siargao in a positive way in the long run, but so much more needs to take place. It's increasingly clear that if the government continues to put in place the right infrastructure, if the local community and developers make environmental conservation a top priority and if local NGOs like the SEA Movement and Nature Kids of Siargao continue to get a say in the island's development plans, then Siargao will have a fighting chance of growing in a sustainable way.

CHAPTER 14

Scaling Antarctica's Vertical Limits—2018

Four months after my surfing trip to Siargao, in January 2018, I was getting ready to embark on a very different kind of expedition. This involved being away from home for almost a month and travelling 10,000 kilometres to the ends of the earth. I was heading to Antarctica with an all-female team to climb new peaks. This was something I had always dreamt of doing. I remember it like it was yesterday and the experience will count, without a doubt, as one of the proud moments of my life.

Landing in Union Glacier

Goaded by a mighty tailwind the massive Ilyushin IL-76 TD aircraft hurtled southwards at a velocity approaching 495 mph (800 km/h). The Drake Passage below sparkled to a far horizon as we made our way westward from Punta Arenas in Chile, to the Antarctic Peninsula and finally to Union Glacier, a private airbase operated by Antarctic Logistics and Expeditions (ALE), located in the Heritage Range, below the Ellsworth Mountains.

After four and a half hours in the air, we landed on the Blue Ice Runway, a rare and naturally occurring ice strip that is solid enough to support the weight of this monstrous Soviet military aircraft. It was a freezing −15° Celsius as we got off the plane and took our first steps on Antarctica.

The vast ocean of white unfolding before my eyes looked simply magnificent. I could see the sun ablaze in the blue, polar sky while the fierce wind made me literally moonwalk on the frozen runway as I tried to move from the plane to the four-wheel drive waiting to take us to the main camp.

'January is the heart of summer in Antarctica,' we were told by one of the ALE staff, 'it's the best time to visit, because the weather is the least hostile.' Indeed, man has never permanently inhabited this remote landmass. Accessible only during its warmest months, from November to March, it has no metropolis or village to speak of, no habitat except perhaps the odd expedition shed or research station. It's all just massive, desolate, glacial emptiness and bone-chilling temperatures that can range anywhere from −10° to −80° degrees Celsius during the colder months.

Our all-female team reached Union Glacier Camp in ten minutes, and after a quick tour of the main facilities, we were assigned to the dual occupancy 'clam' tents. Each tent is named after a polar explorer: mine was named Worsley, after Henry Worsley, a British explorer and Army Officer who was part of the successful 2009 expedition that retraced Ernest Shackleton's footsteps in the Antarctic. Worsley died in 2016, just two years before we arrived, while attempting to complete the first solo and unaided crossing of the Antarctic. I earnestly hoped this was not going to be a bad omen.

Most of us had come from equatorial Singapore and it had taken us over forty-eight hours to get here. No wonder settling in felt so good. I found the tents to be surprisingly comfortable, with their double-lined insulated walls, large 'doors' and tall interiors, which allowed us to stand upright and move around easily, as we sorted out our gear. I was beyond excited and couldn't yet process that I had actually made it here. Looking outside the tent, I could see the Ellsworth Mountains in the distance and behind me the 1,450-metre Mount Rossman, which was a lot further than it looked. Apart from the other tents, all around me was just ice, snow and rock—no trees, no plants, no anything else.

We spent the first few days at Union Glacier brushing up on our climbing skills and getting acclimatized to the Antarctic conditions. The team practised rope work, crevasse rescue, navigation, weather observations and polar camping skills. During this period, we also discussed our objectives with our guides, two incredibly qualified female climbers who had extensive mountaineering experience in polar conditions.

I felt we were in very good hands as they had both climbed in Antarctica many times before and I had no doubts that the next few days, as we went further inland to explore unchartered territory, would be nothing short of extraordinary. In addition to our thirst for adventure, we had a very clear goal in mind. Our group of six was on a quest for new routes and peaks in the surrounding mountain ranges. The bottom line was, I wanted my HER Planet Earth team to use this pioneering challenge to raise awareness and funds for UN Women's Lead Climate Action programme that empowers and educates underprivileged Asian women most affected by climate change—ultimately helping them build climate change resiliency. This UN initiative was focused on rural women in developing countries that were already feeling the brunt of climate change, and the first country on the agenda for this programme was Cambodia, considered one of the most vulnerable to the impacts of climate change such as droughts, floods and sea-level rise.

I chose Antarctica because it is a powerful symbol of this struggle as it is also fighting for its own survival. Not only are geopolitical pressures and interest in its natural resources escalating, but Antarctica's incredible biodiversity is threatened by climate change. In fact, Antarctica, the world's largest desert, which is 98 per cent covered in ice, is melting at an alarming rate. The continent is losing large chunks of ice the size of cities from its coastline as a result of global warming, and when these icebergs melt and raise sea levels, this could have catastrophic consequences for our planet. To put this into context, although predictions for the extent and rate of sea-level rise vary greatly, if all of Greenland were to melt, it would raise sea levels by six metres, but if Antarctica were to melt, this would raise the sea level by sixty-five metres. And at this current rate, a land area housing 300 million people will be flooded annually by 2050. Indeed, this cause becomes more urgent every single day.

After a few days at Union Glacier, we were ready to explore. We were planning to drive half a day away on a massive snow tucker and explore from there. The whole Heritage mountain range is spread over multiple glaciers with many hidden crevasses. So, before we headed out, ALE used a thermal scanner over the area to check that it was safe enough to traverse.

'Only once did a vehicle fall in a crevasse not far from Union Glacier camp,' we were told. 'No one died, the driver managed to be pulled out unharmed.' This made us wish we hadn't asked. The views from the truck's window were just awe-inspiring, all around us were virtually untouched alpine peaks. Since Antarctica is a desert, it does not rain or snow a lot there. When it does snow, the snow does not melt and builds up over many years to make large, thick sheets of ice, called ice sheets. I was fascinated to hear from our guides that the terrain is covered by as much as 3,000 metres of ice. Entire mountain ranges are buried under this ice and for the few peaks that are visible, only the very tops break the surface.

Despite our reservations about the crevasses lurking below us, our team set out in high spirits with a generous supply of food, our camping gear and climbing equipment. We knew that, depending on how the weather behaved, we could be out there for several days. We were all aware from our research that the climate in Antarctica is extremely volatile and conditions can often change dramatically and very suddenly. So, as we prepared to leave, we hoped for the best but planned for the worst.

Setting Out

As soon as we reached the Larsen Valley, an area which is largely unexplored, we pitched camp for the night. This time the tents were very basic, unlike the clam tents at Union Glacier, which now felt like the Hotel Shangri-La in comparison. We shovelled snow over the flaps all around the base of the tents to ensure the glacial wind would not get through as we prepared for our first night, out alone in the wild. In all this landscape, in this vast space, we were the only living things for miles around, with not a single animal in sight. Like tiny dots in the middle of nowhere, our location was the very essence of remote. I felt isolated but also filled with an incredible sense of freedom. The air was so pure and clean; I filled my lungs and was overwhelmed with a sense of gratitude to be able to experience such an adventure. Antarctica, being the only continent on earth without a native human population, allows you to disconnect like no other continent can. I could shout as loud as I wanted, and it wouldn't matter; apart from my teammates, no one would notice because there is absolutely nothing alive out there, just snow and ice.

Over the next few days our team set out on multiple exploratory climbing trips that varied from hard technical ascents to magnificent ridge traverses with views over the Ronne Ice Shelf and Polar Plateau. We attempted steep ice and snowy couloirs, classic ridge traverses, icy crests, rock pyramids, hidden valleys, and finally, unclimbed peaks! It felt incredible to know that no one had ever trodden on the place where we were standing.

We were blessed with good weather for the most part and therefore our determined group was able to establish several new routes, claim the first female ascent of one peak and the first ascents of two unclimbed mountains. As a result, we earned the right to name these two new peaks. The first, a beautiful mountain with incredible ridges was christened Mount Gaia in celebration of HER Planet Earth. Gaia is ancient Greek for the Goddess Earth. The second mountain was named Mount Malala in honour of the Nobel Peace prize winner, Malala Yousafzai, who embodies courage and female empowerment in the face of injustice and violence. I had read her book *I am Malala* and had been inspired by her incredible story and ordeal at the hands of the Taliban. She had survived a gunshot wound to the head when she was just fifteen and refused to be silenced then went on to fight for her right to an education. Indeed, Malala represents everything I want to champion.

After several days camping and climbing under the 24-hour Antarctic sun, I lost all sense of time and space in this immense white expanse. The days were endless and the light was like no other light on Earth, because the air is so free of impurities in Antarctica. During our climb, we confronted both the physical challenges of the adventure and our own human vulnerabilities. The scale of the emptiness was at times almost too much to absorb and the sense of isolation, overwhelming. I felt my emotions welling up to the surface and despite being aware of the feelings of happiness I was experiencing, tears would slowly course down my cheeks sometimes, while I was climbing, because I was so deeply touched by the enormity and beauty of this experience.

Our days of climbing were long and arduous and we were constantly alert for hidden crevasses on the route. On two occasions, one of us fell partly into the throat of a crevasse, but we were roped together at all times in groups of three, fifteen metres apart, so thankfully, no one was lost to the depth of the ice.

We encountered unpredictable weather on occasion, with icy winds and low clouds forcing us to turn around on several occasions. Even when the summit ridge appeared so close that we thought we could almost touch it, we knew that distances were deceptive and things could appear closer than they really were in such conditions. If the weather continued to degrade as we climbed higher, it could endanger the whole team, so we did the right thing and descended back to camp. Indeed, in those instances, poor judgement kills, adaptability is key. A topographic map only tells you part of the story; it does not show you the changing weather, transitory snow, recent glacier movement and human exhaustion or injuries. No matter the terrain, unpredictable factors, especially in Antarctica, are inevitable, therefore we needed to be flexible, cautious and know when to pivot.

On the days that the weather held and we were able to summit, the sense of achievement and pride was truly indescribable.

The team was ecstatic and felt that the spirits of legendary female explorers were cheering us on pushing us forward to new frontiers on our Antarctic sojourn. Despite the exhaustion, the painful sprains and bruises, the frost nip on our extremities—cold injury due to vasoconstriction—and the fact that on one occasion, part of the team got stuck on a very steep and technical mountain face for close to twenty-four hours; the whole experience turned out to be unbelievably rewarding. It taught me, in particular, how to get difficult things done in a challenging environment and showed me that no matter the challenge, the fear and self-doubt, in the end, you are the only authority on your own potential. Antarctica, subject to such extreme conditions, has a natural beauty and raw exquisiteness that draws you in, and pushes you to surpass your own expectations.

What Antarctica Means for our Planet's Survival

Our mission accomplished, we headed back to Union Glacier camp, where we met renowned climbers and polar explorers. One of the highlights of the trip was meeting Sir Robert Swan, the first person to walk to both Poles and one of my own personal heroes. Robert was sitting in the main dining tent with his son, Barney, when we walked in. He stood up when I approached to say hello and was friendly and warm when I introduced myself. Apart from having an incredibly charismatic presence, Robert has striking, ice-blue eyes, the result of his walking through a hole in the ozone layer during his trek to the South Pole many years ago, which permanently changed his eyes from dark to light blue. Robert is deeply passionate about adventure and about protecting the integrity of Antarctica and, in fact, when I met him, he was just getting ready to ski with Barney and his team to the South Pole using only renewable energy, to promote the development and use of clean-energy solutions.

As we got chatting, he reminded me that, 'the real Antarctic explorers of seventy-five years ago, Scott, Shackleton and Amundsen used ponies and dogs. They had teams of fifty people or more. It is much easier to explore Antarctica today, but it also means that we have to listen to what the region is telling us; and if we don't, we will end up putting our own survival at risk.' Conversing with him reminded me that Antarctica, this vast continent at the very edge of the earth, while generally inhospitable, is also a place of hope. The youth of today are the ones who will continue to inspire and teach us new lessons. They will be the ones to come up with innovative solutions for our planet's well-being. To underscore, we all need to recognize that dreams can come true and that small actions together can result in massive change and movement. Robert's biggest piece of advice was to continue to inspire the youth and people of all ages to do their part, no matter how small. 'It takes commitment to make anything happen. It's really that simple,' he said, with a twinkle in his eyes.

Uniquely, Antarctica remains the only landmass that humans have yet to exploit for its resources. No one actually owns Antarctica. It is the last real great wild continent and is protected by the Antarctic Treaty, signed in 1959. The twelve countries that regulate the continent today are adamant that it should remain free from pollution and bacteria. This means that all waste, including human waste, is taken out of Antarctica where nothing decomposes because of the freezing conditions.

Looking back on our expedition, I now see that Terra Antarctica, as it is also known, has a way of cutting you down to size and making you ponder your own insignificance. Becoming the first to summit unclimbed peaks as an all-female team was such a transformational and empowering experience. While I was still absolutely committed to support women affected by violence via my WOAM expeditions and advocacy, my dedication to women impacted by climate change was equally strong and co-existed in parallel.

The expedition to Antarctica forced me to re-evaluate everything I knew and felt about myself and my place on this planet. I realized that I had to continue to live and breathe my advocacy, and find ways to contribute and make a difference. That mission was crystal clear. It also made me see that one of the most valuable lessons of the journey was the realization that the preservation of Antarctica is completely linked to our survival and health here on Earth. If we develop innovative solutions or use more renewable energy in the real world, there will be no financial reason to go out and drill for those resources in Antarctica. Sooner, rather than later, humanity needs to find a way stop this great melting of the ice that threatens us all. It is a big challenge and we are all responsible. Perhaps the fact that no one owns Antarctica means that we can be successful in this endeavour of protecting it. As Robert succinctly put it, 'Antarctica is a moral line in the snow,' and on one side of that line we do nothing and stand idle while others try to exploit it, while on the other, we fight so that this beautiful, virgin, hypnotic place be left alone. No wonder they say, Antarctica gets under your skin, and when that happens, your soul is changed forever.

CHAPTER 15

Sailing for Conservation in the Philippine Islands—2018

It took me a few months to recover from my expedition to Antarctica. I returned home to Singapore physically, mentally and emotionally exhausted despite being elated by the achievement. Perhaps, I was just overtired . . . Furthermore, for a few weeks, my extremities were slightly numb from the tail end of the frostbite. Also, going from twenty-four hours of unremitting sunlight and a desert of snow, to the concrete jungle of the equatorial city state of Singapore was, to put it mildly, a shock to the system. I would be waiting in the street for a cab after work, and the city's noises would be overwhelming, almost offensive. From being the only people for miles to being back in a bustling, congested city, the stimulus was just too much. I realized that I had a mild case of post-expedition depression—something I had never experienced before. After the intensity, the promise, the blisters, the hurdles, the challenge and the focus of having a daily target, life back home just seemed a little anticlimactic. Of course, I was happy to see my family, and they were happy to have me back, but no matter how much I told them about my trip, they couldn't really relate. Thankfully I had another exciting expedition planned in a few months, back to the Philippines, and this was exactly what I needed to concentrate on to get my groove back.

This time I was taking my HER Planet Earth team sailing through the islands of Palawan, one of the most remote and astounding corners of the Philippine archipelago. I had been to this part of the country before as a child on holiday with my parents, and even as an adult a few years ago, but I had never done the kind of sailing we were about to embark upon. I was thrilled to return to a country so close to my heart, and especially to support another grassroots NGO, called the Tao Kalahi Foundation, which empowers local communities and teaches them to care for the land and grow organic fruit and vegetables, as a solution to over fishing.

They say the best journeys run deep and reconnect us with what it means to be human. Our sailing expedition to Palawan, turned out to be exactly that—a deeply inspiring and revitalizing voyage of self-discovery and exploration. We spent an adventurous week sailing on a stunning traditional 74-foot paraw sailboat, the largest in the Philippines, which is a revival of an almost forgotten Filipino maritime culture dating back to more than 1,000 years. Natural splendour abounded as we camped on deserted, white-sand beaches, swam through turquoise waters peppered with brilliant tropical fish, snorkelled around World War II shipwrecks, sampled native delicacies and simply revelled in the purity and wild wilderness of one of Nature's last ecological frontiers. I enjoyed myself tremendously on this journey and reconnected with my childhood love of feeling like Robinson Crusoe.

Our HER Planet Earth team of explorers was formed by ten intrepid women from diverse careers and backgrounds, who hailed from all corners of the world. Some of them had never been to the Philippines and so I was particularly proud to show off my home country through this unique sailing experience. And once again, as with my other HER Planet Earth expeditions, what brought us all together in the first place, apart from our adventurous spirit and a yearning to push our boundaries, was a genuine desire to empower underprivileged women and to protect our beautiful planet.

We began our expedition in El Nido and made our way to Coron, meandering through the beautiful Linapacan island group. From the outset, the weather and tides dictated the itinerary and schedule. The wind, in this part of the world, blows strong and steady. It is sunny almost all the time, and there are literally thousands of islands in the Philippines—7,107 at the last count. Just a few days prior to our departure, a storm had prevented boats from setting sail from El Nido, so I was keeping my fingers crossed that this would not affect us. Luckily, the weather gods were on our side and as we embarked on our journey, the sun came out and shone brightly in the pale blue sky.

The fair weather lasted throughout most of our trip, allowing us to combine stretches of pure, calm sailing with exploration of the islands, the reefs and even the caves that were carved into towering grey limestone cliffs, that our boat's captain, Gener, estimated to be over 250 million years old. Palawan, a UNESCO Biosphere Reserve, literally looks like a Jurassic world, with its dramatic, jagged-rock faces and lush green, tropical foliage. When we arrived at our base camp on the first night, we left the boat safely anchored in the bay, while we swam noiselessly ashore with the full moon suspended in the pitch-black sky above our heads to guide us. It felt absolutely magical, and I was transported right back to those first years in Boracay when I had found my fireflies on the deserted beach.

Around the campfire that night, Captain Gener shared with us that Tao, the company that owned our paraw boat, had been founded by eco-conscious British and Filipino entrepreneurs, almost a decade ago. They started out by running sailing trips across the islands, establishing a network with local families and fishermen. Today, they have grown it into a social enterprise that aims to immerse participants into the true Filipino island life, while at the same time supporting the remote communities of northern Palawan. In Tagalog, the official language of the Philippines, *Tao* means 'human', and on their website it says that they aim to use tourism as a tool to build a world that they share with other dreamers and adventurers. Their mission is to empower local communities in a sustainable way, and this is why they set up the Tao Kalahi Foundation, as their philanthropic arm. This especially resonated with me and HER Planet Earth's values. Having grown up in the Philippines and travelled to many parts of the country, their expeditions, although not for the faint of heart, are probably one of the most authentic things you could ever experience in these parts.

Women in Agriculture

The highlight of the trip was discovering Tao's Kalahi Foundation and farm projects—all of which focus on the advancement of women, children's education, organic farming and local traditional crafts for this precious region of Palawan. As I had found through my research prior to setting up HER Planet Earth, in many countries around the world, local laws and entrenched biases result in women farmers having fewer resources and support from their governments. In some countries, women are not even allowed to own land, which makes it impossible for them to use land as collateral for a loan or to buy farming equipment. In other places, I was frustrated to discover that women are not even able to borrow money without a man's signature. These restrictions hamper their ability to run their farms efficiently, leading to lower yields.

One evening, we got chatting with the team and our guides, and learnt that certain landmark laws in the Philippines have caused the agricultural industry to be fraught with gender issues that have made it more difficult for women to attain equal access to resources such as land, farm equipment and loans. I realized that this is a problem not just for the women farmers, but for the earth.

As I had learnt from reading up about this topic, every year, humans cut forests to create more agricultural land to grow more crops to feed the world's growing population. In turn, this deforestation increases the rate of climate change. This is why, via HER Planet Earth, I want to support women in agriculture and make existing farms run by them more efficient. In fact, a piece of research I came across not long ago, conducted by an environmentalist called Katharine Wilkinson, demonstrated that, if we make progress on gender equality, we will be able to mitigate climate change significantly. Indeed, increasing women's farm yields could stop about 2 billion tons of CO_2 from entering the atmosphere between now and 2050.

Along the journey we stopped at several centres of the Tao Kalahi Foundation and learnt that they function like an extended family in a sustainable micro-economy across a 200-kilometre stretch of islands. The foundation creates jobs and provides opportunities for women in food production, water security, schools and via scholarships. This way they offer alternative means of building livelihoods as well as access to education to families challenged by isolation and the collapse of the fishing industry. I was impressed to find out that the foundation also works with what is already available in the islands; utilizing abundant resources and harnessing existing skills to come up with sustainable solutions.

Along the way, we got to meet the local island communities of fishermen and we would sometimes stop and swim to the shore and chat with them about life in the islands. Some of them would share that fish was scarce because of the dynamite that had been used in the past in these parts, so this meant they had to sail out much further every time. We sometimes encountered women on the beaches and chatted with them while they dried their coconut husks as their children played in the sand not far from there. We asked them about what crops they were planting inland and how the recent storm had affected them. These people's lives were truly at the mercy of Nature and the changing climate, and yet they always had a warm welcoming smile and were optimistic about the future.

Tao's main base camp is on Culion Island, where we stayed for one night. While we were there, we discovered that they run a wonderful children's school and a women's association that focuses on teaching how to give massages, weave and make organic soaps and shampoos. The foundation also educates the islanders on responsible and sustainable farming, from maintaining an organic farm to domesticating animals and producing their own vinegar—one of the main ingredients in Filipino cuisine. I fell in love with their sustainable programmes and the way they supported the local community. It felt good to be travelling with Tao and see how our tourism dollars and donations were helping the livelihoods of the islanders.

A Robinson Crusoe Experience

During our trip, we slept in bamboo huts on the beach. The huts, or *tukas* as they are called locally, are built to survive strong winds and even typhoons. I thought they were such clever contraptions because, not being anchored to the ground by concrete bases, they tend to bend with the wind and occasionally get blown away during typhoons—hopefully not too far—so that they can be retrieved, straightened out and re-used after the storm has passed.

For showers on the islands—if we had access to fresh water—we would wash using a bucket in makeshift outdoor showers or at a local spring. At night, the crew, who were nicknamed 'The Lost Boys'—because they truly were the heart and soul of this adventure—would build a bonfire and bring out their guitars to sing along with everyone. They were kind and generous, and always had a smile for us and a warm greeting. They didn't have much in terms of worldly possessions, but I could sense they enjoyed their job on the boat and meeting people from other parts.

One very important member or the crew was a pet Jack Russell named Amo, who answered to no one but his master, Captain Gener. Amo was our expedition's little mascot! He would often patrol the horizon, watching out for intruders and making sure he was always the first to get off the boat when we came ashore—leaping eagerly into the transport kayaks before anyone else.

Everything we ate during the expedition was delicious and prepared with the freshest ingredients found on the islands, either farmed or grown in the wild. A typical meal consisted of fresh fruit and greens, rice and fish or pork. Seafood was bought every morning from the local fishermen, livestock used for consumption were always the ones raised on the Tao farms and surrounding communities. Most importantly, fruit and vegetables are grown without harmful chemicals so as to minimize the ecological footprint of the whole operation. Every detail had been thought through by the founders and the whole experience felt so personal and authentic.

Sustainable Development

As I reflect on our expedition, I realize how important such journeys are to open up new perspectives and recalibrate our priorities. They force us to step out of our comfort zone, grow as adventurers and empower ourselves so that we can, in turn, empower others. I am deeply grateful for these unique life experiences because, every time, I learn so much about the issues many underprivileged people face around the globe, especially women—making me realize how fortunate I am and how much more I should try to support and encourage this kind of sustainable and responsible tourism.

Indeed, at the heart of sustainable development is a deep respect for the earth and future generations. No matter how remote we feel from the problem, our actions in our everyday lives affects our planet's fragile ecosystem. Climate change and environmental degradation are barriers to sustainable development, augmenting existing inequalities. And once again, as Isabella Lövin, the deputy prime minister of Sweden once shared,

. . . gender often remains the untold story in this dilemma. The destructive forces of Nature, warped by rising global temperatures and manifesting in typhoons, floods and other extreme weather conditions, can act as negative force multipliers in societies already riven by inequality. While climate change is a global phenomenon, its impact is not spread across a level playing field. In fact, its effects are felt locally, and poor people suffer the most . . .

—and nowhere is this more apparent than in places like the Philippines.

During our time there, we were privileged to meet authentic and untouched communities. We learnt about their many life challenges, hopes and dreams. It only confirmed what I knew already, that to truly support and help them thrive, we needed to create opportunities that would make them more resilient to the changing climate and circumstances. And this is exactly what is at the heart of HER Planet Earth. Our mission is to help communities, and women especially, build livelihoods that are eco-friendly and compatible and in harmony with Nature, so as to strengthen their resilience in the long term.

All said and done, such expeditions are exceptional because they are made up of what each traveller brings with them on the journey, and this gets intertwined with the stories of the people we meet along the way. And while 'The Lost Boys' always did their utmost to anticipate our every need, it was truly an extraordinary voyage through some of the most isolated and hidden frontiers of the Philippine archipelago, where each new day is an adventure and where new discoveries await explorers at every turn.

CHAPTER 16

A Journey to the Lost World—Vietnam's Son Doong Cave—2019

After our exhilarating sailing expedition to Palawan, where we discovered how educational programmes in agriculture can uplift local communities, I was keen to look at sustainable solutions in other parts of Asia, and so I turned my attention to Vietnam. I had been there a couple times before, when I had travelled on business with Nike to Hanoi and Ho Chi Minh City, but I had never spent time travelling around the country. While there, I had learnt that Vietnam is the Asian country most affected by climate change and disasters. Due to their gender-defined roles in society and increasing feminization of agriculture as men moved to the cities for better jobs, Vietnamese women were the ones more likely to carry the heaviest burdens and suffer the most from environmental degradation. I reached out to my UN Women Singapore contacts, who put me in touch with their Vietnam office and to my delight, I discovered that they had a robust agricultural programme that focused on making Vietnamese women more resilient to climate change by helping them grow crops better suited for the soil in their region—exactly what I wanted to support via HER Planet Earth. Coincidentally, I also had a unique challenge in mind there, a mind-blowing place that had been on my expedition wish-list for a while—Son Doong Cave.

The siren call was simply impossible to resist. The moment I first heard about its existence, I simply knew that I had to find a way to see it with my own eyes. Indeed, Son Doong Cave, or Hang Son Doong as it is also known, is the largest cave in the world. It is an otherworldly place full of wilderness and grandeur, a true masterpiece of Nature with awe-inspiring landscapes, statuesque stalactites and enormous stalagmites hanging from the ceiling and rising from the ground, all of which produced the impression of an alien terrain. I believe we are all meant to be explorers so as to discover our planet's most unique and beautiful vistas.Our week-long jungle expedition to the heart of Son Doong Cave in Vietnam turned out to be precisely that, an unforgettable journey to a magical place as ancient as time, where we found ourselves constantly at a loss for words in the face of so much stunning beauty and splendour, as we solidified friendships.

We flew from Singapore to Ho Chi Minh City, changed planes, before continuing on to Dong Hoi, the capital of the Quang Binh province. There we met up with the UN Women Vietnam team, so that we could have a working session with them, to better understand their initiatives for women and the agricultural programmes our funds would support.

The next day, we drove to the heart of the UNESCO-listed Phong Nha-Ke Bang National Park, within the Quang Binh province where Son Doong Cave is located. We learnt from our driver that the cave was initially discovered by a local lumberjack named Ho Khanh in 1991. Apparently, he did not dare venture into it because he thought the powerful and mysterious wind blowing from inside the cave came from monsters of local mythology. The cave was then explored in 2009–10 by the British Cave Research Association. It is now open to the public, but officially only since 2013.

In Vietnamese, Hang Son Doong means 'Mountain River Cave', and the grotto wears its name well as it has its own underground jungle and ecosystem, with trees rising up thirty metres above ground and a sinuous river that rushes through its gigantic chambers—

distinct features that set the cave apart from many other grottos around the world.

The journey to the entrance of Son Doong Cave involved two days of intense trekking through thick jungle, multiple river crossings and one night of camping in Hang En Cave (the third largest cave in the world). As soon as we arrived at the entrance of Song Doong, we harnessed up and abseiled down about eighty metres through tight and slippery passages, scrambling over huge boulders into the cavernous belly of the mother of all grottos.

Travelling through the cave's depths required intense concentration. We had to stay alert at all times lest we tripped on the slippery rocks and tumbled down into a ravine lined with razor-sharp stones. Up and down we went, using the wooden ladders wedged between the rocks; sometimes removing our backpacks so that we could squeeze through tiny crevices, splashing across icy rivers, wading through muddy streams, pulling ourselves up with ropes or sliding down on our muddy bums over sloping stone walls and balancing precariously on narrow and rickety bridges to cross wide-open echoing spaces.

The Largest Cave in the World

The cave's proportions are extraordinary. Its main chamber is the largest in the world by volume (38.5 million cubic metres), measuring more than five kilometres in length as the crow flies and running approximately nine kilometres in total on its winding route. Its largest section peaks out at 200-metre-high and 150-metre-wide. The only way to get a real sense of perspective on the sheer size of Son Doong is to have fellow trekkers scatter throughout the limestone galleries. Even then, it's hard to properly comprehend the enormity of a place that could house an entire New York City block or could even store sixty-eight Boeing 777 aircrafts in its main passage. It felt larger than I had imagined, and I was constantly in awe of its sheer beauty and proportions.

I was surprised at how cool it was inside the cave, about 21° Celsius or 69° Fahrenheit. The difference in temperature between the air inside and outside of the cave creates hovering clouds of mist that give rise to a mysterious and surreal atmosphere, enveloping many areas of the cave in a dense fog and contributing to the eerie, prehistoric sensation. At times, I felt as if I were walking into a scene from Jurassic Park, as the shrill calls of birds and macaque monkeys echoed off the limestone and drifted in from the unseen world beyond the skylight. The vegetation is extremely diverse with lush and green foliage in parts where sunrays break through the openings; and practically non-existent in the inner sanctum of the cave.

Because of its colossal size and the high levels of rainfall in the region, erosion happens at an accelerated rate. Occasionally, the weight of the limestone gives way and collapses, creating what is known as a 'doline'. Derived from the Slovenian word '*dolina*', meaning 'valley', these sinkholes form huge gateways to the outside world and allow incredible sunbeams to penetrate into these exposed sections, creating a mesmerizing light show which I found absolutely magical and hypnotic.

On occasion, during pauses in our itinerary, I would look up and shine my helmet's torchlights on the colossal limestone ceiling above my head and marvel at the awe-inspiring majesty and beauty of this underground cavern. In those moments, I would be reminded of how unbelievable and rare this whole experience truly was. Josh, our British guide and caving expert, told us that, in reality, more people have stood on the summit of Mount Everest than have witnessed the surreal beauty inside these enormous chambers.

Our Vietnamese guide, Vu, added that the cave was estimated to be about two to five million years old and was initially formed by river water eroding the weak limestone beneath the mountain, creating huge skylights. In many parts of the cave, we saw fossils believed to be millions of years old and thousands of cave pearls neatly packed into terraced compartments on the grotto's floor. Cave pearls are a natural phenomenon formed over hundreds of years when dripping water creates layers of calcite that build up around grains of sand.

At times, we would encounter crawling white insects, almost transparent in hue, that had probably never seen the light of day.

At other times, we would step over the remains of small animals such as deer or rats, their bones mixed with mud and dust. One morning, on the first day of the expedition, I was awakened by the chirping of hundreds of swifts sweeping across the cavernous hall above our heads. The whole experience was amazingly mystical and surreal. I felt transported to another, more ancient world, and if a dinosaur had suddenly emerged from one of the corners of the cave, I would not have found him out of place in this dreamlike setting.

In truth, it was a spectacular adventure from start to finish. I was mesmerized at every turn, discovering new and intriguing phenomena and mind-blowing sceneries that literally made my jaw drop. The trek was challenging and even scary at times as we abseiled into the dark or climbed through slippery cracks in the cave's wall. We used ropes once again, to climb out and exit the cave via the Great Wall of Vietnam, a calcite wall totalling ninety metres in height. Apart from our guides, Josh and Vu, this expedition required an additional twenty-six support staff, consisting of seventeen porters, two chefs, one national park ranger, one porter team leader and five safety guide assistants, who really were the backbone of this fantastic journey. In the same way that the Sherpas of Nepal are key to a climber's success in summiting some of the highest peaks, the local porters of Son Doong are the true heroes of this multi-day, caving expedition. All these men hail from Quang Binh, one of the poorest provinces in Vietnam, and come from a variety of working backgrounds such as farming, hunting and logging. One thing they all have in common is their astounding ability to survive and thrive in the jungles and caves of Phong Nha. Without a doubt, we could have never experienced this remarkable journey inside the world's largest cave without their implacable energy, support and guidance.

Leading from the Back

On all my expeditions I work with guides and local support crews who know the area well and are experts in their fields. On technical treks that involve rock climbing or in this case, caving, our expedition leader is always the safety expert. My role as a leader is more in the overall curation and organization of the whole expedition, team selection, fundraising, communication and training, etc. And while on the actual trek, I defer to the local guides and work closely with them to ensure my team is well and thriving, and that the expedition proceeds smoothly and safely. Because of the sheer numbers of people involved in this expedition, once again, I found myself leading from the back. This meant letting the local guides and caving experts take us through the cave, as we navigated the treacherous passages, rock façades and rivers, and harnessed up on several occasions.

Leading from the back means that you don't have to be the official leader of a group at all times. It means you can be part of a team and still have a lot of influence. In his autobiography, Nelson Mandela equated a great leader to a shepherd, who

. . . stays behind the flock, letting the nimblest go out ahead, whereupon the others follow, not realizing that all along they are being directed from behind.

Leading from behind doesn't mean ceding one's leadership responsibilities. For me, leading from the back demonstrates adaptability to the situation and ensures the whole team moves together, forward, in the right direction. I check in with each of my teammates at different moments of the trek. I chat with them casually to see how they are faring. I make myself available if they need to discuss anything related to how they are feeling or what might be concerning them, the itinerary, the food, their blisters, anything. I ensure they know I care deeply for them, their well-being and their safety. In some ways it's a very motherly kind of leadership, and being a mother of four, I am quite comfortable leading this way because I feel I have a better perspective of the situation.

Many leaders are always looking forward—but with only the occasional report from the back, leaders can often get blindsided. Through my numerous expeditions I've learnt that, rather than staying at the front at all times, leaders can create space for others to go forward. From the back, you can see those who are straggling, disengaged and discouraged, and then deal with the problems right away. And because I take women from all walks of life with me, I have had experience with a wide range of personalities on my treks, so I can often sense who wants to be ahead and who might need more encouragement and prefer to stay at the back.

When leading from the front, it is about injecting energy, providing guidance and rallying the entire team. Without a doubt, an effective team leader is one who can lead from either end, rather than excel solely from the front. But most importantly, without a team's trust and respect, it is difficult to lead from the back because, after all, it is always easier to 'manage', but harder to 'lead' from that position. And so, I've learnt that trust is the glue that binds the leader to her team. That is the most important ingredient of leadership and key to a successful expedition. As I prepare my teammates for a trek in the months leading to our departure, I communicate with them often to ensure they have the tools they need to get ready, and this in turn builds their confidence in me, in my organizational skills and allows them to see the honesty of my intentions and sincerity of my words.

Humanity's Relationship with Nature

As we left the cave at the end of our journey and made our way back to civilization, my heart sank because part of me wanted to stay back and remain in this precious Garden of Eden. I felt as if this past week we had travelled back in time through a magical portal, deep into the earth's inner core. Or perhaps even, taken a trip to a lost world millions of years old.

As I pondered humanity's relationship with Nature and finally returned to my daily life in Singapore, it took me a while to readjust. That's when I came across a quote by the author, Antoine de Saint-Exupery,

The earth teaches us more about ourselves than all the books in the world, because it is resistant to us. Self-discovery comes when man measures himself against an obstacle.

The excerpt from his memoir, *Wind, Sand and Stars*, which deals with the themes of friendship, death, heroism and what makes life worth living, helped me better understand this relationship humans have with Nature. Saint-Exupery was someone with a feverish passion for life although, at first glance, you wouldn't guess it from his seemingly daredevil lifestyle. During the early twentieth century, he flew commercial planes over airmail routes in Europe, Africa and South America. These were dangerous journeys fraught with uncertainty as was demonstrated by the near death of him and his colleagues on a number of different occasions when their aircraft inadvertently went off course or when they were forced to crash land in remote places. Saint-Exupery's message is clear, our human ego tends to make us think of Nature in terms of how useful it is to us, to test our own limits, or useless in general, if we have no need for it.

Truly observing, learning and appreciating Nature teaches us that everything under heaven has its own purpose, regardless of what humans want, and we should value her wisdom and how each creature is meant to exist, even if it doesn't aid us in our own survival or conquests. Ultimately, pegged against Nature, we humans are truly insignificant in the whole scheme of things, and surely, it's better that way. Son Doong Cave showed me that the solution to many of life's problems is to simplify things and not overcomplicate them. It's often better to remove things than to add things. Nature is a recurring demonstration of this: the purer and more pristine she is, the more beautiful she is. When I look back at this expedition, I feel deeply humbled by the experience and privileged to have glimpsed what the world must have looked like when dinosaurs roamed the earth and humanity was not even in its nascent stages. Somehow far from civilization's hustle and bustle, everything seemed so much purer and simpler down there.

CHAPTER 17

In the Land of Fire and Ice, Iceland—2019

After the February caving expeditions to Son Doong Cave, where we climbed below the surface of the world into the mouth of a grotto, I was looking for peaks and different vistas all together. I was keen to organize another HER Planet Earth expedition to Europe, which I had never done before, to drive home the intrinsic connection between melting glaciers, sea-level rise and the existential danger this caused to coastal cities in Asia.

For continuity, I also wanted to keep supporting UN Women's impactful programmes in Asia, empowering women and helping them become more climate-change resilient but this time, I looked to expand the scope to include Bangladesh, Nepal and once again, Vietnam. Indeed, while climate change is a global phenomenon, I knew that its effects continue to disproportionally affect women, in those countries especially. Many of us don't realize that up to 80 per cent of people displaced by climate change are women. Roles as primary caregivers and providers of food and fuel make women more vulnerable when flooding and drought occur. It is not just women in rural areas who are affected. Globally, women are more likely to experience poverty, and to have less socio-economic power than men. The cause was becoming more and more urgent for me. I was keenly aware that these discrepancies were making it harder for women to recover from disasters, which affect infrastructure, jobs and housing. I felt passionately that these were facts and stories that needed to be shared more widely, and our expedition was a meaningful way to do this.

After extensive research, I chose Iceland because it is one of the countries already feeling the brunt of climate change. In fact, Iceland is rising a few inches every year because of climate change. As the country's glaciers melt, the pressure on the land is reduced, and this causes the surface to rise. This changing geography is another tangible showcase of the effects of global warming. I felt Iceland would be the perfect place to inspire my team and push their limits, while raising awareness and funds for underprivileged women affected by climate change.

Landing in Iceland made me feel like I was arriving at the very edge of the world. For an avid trekker like me, this place is paradise because of the incredibly rich topography and varied landscape. Also known as the Land of Fire and Ice, it has stunning blue glaciers, black sandy deserts, over 130 volcanoes, obsidian lava fields, multicoloured snow-capped mountains and explosive geysers. Indeed, Iceland's very existence is a geographical oddity. It marks the point where the European and American tectonic plates meet, and are pushed apart by volcanic activity, making it one of the most geologically active places on earth.

In an area approximately the size of New York, but with a population of just over 360,000, Iceland is the most sparsely populated country in Europe. Through my reading I had learnt that the first permanent settlement wasn't established until 874 AD, when a Norse Viking Chieftain called Ingólfr Arnarson arrived off the coast with his family. According to local lore, he threw two carved pillars overboard vowing to set up home where they landed. The pillars washed ashore on a coastline dotted with steam vents, so he called the place Reykjavik, which means 'Bay of Smoke' in Norse. His settlement is still the capital today, and home to two thirds of Iceland's tiny population. I also learnt with interest that Reykjavik is one of the cleanest, greenest, and safest cities in the world.

My HER Planet Earth team and I arrived in Reykjavik on an August day in 2019, towards the end of the Icelandic summer. No one in our group had ever set foot there, except one person who lived in Denmark, my friend Isabelle, whom I had grown up with in the Philippines, and who had also been with me in Boracay with her family in those early days when it was still an untouched and relatively unknown place. So, it was very special to be reunited with her after so many years apart and to have her join me on this expedition. The whole team was excited about the journey ahead and looked forward to spending five days traversing one of the most active, volcanic and alien landscapes on earth, Laugavegur, a trail in the Southern Highlands of Iceland, originally formed by an eruption in 1477.

Just a few weeks before our trip, Iceland held an actual funeral for the first glacier 'killed' by climate change—the 700-year-old Okjokull, which was the first of Iceland's major glaciers to die. If a glacier melts and becomes too thin, it stops moving and then it is declared dead. Actions like Iceland's glacier funeral are a vital part of the mourning process. It demonstrated the Icelandic people's close ties to Nature and their commitment to trying to preserve their environmental wealth.

Laugavegur

After a bone-shattering three-hour drive east of Reykjavik on the rough dirt road, we reached our first camp in the late afternoon, at the start of the Laugavegur trail. The area is only open to trekkers from June to August, because the rest of the year, the weather is simply too ferocious to risk hiking. As I stepped out of the van and took in the magnificent view of the mountains, I breathed in the crisp 6° Celsius air, and couldn't believe it was this cold in the middle of summer. Nevertheless, the camp had a great surprise in store for us—a natural geothermal hot spring for campers to bathe in.

This first evening, the team was in high spirits. In the summer, Iceland never really gets dark, so we were tempted to stay up late, despite the early start planned for the next morning. The trail awaited.

Considered one of the finest walking routes in the world because of its staggering beauty and diversity, Laugavegur ranks right up there with the Inca trail in Peru and the Milford track in New Zealand. I was so eager to get going and discover the sights.

We set out the next day under clear blue skies, and as soon as we stepped out of camp, and turned the corner behind the first few hills, we were greeted by the most extraordinary, heart-stopping landscapes. The mountains were breathtaking, barren with more than fifty shades of brown. I had never seen anything like this, the rolling hills around them had multicoloured layers of earth, stacked on top of each other, and it created the impression that we were about to journey into a great big chocolate kingdom. And as we climbed higher through this magical landscape, the wind started to bite.

This place made me feel as if I was a character in the *Lord of the Rings* on my way to Mordor. It is no accident that J.R.R. Tolkien was fascinated by Iceland. They say this part of the country is as close as you will ever get to Middle Earth, the fantasy land he described in his novels.

As the day progressed, we made our way to the heart of this geothermal wonderland and came across stunning sceneries at every turn: incredible lunar surfaces, volcanic rocks, majestic waterfalls and steaming hot geysers with their bubbling sulphuric acid pools. I was taking it all in and documenting as much as I could on my iPhone.

My respect for the landscape grew deeper with every step. Our guide, Helga, shared with us that it was this otherworldliness that brought NASA to Iceland on numerous occasions to train astronauts for the geological conditions they would encounter on the Moon and Mars. Across most of Iceland, people live mainly on the coastal areas; because of this, you could walk for miles inland and see no sign of human life, no roads, no houses, nothing.

'In the thousand years since Iceland has been inhabited, there have been over 250 eruptions in a volcanically active zone covering a quarter of the country,' said Helga. Our trail ran through the heart of this zone, which made me wonder just how dangerous it really was to trek here.

'Surely they would close the trail . . .' I thought to myself, 'if there were any signs of an impending eruption.'

We soon came across a sobering reminder of why we should never underestimate the risks on mountains. It was a memorial for a young Israeli man called Ido Keinan, a modest pile of stones with a metal plaque that said: 'In loving memory of Ido Keinan who passed away in a blizzard so close to the safe hut nearby yet so far at only 25 years old June 27, 2004.'

A chill ran down my spine as I looked at his memorial, indeed, I thought, 'There but for the grace of God go I.' Something like this, could easily have happened to anyone. The saddest thing for me was knowing just how close he had been to safety. This tragedy took place at the height of summer. We were walking in August, and it didn't feel like it. Just a few hundred metres later, we reached the Hrafntinnusker campsite and broke for lunch, reflective about life and the grave we had just walked past.

Throughout the trek, we camped outdoors and experienced a range of temperatures from beautiful sunny days to cold, windy and rainy spells, with 5–6° Celsius temperatures. We hiked about ten hours per day and the team felt relieved and joyous when at the end of each day, we finally reached our campsite for the night with warm food and rest. I enjoyed waking up in the early hours of the morning and unzipping my tent to look out into the misty mountainous views that surrounded us. It was simply beautiful and such a privilege to be here.

As we progressed on the Laugavegur trail, the landscape was ever changing. Descending into the valley, we went from slopes covered in electric green moss, to lunar landscapes and arctic trails, before entering a thick fern and birchwood forest called Thorsmork, named after the Norse god of thunder, Thor.

As we hiked through the woods, our intrepid and experienced guide, Helga, shared with us, 'We do have trolls who live in these mountains. They only come down to forage for food at night. If they are caught in the sunlight, they immediately turn to stone.' I found it amusing and enchanting that according to Helga, the majority of Icelanders believe in, or at least refuse to deny the existence of elves, trolls and other other-worldly beings. This only reinforced the mystical quality of our expedition and along the way I would inadvertently scan the horizon in case I got lucky enough to spot one of these magical creatures.

On the third day, the weather caught up with us. The showers came and went as we marched on through black volcanic rock covered with a thick layer of dust and sand. But this wasn't ordinary dust. This was the stuff that caused chaos all over Europe when in 2010 the volcano under a glacier known as Eyjafjallajökull began erupting for the first time since the 1820s, spewing ash 9,000 metres into the air and causing the largest international airspace shutdown in years. I tried to imagine what it must have been like and the only comparison I could relate to was the time when Mount Pinatubo erupted in June 1991 in the Philippines, and spewed out more than five cubic kilometres of magma and sent an ash cloud 35,000 metres into the air, which eventually covered Manila in a blanket of grey ash.

Mountains Deserve Respect

On the last day, the weather conditions worsened. Clouds closed in and became quite menacing, quite fast. The wind and rain were relentless and intensified in strength. I started to anticipate that we might have to change our itinerary and consulted with Helga to discuss our options. The weather continued to worsen, and this forced us to seek shelter and descend from the mountain slope we were on, and plan for an early evacuation. Gale-force winds at fifty-one kilometres per hour started battering the mountains. This was another reminder that mountain weather is fickle and no matter how warm it is one moment, it can turn into a raging storm in minutes. Of course, I was disappointed that we had to cut our trip short by one day, but safety was the priority and there was no other way around this.

As we rode back to Reykjavik in the all-terrain vehicle sent to pick us up, while the storm raged on outside, I pondered the lesson in humility the mountain had handed to us that day. In truth, climbers should always approach a mountain with respect, recognizing that Nature is so much bigger and mightier than us mere mortals. It sometimes seems hard to believe that something as awe-inspiring and beautiful as a mountain can be so dangerous and lethal at the same time.

The author Andy Andrews summed it up best when he said,

> Everybody wants to reach the top of the mountain, but there is no growth at the peak. It is in the valley that we slog through the lush grass and rich soil, learning and becoming what enables us to summit life's next peak.

Indeed, mountains remind us that the world is not entirely man-made, controlled and predictable. They flag up our need to be durable and prepared without rigidity and inflexibility. It is not so much about getting there, as it is about reaching new heights with each step because when you get to the top of any mountain, you are simply at the bottom of another greater climb.

The Importance of Good Communication

Another important lesson from this expedition, which came to the forefront for me, was the importance of good communication. Often on such treks my teammates and I spend many hours chatting on the route and we get to know each other quite well. Sharing shelters or sleeping in tents with a group of humans requires good-communication and conflict-resolution skills. In my years of experience organizing these treks, I've learnt the importance of clarifying boundaries, routines and pet peeves. The understanding and respect that you build with your team can easily translate to life and relationships back home. Thus, I've found that learning to communicate our boundaries and expectations is key for any strong relationship. And the more remote we are, the more our ability to communicate openly, honestly and frankly becomes a lifeline.

My teammates are often made up of women anywhere between 22 to 60 years age. They could be from Hong Kong, Singapore, Dubai, Cape Town, Paris or London. Their careers and profiles are diverse and far ranging. I've had CEOs and new graduates, pilots and artists, engineers and marketers, stay-at-home mums and consultants, to name a few. The women are of all nationalities, races, marital status, sexual and religious orientation. Our unity of purpose has always been a great strength, but it is our diversity that has been at the heart of our powerful sisterhood, and which has made our time together so precious.

On this particular expedition to Iceland, I had a few strong and opinionated personalities, and at one point, I had to speak in private to a couple of them about the way they voiced complaints about the food, or about the accommodation. It was important for me to get this in check so that their attitudes would not to ruin the team spirit or atmosphere on the trek. Doing this requires you to be firm but also fairly diplomatic, it is sometimes tricky to navigate and not always easy to manage, but with experience, I have gotten better at it. I usually try to reframe the situation and remind the person why we are on this journey together. It's not a holiday. We have a bigger mission, and instead of focusing on annoying details, we need to look at the bigger picture—we are here to push our limits to empower others.

An expedition is a group process, not a random group of individuals on the same trail. It provides a framework in which each person understands the importance of relationships and the role of each individual in the accomplishment of the expedition. This is why I insist that the team come together either physically or virtually a good 6 to 9 months before the start of any expedition so that we can get to know each other as we prepare, train and fundraise together. Essentially, a shared purpose and a common goal creates a stronger bond within a team—contributing greatly to the success of any expedition.

Overall, the journey was phenomenal. Despite the poor weather conditions at the end, Iceland and its beauty drew us in. The team covered close to eighty kilometres of undulating mountainous terrain, crossing numerous freezing rivers in the process and enduring unpredictable and capricious micro-climates. It certainly deepened my appreciation for Nature and its volatility.

The whole experience and mystical landscapes were surreal, and for many of us almost spiritual. Travelling together as an all-female team was a powerful bonding process, and for me as a team leader, another formative, even if at times challenging, experience in team management. The stunning beauty and dramatic lunar landscapes of Iceland kept us transfixed throughout the journey. Best of all, pushing our limits for a very worthy cause had made the whole experience even more meaningful. We returned home with a deeper respect for the formidable forces of Nature and with an unforgettable impression of this truly wild and awe-inspiring Land of Fire and Ice.

CHAPTER 18

On the Trail of the Samburu People of Northern Kenya—2019

2019 was one of my busiest years in terms of expeditions. I organized three of them with HER Planet Earth and put WOAM on pause that year because I was increasingly receiving requests from women wanting an expedition that had an environmental mission. So, after Vietnam in February and Iceland in August, I prepared for my third trek, this time to Kenya, in October that year.

I chose to partner with a charity called Conservation International or CI, as I had met the team in Singapore and was impressed by their professionalism and ambitious projects focused on transforming countries' climate resilience by promoting green economies. I knew they had some great partnerships with local NGOs in Kenya, and solid programmes aimed at building the resilience of local women by involving them in wildlife conservation.

So, we set out to plan the expedition together and aimed to raise $150,000 dollars for CI's work in Northern Kenya. They recommended a tour operator that I could work with to deliver a pioneering experience. After consulting with them, I decided on a trek across Northern Kenya's remote Karisia Hills. The trail had never been attempted before and would take the group on a new passage across the mountains. In no time, I had recruited sixteen women from across the world, and soon, we were all set to begin our journey to Africa.

A Samburu Sojourn

A century ago, up to 12 million of the world's heaviest land mammals, elephants, roamed the earth. Today, there are only about 500,000 left. Despite a 1990 ban on international trade in ivory, and even if the demand for animal tusks has decreased over the last few years, these majestic animals are alarmingly close to extinction.

In October 2019, my HER Planet Earth team and I had the great privilege of trekking 100 kilometres with Samburu warriors in the Karisia Hills of Northern Kenya. The Samburu are nomadic pastoralists who have lived harmoniously with Nature in this region of Kenya for centuries. I discovered that they have a love of and a deep respect for elephants. These beautiful mammals have influenced Samburu tribal culture since the dawn of time. Elephants create paths to water and break branches that can be used for firewood, two functions that benefit the Samburu people's survival. Following patterns of rainfall in search of fresh pasture and water for their cattle, camels, goats and sheep, Samburu people have also developed a special relationship with the environment, and this has created a biocultural landscape that promotes both their culture and biodiversity.

During our week-long sojourn in this remote part of Kenya, I witnessed incredibly stunning landscapes and ever-changing sceneries, from dry deserts and rocky volcanic terrain to lush green forests and meadows as we climbed higher in altitude to 2,550 metres above sea level. Our main guide was an expert tracker called Kerry Glen, a British lady who grew up in Kenya and who walked on the trail carrying a rifle on her shoulders. Her signature outfit, a khaki safari skirt that arrived at the knee, was the envy of all the ladies on the trek. Kerry knew the area like the back of the hand and was the founder of the company that organizes these walking safaris.

Travelling with a full safari train, made up of twenty-eight transport camels loaded with our tents and supplies was a surreal experience. Having those gentle giants follow us on our journey, with their long legs, big-lipped snouts and humped backs was novel and at times quite entertaining. When we would get to camp, the camels would sometimes come by our tents and drink from our water holders, which were little satchels of water that the guides had placed in front of our tents, for us to wash our hands and faces with. And if the camels sensed a predator nearby, they would get agitated and make wild and anxious noises.

Our team walked side by side with an armed Samburu escort, composed of proud local warriors, trackers and rangers. Our main local guides, Paul and Gabriel, two strong Samburu warriors, were decked out in their traditional dress. For the Samburu this consists of a striking red cloth wrapped like a skirt and a white sash and further adorned with colourful bead earrings, bracelets, anklets and necklaces. Each piece of jewellery represents the status of the wearer. Both men spoke English fluently and regaled us with stories of the rich culture and traditions of their people.

As we journeyed through their territory, they shared how the Samburu, who had always lived in tribes, had to adapt because of dire circumstances and changes in the climate. They always envisioned life as one great, interconnected web, convinced that our actions directly impacted and influenced the natural world around us and vice versa; this shapes their leadership practices and social hierarchy significantly. I appreciated how they understood that each action has a consequence, especially as it relates to the environment. Like ripples on a pond, they knew actions spread out and affected others because everything is interconnected.

Each day, we covered about eighteen to twenty kilometres on foot, leaving camp just as dawn broke, and arriving at our next campsite by early afternoon. Our guides kept us safe throughout the trek, scanning the path ahead meticulously, constantly on the lookout for signs of wildlife or other visitors. They were attentive to every detail and looked after us with sincere and generous hospitality, which made all the difference.

The objective of our trek was to increase awareness of the impact of climate change in this region and raise valuable funds for women's livelihood programmes. I learnt from Robert, one of CI's managers based in Singapore, that in Kenya, women are the natural custodians of the environment and the first to be affected by environmental degradation. This is because they are the ones who walk for hours looking for water, who fetch firewood and who provide food for their families. It felt good to know that our team's funds would create more opportunities for women in this area—focused on wildlife conservation.

As we soaked up the beauty of the region during our long days of walking, our guide, Gabriel, shared with us a local legend that tells the tale of how elephants and the Samburu are closely interlinked.

'In the beginning of time, the Samburu people and the elephants lived together. In fact, the elephants used to help women find firewood; but because of an argument one day, they, the elephants, got upset and stormed off to live in the bush. Since this happened, the Samburu and the elephants have lived apart. Yet, today, the elephants still help the Samburu women, by making paths leading to water, by breaking branches, making it easier for women to collect firewood,' he recounted. This story helped me understand the special love and connection the Samburu have for these beautiful mammals.

The Impact of Climate Change

I soon also realized however, that the Samburu way of life was being severely threatened by the impact of climate change. Droughts are leading to conflicts, human and livestock displacement, animal diseases and food insecurity. Kerry shared with us that the nomadic herders frequently have to dig deep holes to find water for both themselves and their livestock. They call them 'Singing Wells' because they sing to their livestock as they dig, and the cows recognize their family's song and come down to the well to have a drink. The difference between each family's song is usually clear but can be very subtle. At night, thirsty elephants seek out these wells. We got to see those wells as soon as we arrived at Sarara Safari Lodge, towards the end of our trek. Our guide explained that adult elephants, with great long trunks, have little problem reaching for the water, but the younger, inexperienced elephants can tumble in. If the animals can't be pulled out, the elephants are forced to abandon their young.

Over twenty of these abandoned elephants now live at the nearby Reteti Elephant Sanctuary, the first community-owned elephant reserve in Kenya, which we also had the opportunity to visit. At Reteti, we learnt that the baby elephants are being devotedly taken care of and bottle-fed, until they are big enough and old enough to be re-introduced into the wild. It's a unique form of conservation, where the local Samburu people collectively own and manage the 3,400-acre property. On average, elephants stay with their mothers for sixteen years—just about the same amount of time that human children rely on their parents. I found it incredibly touching to see how the women at Reteti care for these abandoned baby elephants as if they were their own. Feeding them, caressing them, staying by their side if they are ill, even singing to them, and the little elephants really warm to them as substitute mothers, and survive and thrive only because of the love and care they receive from them.

As the largest of all land mammals, African elephants play an important role in balancing natural ecosystems and this is why part of our HER Planet Earth team's fundraising went to support this elephant sanctuary to help them grow and develop the programme, so as to employ more local women to care for these beautiful creatures.

Female Empowerment and Eco-Livelihoods

An additional programme we funded was CI Indigenous Leaders Fellowship, which focuses on supporting indigenous women and elevating their voices in the dialogue around climate resilience and conservation. The fellowship offers individualized support to fellows, in an effort to enhance and expand leadership, as well as to provide learning opportunities and connections for personal and professional development.

One of those beneficiaries was Rufo Halakhe, whom we got a chance to meet during our visit to Lewa Wildlife Conservancy at the start of our trek. Rufo literally lit up the room when she walked in with her bright eyes and overflowing positive energy. She told us all about her plans to use her fellowship to explore how women are affected by tribal clashes involving communities in her region and how they could become champions of peace through their existing cultural structures. Rufa's passion was contagious, and I found a kindred spirit in her.

Another very special beneficiary of the programme was Josephine Ikuru, a community leader and the first female peace coordinator for the Northern Rangeland Trust, a local partner of CI. Josephine exudes confidence and authority. She is very tall and looks you straight in the eye. When we met with her, she shared her incredible life story with us and we learnt how she had been a champion for women's rights in Northern Kenya since her teen years, defying gender norms to attend local meetings traditionally dominated by men. Josephine gained a passion for conservation through her efforts to reform poachers, working to end both the devastation of her beloved wildlife and the poverty that has given rise to it. By the time she was twenty-two, she was elected the chairperson of the Nakuprat-Gotu Conservancy, bringing together rival tribes to curb poaching and conserve the native wildlife. Throughout her career, Josephine successfully reformed dozens of poachers, helping convert several of them into conservationists and peace ambassadors. Meeting Josephine and Rufo and hearing their life stories and their hopes and dreams for the future of women in Kenya was a genuinely moving and uplifting experience for our team. Even if we played a very small part in supporting their work, it was an honour to meet such role models and hear about their mission.

It's About the Journey Together

Overall, our time in Kenya was a truly enriching and insightful experience. This magnificent country of epic landforms stirred in me a deep longing for the rest of the African continent. Our beautiful walking safari expedition in the Karisia Hills with the Samburu warriors, learning about the issues that women face in Kenya and the effects of climate change on their livelihoods, discovering the Reteti Elephant Sanctuary and how they care for rescued baby elephants; all these elements contributed to making our visit to Kenya unforgettable.

When we departed, as the plane lifted, I felt that more than leaving a continent, I was leaving a state of mind. As I gazed through the aircraft's window, my heart was full with the staggering beauty of the local people whom I came to know during our journey. They brought soul and colour to the earth. I know that I will always treasure the vast multicoloured grasslands peppered with immense herds of wildlife that we traversed during our time to this amazingly beautiful and epic land.

As with many of my expeditions, it's not so much about the destination as it is about investing in the journey itself. I used to see success as a finish line, achieving a goal, a literal threshold at some point in time in the future. Kenya and the Samburu people taught me that success looks more like a continuous journey, everything is interconnected and it's more worthwhile and important to strive forward at a steady pace and enjoy the ride.

The conservation mission is difficult and urgent, and the odds are seemingly stacked against us. The path is rocky, steep, hard and dusty. At times I feel overwhelmed; it's difficult to take even one more step forward, but then I see my teammates, who are just as thirsty and tired as me, and then I know that I am not alone in this journey. Together, we can lift each other up and it inspires all of us to keep going, because this pursuit is too important. We must never give up.

CHAPTER 19

Fat Tyres in the Frozen Lands—
Greenland—2020

After Kenya, I came home to Singapore on a high. The expedition had been a roaring success, we had succeeded in hitting our fundraising target and my sixteen teammates were over the moon, full of amazing memories of our trip, with a stronger and renewed commitment to conservation. I had another epic HER Planet Earth journey to Greenland planned in early 2020, a place I had always wanted to visit, and later in September of the same year, a WOAM expedition to Kyrgyzstan, which already had twelve women signed up and many more on the waitlist. Little did I know that the universe had other plans . . . because the COVID-19 pandemic was about to erupt.

Into the Arctic Circle Trail

There is no doubt that traversing the full length of Greenland's Arctic Circle Trail in the depths of winter on a fatbike will stand as one of the most extraordinary and unique experiences of my life. The journey saw my team and me push our limits to the brink of total exhaustion on multiple occasions in extreme conditions across one of the most awe-inspiring and remote places I've ever witnessed.

The expedition took place in early March 2020, at the start of the coronavirus pandemic. Yet when we landed in Kangerlussuaq, a small town in western Greenland, on 4 March 2020, there were no cases of the deadly virus in this remote and faraway island, located east of the Canadian Arctic Archipelago.

We had just flown in from Singapore via Denmark the night before, and at the time, the Asian island nation had 112 COVID-19 cases and Denmark, just eight in comparison. I felt lucky to be able to push through with our expedition—a unique challenge which I had been planning for some months. One of the aims of this adventure was to cross a section of the world's largest island, Greenland, on fatbikes, off-road bicycles with oversized tires, in the middle of winter, as the first all-female team. Up until our departure date, the team and I had been monitoring the situation carefully, keeping our fingers crossed that this fundraising and awareness-building expedition could still go ahead. Once again, the objective was to raise funds for underprivileged women affected by climate change in the Asia region. I chose Greenland because after trekking far away to Siberia and Antarctica, I knew I had to seek out this last final frozen frontier.

Greenland and Asia: What's the Connection?

Through my research, I learnt that Greenland is 80 per cent covered in ice, and its glaciers are contributing to a rise in the global sea level faster than was previously believed. In fact, many of the processes that control sea-level rise are amplified in Asia. A lot of people think that what happens in the Arctic and Antarctic does not really concern Asia, but China, Bangladesh, India, Vietnam, Japan, Indonesia, Thailand and the Philippines account for some 70 per cent of the people living on land at most risk from rising waters. Speaking with Professor Benjamin Horton, the director of the Earth Observatory of Singapore, one of our HER Planet Earth partners and leading experts in sea-level rise, I discovered that as the rate of climate change accelerates, many coastal cities will be affected and Asian cities will be hit much harder than others given their population, economic activity and landmass. As a result, about four out of every five people impacted by sea-level rise by 2050 will live in East or Southeast Asia.

I was alarmed to learn that 99 of the 100 most risk-prone cities in the world are in Asia, with the Indonesian capital, Jakarta, topping the list and cities in India close behind. In fact, Jakarta, with a population of more than 10.5 million people, is sinking. Like many coastal cities around the world, it is vulnerable to sea-level rise. Built on what was once a swamp, the city has serious water supply problems as well, and the air is severely polluted. It is one of the fastest-sinking cities in the world. If this goes unchecked, parts of the megacity could be entirely submerged by 2050. As a result, the Indonesian government plans to move the capital to East Kalimantan, on the island of Borneo.

Furthermore, I heard from Professor Horton, that a one-metre rise in sea level over the next century would submerge many small island nations in the South Pacific, such as the Solomon Islands, Micronesia, Palau, Kiribati and the Maldives in the Indian Ocean to name a few, most of which are just one or two metres above mean sea level. You get the picture? the data is actually quite frightening. This expedition to Greenland and learning more about the connection between its ice sheet melt and Asia, really put this frightening reality into focus for me. It made me all the more determined to put all my energy on supporting initiatives that can mitigate and slow this process of sea-level rise.

Arriving in Greenland

As we arrived in Greenland, we were conscious that because of the increasing fears about the pandemic, we might not be the most-welcomed tourists. Nevertheless, we experienced no such prejudice and anyway, over the next few days, we would be biking across, the 200 km Arctic Circle Trail, which connects the Russell Glacier with the western coast of the island.

When I stepped off the plane at Kangerlussuaq in Greenland, the −33° Celsius temperature hit me in the face instantly. The dry air filled my nostrils and lungs, and the ice particles I inhaled made me feel like I was being frozen from the inside out.

Standing there, waiting for our team at the tiny airport terminal, with a warm and welcoming smile, was a giant of a man, the Greenlander, Bo Lings. With his impressive 2-metre tall, muscular physique he was, quite literally, the largest man I had ever shaken hands with. He immediately inspired a deep sense of confidence and calm in our team. I had been a little anxious on the flight there, given it was my first time to Greenland, and because I really didn't know what to expect. But now, seeing Bo made me relax. I could sense his protectiveness and an overwhelming feeling of trust enveloped me. I understood that we were in very good hands. In truth, I am fairly certain that, in that very instant, I would have followed him anywhere—without question—if he had simply asked.

After a short drive from the airport, we checked into our shelter for the night, which looked more like an army barracks than a hotel and changed excitedly into our biking clothes. This is the moment we'd all been waiting for these past few months. We pulled on layer upon layer: thermals, fleeces, soft-shell jackets, windproof jackets, balaclavas, inner gloves, outer gloves, woollen socks, insulated boots, helmets and goggles. The list of items was interminable, yet each piece had its precise function, necessary to safeguard us from the arctic conditions out there. I felt a growing sense of excitement but was also a little nervous about the savageness of the biting cold outside.

The First Leg

We collected our fatbikes, adjusted our saddles and installed our pogies—jumbo mittens that fit over the handlebars for added warmth—and by the time we arrived by bus at the foot of the Russell Glacier, the starting point of our 200-kilometre journey, it was already 4 p.m. and a sobering −35° Celsius.

The glacier was magnificent, a sharp contrast to the surrounding land and icescapes. It had an impressive, jagged ice wall soaring to a height of sixty metres in parts and stood before us against the deep blue sky like a white giant with gaping, turquoise cracks and crevasses.

'These structures can calve and break at any time,' shared Bo, 'therefore, it is important we remain at a safe distance from the glacier.'

I took in the view, but my mind was on the biking. We had twenty-six kilometres to ride back to our shelter for the night. This should be a piece of cake, right? Wrong. From the first few pedal strokes, I realized it was going to be a real struggle. The snow around the glacier was powdery, thick and slippery, so we skidded, swerved and fell multiple times like clumsy, circus clowns, before finding our footing. It was not a good start.

The cold was quite daunting this late in the day and as the wind picked up; −35° Celsius felt more like −45° Celsius. When not pedalling, we were aware of the icy cold in our bones and in our extremities. Luckily, after a while, we hit harder snow on the dirt road, which was much easier to pedal on, and finally, we picked up speed and settled into a good pace—and with that came more body heat.

That first day, we cycled up and down over the rolling hills for what seemed like an eternity. Soon, the sun set and the temperature plummeted. We noticed that the team was quite spread out. Everyone was finding their own pace, getting used to the snow, the bikes and taking it all in. Thankfully, despite the growing darkness, there was a beautiful full moon welcoming us to Greenland on our first evening. This meant the path was still visible. We took off our goggles. Ice formed on our eyelashes and around our balaclavas because our breath connected with the cold and wind around our faces. Finally, four long hours later, just before 8 p.m., we reached our shelter for the night.

We were spent. We thought this would be a warm-up day, instead with the jetlag and no lunch, this first leg was intense and draining. I was particularly exhausted that day because I had not eaten much and had slept very little in the last twenty-four hours, perhaps because of the heightened excitement, and found it very hard to finish this first leg.

The Killer Day

The next day, we knew we had sixty kilometres on the itinerary, and there would be no road this time, just a path in the snow. That evening after a hearty meal, we crashed into our beds exhausted, wondering, with some apprehension, what tomorrow would bring.

The next day was a killer. It turned out to be tougher than I ever imagined, but we survived it—just. It seemed to drag on, long and interminable. My energy stores, which had not been completely replenished after the previous day's exertion, seemed empty by mid-day, and we still had thirty kilometres ahead! I thought we would never make it, I was running on fumes. The cold was chilling me to the core, and as soon as I stopped, I shivered uncontrollably. I started to think, 'What the hell did I get us into?' It was miserable, for most of the way. Yet, we kept going. I divided the day into smaller chunks of one or two hours to make it easier to get through. At least we were making progress, but by God was it hard! We cycled our hearts out, to the brink of exhaustion, and advanced across this gigantic white desert. Finally, after ten hours out in the cold, biking in single file, with just our thoughts in our heads for company, we reached our hut in complete darkness, and arrived shattered, cold and wet.

Every bone and muscle in our body hurt. This was the day that never ended. We longed for Bo's support vehicle to appear on the horizon, with some hot tea or soup, to give us hope, a much-needed boost of energy and words of encouragement. During those precious breaks, it was important never to stop for long, because despite the added down-jacket we quickly threw on, we got too cold, too fast.

That night at the hut we slept like the dead.

Carrying On

The next morning at dawn, we woke to the howling of dogs outside our cabin. I looked out the window and saw that a local, Inuit couple had arrived on a sled pulled by ten dogs. Bo told us later over breakfast, that the Inuit, who are the indigenous people of Greenland, make up 90 per cent of the population and originally migrated from Alaska through Northern Canada. This couple was probably on its way to hunt caribou, muskox, seal, or fish. He said, 'Inuit don't wander aimlessly in search of meat, they visit the same seasonal hunting and fishing camps each year to harvest food.' Indeed, with the use of sled dogs, kayaks and the toggle-headed harpoon, the Inuit were able to thrive along the majority of Greenland's coastline. Their remarkable nomadic lifestyle revolves around hunting, fishing and a rich oral tradition of storytelling passed down from generation to generation.

After breakfast, we got on our bikes again, and started across a vast frozen lake. Our expedition guide, Paul, an ex-British military officer who had fought in Iraq and Afghanistan, reminded us, 'Be bold, start cold! Not too many layers, ladies!' Advice that was not easy to follow when we were stepping out from the warmth of the hut, into the glacial morning air.

We cycled in silence for a couple hours across the lake. The clouds were low and visibility was poor. We focused on the tracks of the person ahead of us, and in those instances of deep concentration, it was easy to think of absolutely nothing and just simply be present in the moment. Then, as we reached the other side of the lake, we began to climb towards a mountain pass, sometimes getting off our bikes to push when it got very steep in parts.

Getting up mountain passes while pushing a 13-kilogramme fatbike, carrying a 6-kilogramme pack and breathing through a balaclava is an exhausting job. To encourage myself when I got dog-tired, I would count fifty paces in my head, then stop to catch my breath, then start again to break down the task into smaller bits. As soon as we reached a peak, we were always rewarded with breathtaking views. The valleys and frozen lakes below were spectacular. As I gazed in awe, the vast emptiness, desolation and barrenness that enveloped us inevitably made me ponder our own insignificance. Subsequently, from these heights, the downhills were formidable, a much-deserved reward after the long and hard slogs. Descending a snowy trail at full speed on a fatbike, with towering mountains all around, in the remote wilderness of Greenland, made me feel more alive than I had felt in a long time.

The next four days varied in distances from twenty-two kilometres to thirty-three kilometres each day. Some days were harder than others, but after the sixty kilometre leg, we felt we could tackle anything. The journey unfolded and we made good progress. Each day we pushed our limits even further as we battled extreme and bitterly cold conditions, with temperatures ranging from –20 to –40° Celsius.

We rode on all types of terrain, from hard-packed and powdery snow, to ice, mud and rock. The days on the trail were long and tiring, with no shelter from the cold and wind for up to eight hours each day. Despite the gruelling conditions, the esprit de corps was strong. The team looked after one another with kindness and compassion, and that made all the difference. We encouraged each other, made each other laugh, a lot. The faster ones learnt to slow down, to wait for those who were catching up. The team was tight and gradually became a high-functioning unit. The extreme conditions emphasized the importance of looking after each other—there was no room for mistakes or complacency, the risk of frostbite was all too real. We disciplined ourselves to stay close together despite the different biking paces, because if someone got lost, hurt and left behind, they could freeze to death or die of hypothermia within hours. Indeed, in the Arctic, survival time is measured in hours.

During the long days on the trail, we had no contact with the outside world. We often thought about our loved ones at home in these uncertain times. However, if truth be told, the lack of connection was a welcome reprieve from the onslaught of news about the coronavirus during the weeks leading up to the expedition.

The last day on the trail seemed like one of the hardest physically. We were so close to our goal, yet so far, and even though we were looking forward to a warm bed and a hot shower, there was a bit of sadness in our hearts because it felt like the journey had come to an end too soon.

The snow had changed and had gotten softer and more slippery as we approached the coast. The sky was grey and visibility was very limited once again. We needed to stay focused. There was a very steep ascent to start, and the first few hours were difficult and slow. The descent after that was tricky and we experienced many falls and wipe-outs but, so close to our finish line, we were determined to be cautious and avoid breaking any bones.

Arriving in Sisimiut and Celebrating the Team

By mid-afternoon, we rode triumphantly into the coastal fishing town of Sisimiut. With a population of 5,500 people, it is the second largest city in Greenland. Suddenly, we were back to civilization. It was a very strange feeling after days of isolation in the vast, white emptiness of the Arctic Trail. There were cars, snowmobiles, dog sleds, people walking in the snowy streets, staring at our convoy of bikes. I felt completely disconnected from this first sight of civilization, as if I was watching a movie and was not actually living this experience. Biking through Sisimiut felt alien and surreal, almost banal and ordinary, yet what we had done was, to me a least, extraordinary.

We arrived at Bo's warehouse and suddenly I realized . . . that's it. We had arrived. We had succeeded. The journey was over.

We got off our bikes, still dazed, and then embraced each other and started to celebrate, overwhelmed with emotion, perhaps even relief. It had been one of the most difficult challenges I had ever experienced. We were travelling as a team, yet most of the time, we were alone in our thoughts, behind our goggles and our balaclavas, pushing our limits to the extreme.

The sense of happiness and achievement was palpable, even if still not completely tangible, and our eyes filled with tears of joy. We were the first all-female team to fatbike the frozen lands of the Arctic, connecting the Russell Glacier with the western coast of the world's biggest island, Greenland. Yet it was the experience as a team that bonded us, more than the achievement itself. It proved to me once again that teams with a strong sense of common purpose pull in the same direction and have more resilience. They are able to endure much more discomfort and uncertainty and transform into a far more efficient, consistent and high-performing unit. But most importantly, teams with a mission that is focused on improving the lives of others, on improving society or overcoming injustice and oppression, or more globally, protecting the environment and mitigating climate change, are altruistic. This means we become more concerned about the happiness of other human beings or animals rather than our own happiness. We become more selfless, the opposite of selfish, which is such a beautiful and constructive virtue to have at the heart of a team.

As we reconnected to the outside world after the crossing, and with our families via Wi-Fi, we realized that in the span of a week, the pandemic had exploded. We had returned to a world in carnage with the numbers of infections skyrocketing across Europe and the United States especially. After days in isolation, the onslaught of bad news was almost too much. It was as if we had been cocooned in the Arctic—shielded from the world—a short moment suspended in time.

Coming Home to a Pandemic

The day after we flew out of Greenland, the island shut down its borders. There had been a first positive case of COVID-19 in Nuuk, the nation's capital. As a result, the government decided to take swift action to safeguard its 56,000 inhabitants—90 per cent of whom are Inuit indigenous people—from the spread of the virus. Our team flew home as countries everywhere went into lockdown, grateful for this incredible adventure we had been able to live and experience together.

There is no doubt that Greenland's savage beauty cast a spell on us. This land so wild and remote has a fragility to it that called us to wake up to a new world reality. We understood that we were somehow connected to it and that our destiny was interlinked with Greenland's very survival. Nations, like individuals, come to light at times of crisis. As we sheltered in place in Singapore, my WOAM Kyrgyzstan expedition was put on hold, indefinitely, and at the time, no one would have predicted that I would have to wait two long years, until September 2022, before I could deploy my expedition wings once more . . .

Despite the growing fear of the virus in our midst, we realized, even then, that we could not let our fight to mitigate climate change be forgotten. In a sense, the pandemic may have led us to a deeper awareness of the ties that bind us all together as human beings and helped us get to grips with our biggest emergency and long-term existential threat—the climate crisis. Indeed, what happens in the Arctic, does not stay in the Arctic, but will surely shape humanity's future and survival, sooner than we think. The question is whether each of us will do our part to safeguard our planet and its most vulnerable, or simply be a bystander.

CONCLUSION

The Wisdom of the Wild

The Tales of the Two Wolves

An old Cherokee Indian chief was teaching his grandson about life. He said, 'A fight is going on inside me, a fight between two wolves. The dark one is evil—he is anger, envy, sorrow, regret, greed, arrogance, self-pity, guilt, resentment, inferiority, lies, false pride, superiority and ego.' He continued, 'The light wolf is good—he is joy, peace, love, hope, serenity, humility, kindness, benevolence, empathy, generosity, truth, compassion and faith. The same fight is going on inside you grandson . . . and inside of every other person on the face of this earth.'

The grandson ponders this for a moment and then asked, 'Grandfather, which wolf will win?'

The old Cherokee smiled and simply said, 'The one you feed.'

Every day we make choices, choices that can often be overlooked as trivial decisions—but these choices end up defining our destiny. Every one of our actions reveals what we truly believe. It is a vote for the kind of world we want to live in. It's sometimes so much easier to feed the dark wolf—the dark wolf is there to encourage the easier options in life. It's easier to procrastinate, complain, dismiss, ignore, and give up.

The light wolf is very different; it's harder to feed. It's challenging, tiring and time-consuming to do things like learning, teaching, growing, helping others, inspiring or sharing. These things take energy, effort, showing vulnerability and being generous. They take more time and effort. Which wolf you choose to feed will define who you are, and we all know we should feed the light wolf— even if it's harder. Feeding the light wolf is how we end up feeling a sense of accomplishment, pride and success. It is how we lead a life we can be proud of.

However, it doesn't end there, the story continues. In the Cherokee world, there's another version of the story.

The old Cherokee said, 'If you feed them right, they both win.' And the story goes on: 'You see, if I only choose to feed the light wolf, the dark wolf will be hiding around every corner waiting for me to become distracted or weak and jump to get the attention he craves. He will always be angry and will always fight the light wolf.

'But if I acknowledge him, he is happy, and the light wolf is happy, and we all win. For the dark wolf has many qualities—tenacity, courage, fearlessness, a strong will and great strategic thinking—that I have need of at times. These are the very things the light wolf lacks. But the light wolf has compassion, caring, strength and the ability to recognize what is in the best interests of all.

'You see, son, the light wolf needs the dark wolf at his side. To feed only one would starve the other and they will become uncontrollable. To feed and care for both means they will serve you well and do nothing that is not a part of something greater, something good, something of life.

'Feed them both and there will be no more internal struggle for your attention. And when there is no battle inside, you can listen to the voices of deeper knowing that will guide you in choosing what is right in every circumstance.

'Peace, my son, is the Cherokee mission in life. A man or a woman who has peace inside has everything. A man or a woman who is pulled apart by the war inside him or her has nothing.

'How you choose to interact with the opposing forces within you will determine your life. Starve one or the other or guide them both.'

Why do I like the second version of the two wolves' story better? Because it makes sense. It honours what the Taoists refer to as the yin yang—or the sacred balance of life. The Buddhists also refer to this as the Middle Way, a path that embraces being both human and divine. It means acknowledging the dark impulses we sometimes feel, ignoring or repressing them will only make things worse.

Feeding the light wolf involves learning to love and accept yourself fully. It means listening to your intuition, practising gratitude and using positive affirmations, learning to let go, to forgive yourself and others. It involves meditating and healing your body and soul.

Feeding the dark wolf is addressing any inner pain or trauma you may have. It means exploring negative core beliefs, weaknesses, vulnerabilities, doing inner-child work, dealing with trauma, grief. It involves acknowledging our fears, worries and insecurities.

Feeding Both Wolves and Indigenous Wisdom

Feeding both the light and the dark wolves equally will allow us to create more balance, harmony, peace, joy and spiritual expansion within our own life. There is so much wisdom in indigenous stories and a reminder that to attain peace and happiness can be an arduous journey.

I am convinced that we cannot achieve environmental conservation and wellbeing for people and planet unless we acknowledge those two forces inside us and respect and value the wisdom and lessons of indigenous peoples. Indeed, we are all visitors on this earth—for 80, 90 maybe 100 years at the most—just passing through, and our purpose should be to observe, learn and grow. And during this time, it is right that we should learn from those who came before and strive to leave the world a little better than how we found it.

In the tribal communities I visited during my travels, all people are expected to act as specialists or leaders in their own area of responsibility, and the tribe's survival often depends on each one carrying out his or her role as expected. In conversation with

Emmanuel Mankura, a Maasai leader from Kenya, he shared with me that, 'a good leader must possess, among other things, the following essential qualities: courage, empathy, decisiveness, tenacity and stewardship and needs to set aside personal feelings and anger in order to make decisions based on what is good for the community. The leader must persist in the face of difficult circumstances. When a chief can display these qualities, there is more peace and harmony in the tribe.'

In traditional Maasai communities, in the early days, tribal leadership was primarily a male function. A person could be chief only if he had proven that he could lead and take care of the people. A hunter, for instance, could not eat what he killed. A hunter killed game to feed someone else, then someone else would provide game for the hunter. This is another example of the tribe's interconnectedness. Women were also leaders in some of the tribes, but not in the same areas as men. They had their assigned responsibilities around camp, but everyone's role was essential and stood equally in the circle of life.

The importance of showing vulnerability and authenticity has been one of the greatest lessons from my expeditions. Vulnerability may sometimes seem like a double-edged sword. Those who protect themselves to avoid getting hurt, fail to appreciate intimacy and close relationships. Everyone is vulnerable, no matter how much they try to avoid it. We are born vulnerable and stay that way for our entire childhood then, as we grow up, we start to build a protective shield around our heart, an armour that sometimes prevents us from showing our true nature. To live a wholesome and happy life means accepting vulnerabilities, and when we let our guard down bit by bit, it is a commitment to our personal growth. It is a true act of courage because we unveil our authentic self instead of hiding behind a façade to appease others and our fears.

As often, when stepping into the unknown on expeditions, it is scary and uncomfortable because it is outside our 'safe' zone. Over the years, I've come to realize, as I reflect on these magnificent journeys that I have been so blessed to undertake with teams of women around the world, that the experiences which, at the time, felt like the most miserable and desolate, were, in fact, the most formative and enriching. I understand that our greatest achievements as a team came in the face of the greatest adversity, and that true growth and resilience only come from challenge, from persevering, from having grit, from stepping away from what is comfortable, and having the courage to step into the unknown. This is not simply true of travel—no matter where you are in the world you can seek and find adventure, by opening your mind and heart and testing your own courage.

Embracing vulnerability can be a leader's greatest strength. It makes you aware of your pain points. Retaliation leads to more suffering, since you are likely to defend your pain like a wounded animal. Vulnerability involves healing your broken parts by merging with the wholeness of your being—this is the heart of our whole life story.

The challenge is to find a way to be more comfortable feeling the innate vulnerability of being human. Feeling that rawness from the exposure of our open heart. As author Mark Coleman says,

> If we can hold our vulnerability with a loving attention, the painful feelings can unfold and slowly move through us.

We all need to learn to love ourselves and be compassionate as we acknowledge our own strengths and weaknesses. Only then can we truly appreciate how vulnerability is a commanding act of strength and courage.

Indeed empathy, compassion, having humility, taking responsibility and having the courage to show vulnerability, need to be at the core of our humanity. Basically, it is about using these qualities to empower people around us. It is about lifting others up and helping them progress. The role of a leader is to communicate to people their worth, strengths and potential so clearly and encouragingly that they start to see it in themselves and believe in their capacity to do great things.

I believe that inspiring leadership is about advancing the lives of others and encouraging them to impact the world in a positive way, because this will bring us the most fulfilment and happiness. This is why I often remind myself to try to be the kind of leader that I myself would like to follow—and to reflect those values and qualities that I find admirable in my life.

We Rise by Lifting Others

Throughout the last few years, one of my guiding principles has been that 'we rise by lifting others.' Innately in all of us, I believe there is a desire to be good, to be fully alive and to find meaning in life.

What is that meaning? What is that purpose? Could it simply be, to love what you do, whatever your profession, and to feel that somehow it matters, that you are making a difference to the people around you? Surely that is where it all begins. Winston Churchill once said,

> To every man there comes in his lifetime that special moment when he is figuratively tapped on the shoulder and offered a choice to do a very special thing; unique to him and fitted to his talents; what a tragedy if that moment finds him unprepared or unqualified for the work that would be his finest hour.

Focusing on what you love and are good at and honing those skills will ultimately bring you to the point where you were meant to be all along.

The need for purpose is universal. It is one of the most basic requirements and defining characteristics of human beings. We all crave purpose in our lives and suffer serious psychological difficulties when we don't have it. Purpose is a fundamental component of a fulfiled, happy and healthy life.

Having a strong sense of purpose can have a powerful positive effect. When you have a purpose, you never get up in the morning wondering what you're going to do with yourself all day. When you have purpose, life becomes easier, less complicated and less stressful.

A powerful example of this comes from Victor Frankl's famous book, *Man's Search for Meaning*, in which he describes his experiences in a concentration camp during World War II. Frankl observed that the inmates who were most likely to survive were those who felt they had a goal or purpose. Frankl himself spent a lot of time trying to reconstruct a manuscript he had lost on his journey to the camp—his life's work. Others held on to a vision of their future—seeing their loved ones again or a major task to complete as soon as they were free.

Purpose and *Ikigai*

My purpose over the past decade with Women on a Mission and HER Planet Earth has always been to empower and support vulnerable women. This is what drives me on a daily basis. Both NGOs use sports and adventure as a way to have an impact. In addition to the sixteen expeditions I've successfully run to date, my team and I have also organized major fundraising events with thousands of guests combined. And as of the time of publication of this book, I am very proud to say that we have raised a combined total of US$1.7 million dollars for charities that protect our environment and advance the position of women around the world. As a result, we have directly impacted the lives of hundreds of women and girls and indirectly impacted thousands more. What started as an idea, a movement, has turned into a passion, an obsession and has become my unique way of changing the world, one woman at a time. Indeed, there is real power in purpose, in putting what you care about at the centre and core of your life, so that it ends up defining your path, your career, your life story and becoming something bigger—something that matters.

That realization has given me so much fulfilment, peace and happiness. It is as if everything that I have done in my life thus far has prepared me to do this very special thing, unique to me and fitted to my talents—which ultimately has more significance and meaning than the sum of my experiences to date.

This has become what I like to call, my profession of the heart, or my *ikigai*, which is a term I learnt during my time in Japan. Ikigai means 'a reason for being' or 'the reason for which you wake up in the morning.' It means doing what makes you feel in harmony with yourself and that which allows you to be happy, to grow and to be successful. As a result, I've learnt a tremendous amount about the issues facing women around the world, about the challenges caused by climate change, and also a lot about managing teams under pressure on tough expeditions to some of the most inhospitable places in the world.

And one of the greatest lessons I've learnt through this experience, is that the courage it takes to decide to follow your dreams is so little compared to the strength it takes to wake up every single day stuck in a life that doesn't make you either happy or sad. Think about this. In truth, our achievements grow according to the size of our dreams. And there is no better time than now to set another goal or to dream a new dream.

A Life's Legacy

I believe, without a doubt, that the good work a person does throughout their life can establish a legacy of generosity, kindness and social responsibility. From helping others who are less fortunate or in vulnerable positions, to heroic acts that inspire others, those who do good work throughout their lives establish a positive legacy that helps make life better for themselves and for others.

One of the poignant stories that came out of 9/11 involved a former, high-school football hero named Tom Burnett. On that day, he was a passenger on board United Airlines Flight 93, which was hijacked as part of the September 11 attacks. As Burnett called his wife from the hijacked plane, he had already realized that two other hijacked planes had crashed into the World Trade Centre. 'I know we're going to die,' he said, 'but some of us are going to do something about it.' He, along with other passengers, formed the plan to retake the plane from the hijackers, and led the effort that resulted in the crash of the plane into a field in Stonycreek Township near Shanksville, Pennsylvania, thwarting the hijackers' plan to crash the plane into a building in Washington, D.C., most likely either the U.S. Capitol Building or the White House, and saving many other lives as a result.

If you think about it 'I know we're going to die' is a wholly unexceptional statement. Every single one of us is going to die at some point. But it's Burnett's next sentence that is captivating: 'some of us are going to do something about it.' Those words, to me, express one of the most fundamental question of our human existence. It's true we are all mortals with a finite amount of life years allotted to us. What differentiates us is what we actually do with the time allotted to us.

As I reflect on my life thus far and the choices I've made up to today, the places I've been fortunate to travel to, the initiatives I've begun and the relationships I've forged, I can't help feeling that it's been a wonderful adventure and one made even more special because of the people I've brought along with me on the journey.

I am convinced that we are all meant to be explorers, pioneers and treasure hunters of the soul. We are not supposed to be sleep-walking through life, caught in a routine, ambivalent to the possibilities that lie waiting all around us. The world is a dramatic arena and each of us is meant to experience it in the best possible way.

I believe we are here on this earth to live a grand and exciting adventure made up of a series of smaller adventures. We are here to discover, to grow, to be creative and to have a positive impact on the people and the world around us. Anything less feels like such a missed opportunity.

Whether your adventure is rugged or glamorous, understated or intense, whether it plays out on a global stage, or within the confines of you own neighbourhood, whether your journey involves changing the world, or simply changing yourself, an adventurous approach to life is a prerequisite to becoming the person you are meant to be, making your mark on the world and on the lives of others.

An adventure has to be experienced with eyes wide open, in doubt, fear, wonder or pleasure. It is an existential endeavour, a leap of faith that calls into action every aspect of your existence. In fact, adventure is all about transformation and progress. It's about growth. And, when all is said and done, growth is the core of life.

The route I've chosen has allowed me to become the woman I wanted to be, the leader I hoped I would grow into, while finding meaning and purpose through the many projects my team and I have developed to empower other people, and women in particular, to live their dreams and build a better life for themselves and for their families.

This life experience has taught me that your team will follow you, even to the very ends of the earth, if you have the courage of your convictions and are fearlessly authentic. And there are only two ways to influence this behaviour. You can manipulate it, or you can inspire it.

Inspiring it is the most powerful and effective way to do it, of course, and keeping your values at the very core is absolutely essential. This is a universal truth, not just for volunteer-based organizations, but in big multinational corporations too. The most important lesson about leadership for me has been that a leader is worthless unless he or she empowers and uplifts the pack.

I don't know if I've reached enlightenment yet and I certainly have not mastered leadership, but my hope is that my journey, told with all the honesty and candour that I could find in my heart and in my memory can inspire others to take their dreams and aspirations into their own hands, find their purpose and go for it fearlessly, without limitations.

Another truth is that finding purpose and meaning does not lie in material things, it lies in us. When we attach too much to things like money, prestige, status—we are looking for meaning in things that are meaningless and empty. I've found that our greatest tool for changing the world is our capacity to change our mind about the world, to keep seeing the possibilities and the ways it can be improved and how we can help our fellow human beings lead happier and more fulfiling lives. There is power in spreading positivity and hope. If we want to be happy, we need to make others happy. If we want love, we have to give love. If we want joy, we need to make others joyful. If we want peace, we have to create peace in the world around us. And this desire needs to come from the heart.

Research has shown that the heart sends far more signals to the brain than the brain sends to the heart—and while both the cognitive and emotional systems in the body are intelligent, there are far more neural connections that go from the heart to the brain than the other way around. The only way to truly change and transform your life for the better is by transforming and changing the lives of others. This sometimes means listening to your drum and only to your drum, even if other people cannot seem to hear it, and finding a way to share that vision with others to inspire them to join you on this mission.

The more difficult and perhaps the most valuable sacrifice a person can make is to face the complexity of their life and try to live life to its fullest, morally, spiritually and societally. It is far more difficult to navigate through the challenges thrown up by the globalized economy, the complexities of modern urban life and the utter sense of futility that all of us inevitably feel as some stage of our life. This is the true challenge of a purpose-inspired life.

The global climate change crisis and the epidemic of violence against women in our world are the two issues that keep me up at night. That and the kind of world my four children will inherit. There is this incredible sense of urgency inside of me that drives me to do what I do. Using my time and energy to work on the things that I feel deeply passionate about, in other words, living and focusing on what I love, makes me truly happy and moves me to action. Clearly, I've found my calling. But the call came in slow bursts. I had to listen hard to hear it. I believe some of the greatest journeys start that way, with a simple call, sometimes a whisper—often unexpected, inconvenient, painful and uncomfortable—and of course with our willingness to answer. Answering the call doesn't mean it's going to be easy. In fact, in many cases, it's the road less travelled. It's much harder and more challenging.

As I come to the end of this book, I want to leave you with a letter I wrote my children a few years ago. It represents all that I want them to remember when they finally set out into the world as young adults. I hope it inspires you too.

Ready or not, the day will come when you will leave our home and set out into the world.

When that time comes, as you begin on your own journey of life,

remember to love yourself always, with all the qualities and imperfections, you may have.

Never forget that you are worthy of love, kindness and respect.

Don't settle for anyone who treats you any less than you deserve.

Self-esteem is the key to being whole and happy.

Dare to live life to the fullest, go after your dreams even if you don't know yet what that looks like.

Choose to do something you are deeply passionate about.

You will find joy and fulfilment by living life this way.

Find ways to challenge yourself continuously, and don't be afraid to try new things.

This is how you will grow and blossom as the years go by.

Choosing to do something outside of your comfort zone will ignite talents you didn't know you had.

Live with no regrets and let go of guilt.

Learning to forgive yourself when you don't get it right,

or make mistakes, is the best thing you can do to be truly at peace.

Travel whenever you can because you will come to know yourself better and discover how full of wonders and beauty the world really is.

Apply yourself at your chosen career and always conduct yourself with integrity.

Remember that every single one of your actions shows who you are and what you value.

Be thankful for all that you have and for all that you have received.

The happiest people are not those who wish they had more, but those who feel they have enough.

Strive for goals, but don't choose someone else's definition of success; instead, have the courage to define success on your own terms.

Your uniqueness is your power.

Develop the spiritual side of your life and practise compassionate love, by giving back to those who need it most.

Remember that with great privilege comes great responsibility.

Lastly, invest in the meaning and purpose of your existence, and find a way to live a life that matters—

a life that empowers and uplifts others with kindness and true generosity of spirit,

This is what will give you the greatest satisfaction in life.

It won't happen by chance; the choice will only be yours to make.

So, when the time comes,

dare to make those brave choices and strive to live a life that matters and that is true to your heart.

AFTERWORD

The Future in a Post-COVID World

I often ask myself this question when I look ahead: what kind of future do I want? That answer comes back to me time and time again, loud and clear, without fail: I want a fairer, more just and equitable future, for society and the environment. One where businesses—both companies and investors—non-profits and governments work together more closely than ever to bring ethical, creative, innovative strategies and invest capital to solve the biggest problems of our world.

The COVID-19 pandemic was a reckoning. It has shown me how vulnerable we all are in times of crisis. While exacting a heavy price by exposing and amplifying humanity's problems, it has also given me a chance to take a good look in the mirror and change my behaviour and continue to use my energy to build a better, more equitable world. It has also made me realize that to drive change moving forward, corporate social responsibility needs to be at the heart of big corporations, embedded in their business model, aligned with their values and not part of a separate initiative.

The non-profit sector, which unfortunately is built on the fickle-natured foundation of donor-based funding, has taken a huge blow during this pandemic. The ongoing global refugee, climate change and hunger crisis are no different, and are all experiencing for the first time in recent years a complete overshadowing of funding priorities. Simply speaking, more donors are holding on to their money, and the priority for the funding that is available is going to

COVID-19 responses. It's an understandable shift, no doubt, but it does lay bare the fragility in the non-profit-led approach to helping other vulnerable groups.

This only increases the urgent need for businesses to step up their efforts at a global scale. I believe the biggest problems in our world need trillions, not just billions, of dollars to fix. So, if we are going to make lasting and significant progress, and tackle the challenges of our planet, we need corporations, both the companies and the investors, to drive the solutions. This means thinking about supply chains, working on product design and manufacturing processes and distribution. It involves incorporating social and environmental considerations.

Some companies are already making this happen. Mars is a good example. As the sixth-largest, private company in the United States, they manufacture confectionery products like chocolate and as a result, cocoa is one of their important ingredients. To ensure a stable supply of that crop for the long term, Mars has partnered with non-profits around the world who are working with small shareholder farmers to help them improve crop yields, making sure that they get a fair, premium and liveable wage. The company also ensures that it is minimizing the effects on the environment, like deforestation, and that it is addressing any human rights potential issues in their supply chain. Mars is on a path to 100 per cent certified cocoa, and this means their programme is good for farming communities, for the environment and for Mars, who have solved a significant risk in their supply chain.

Another great example of sustainable leadership in the corporate world is Yvon Chouinard, the founder of Patagonia. He said, 'Who are businesses really responsible to? Their customers? Shareholders? Employees? We would argue that it's none of the above. Fundamentally, businesses are responsible to their resource base. Without a healthy environment there are no shareholders, no employees, no customers and no business.' Patagonia is also a leader in environmentally friendly business practices, committing

10 per cent of profits to environmental projects around the world. Maybe that's why Patagonia has a track record of outperforming its competitors and enjoying continuous growth and unmatched employee retention—leading not only in its industry but also on multiple social causes.

Having more leaders like Chouinard with sustainable practices and more equitable mindsets will ensure the world moves in the right direction. Societies and the environment benefit when CEOs and companies prioritise sustainable leadership and this will mean far greater contribution to achieving a sustainable global economy and society by 2030.

In 2018, I sat on a panel with Swiss luxury company, Chopard's co-president, Karl-Friedrich Scheufele, in Singapore to discuss the company's commitment to sustainability and to using 100 per cent Ethical Gold in its jewellery and watches. Chopard defines 'Ethical Gold' as gold acquired from responsible sources, verified as having met international best practice environmental and social standards. Their sustainable values are the way of the future. It is another option to conserving our planet since consumers would be channelling their purchasing power to where they might do the least harm—by buying sustainable luxury goods. Commitments, such as these, from companies are not only good for the planet but make absolute business sense in the long term.

In many regards, our current way of producing, living and working has proven to be unsustainable. We have to change tack and pursue a path in alignment to environmental, social and economic imperatives. One start-up going in the right direction, and which I had the opportunity to work with in Singapore recently, is Eat Just Inc. This private company headquartered in California produces plant-based alternatives to conventionally produced egg products as well as lab-grown chicken under its GOOD Meat brand. In December 2020, the company became the first in the world to receive regulatory approval in Singapore, for its cultivated chicken. With 23 billion chickens on our planet, raised to feed our human population, chicken are the most numerous land species on earth today. And they are seriously hungry, which means millions of acres of the most biodiverse rainforest have been replaced with field after field of chicken feed. For the first time in human history, we are now living in a world where one, single cell can produce an unlimited amount of meat—all without the disturbance of a single forest, the displacement of a single animal's habitat, or the use of a single drop of antibiotics. And all without a single life taken. Eat Just offers a way for us humans to feed our families and rebuild our planet with a food system that is fair, just and kind—one that reflects the best of our humanity.

In the future, massive change in the way businesses operate will create game-changing solutions such as the products Eat Just Inc. are offering—solutions unseen since the Industrial Revolution. Sustainability leaders of the future will derive value from entirely new business models, from new forms of innovation and system optimization across a fully transparent supply chain. As a result, new winners and losers will emerge who will transform the competitive business landscape and the world.

Another area that is trending upwards these past few years is socially responsible investing. A company in Singapore that I am proud to be involved with as an advisory board member is the Impact Investment Exchange (IIX). Its founder, Durreen Shahnaz, is an inspiring leader who became the first Bangladeshi woman on Wall Street and later, she worked for Muhammad Yunus at the Grameen Bank. Durreen is a true pioneer in impact investing. She had a big dream to connect the under-served communities of the back streets to the Wall Streets of the world. Today IIX is a global organization dedicated to building a more inclusive world as the foundation for sustainable peace and it has impacted millions of lives worldwide while continuing to empower women and help under-served communities. In 2020, IIX launched its third edition of the Women's Livelihood Bonds, aimed at helping women and women entrepreneurs in the Asia Pacific region recover from the pandemic.

Furthermore, it is heartening for me to see that investors plunged nearly four times the amount of cash into responsible investment funds in 2020 than they did the year before. I have been inspired by the growing number of countries, companies, investors and communities that are joining the impact economy to advance the Sustainable Development Goals. From billion-dollar funds to non-profits, the movement to make finance and business a force for good has gained well-deserved recognition for its potential to transform and build a better world.

Tech industry giants like Google, Facebook, Microsoft and Apple, who have emerged from the coronavirus crisis stronger than ever, have also taken steps to more equitable and sustainable practices. In fact, Apple has committed to be 100 per cent carbon neutral for its entire business, manufacturing supply chain and product life cycle by 2030. The company is already carbon neutral today for its global corporate operations, and this new commitment means that by 2030, every Apple device sold will have net zero climate impact. Apple's CEO, Tim Cook, understands the implications,

> Businesses have a profound opportunity to help build a more sustainable future, one born of our common concern for the planet we share. The innovations powering our environmental journey are not only good for the planet—they've helped us make our products more energy efficient and bring new sources of clean energy online around the world. Climate action can be the foundation for a new era of innovative potential, job creation, and durable economic growth. With our commitment to carbon neutrality, we hope to be a ripple in the pond that creates a much larger change.

In truth, one of the best ways for businesses to help ensure their own growth, their success and longevity, is to meet some of the hardest challenges in our society and to do so profitably. And when they do that innovatively, ethically, responsibly and credibly, on a large scale, things finally start to shift noticeably and in the right direction.

The real solution to the world's biggest problems, in my opinion, is more purpose-driven businesses. When companies align their purpose with doing good, they can amplify the company's relevance and create real impact for our planet. There is no doubt in my mind that this is the kind of future we need to move towards.

ACKNOWLEDGEMENTS

Writing a book is harder than I thought and more rewarding than I could have ever imagined. Like so many authors before me, I've had days when I felt like giving up, deleting everything I've written so far and simply forgetting about this whole book project altogether. But a few people, who believed in me, kept me going and gave me the courage to surmount my self-doubt and finish this book.

Firstly, I want to thank my publisher, Nora Nazerene Abu Bakar, from Penguin Random House SEA, for reaching out to me on LinkedIn just as the pandemic was developing at the end of 2020, asking me if I had a story to tell. At the time, I had started writing a sort of memoir, and told her about it, that's when she gave me her honest point of view, 'for sure your edge over others is your amazing expeditions, and there is a lot to learn from each one . . . we'd like you to really focus on the life lessons from these experiences'. After much back and forth and guidance from Nora, I reshuffled my outline and she accepted my proposal for *Wild Wisdom*. Thank you so much, Nora, for your belief in me, for your support and for giving me this opportunity to begin with.

I also want to express my sincere gratitude to my editor, Amberdawn Manaois, who painstakingly worked through my whole manuscript, and who took the time and effort to help me find my voice and dig deep to pull out my thoughts, impressions and ruminations. She helped me improve my manuscript tenfold and I could never have done it without her expert guidance and advice.

To my darling husband, Steve, who is my best friend and partner in life. I am so lucky to have you by my side. You are the most loving father and stepfather in the world. You have my deepest gratitude for always supporting me in all my endeavours; for the countless hours you've spent listening to me reading back my various chapters; for helping me find the title of my book; for always giving me your honest opinion; you have my whole-hearted gratitude and love.

To my mum, who is the woman I love and admire the most in the world, thank you for always encouraging me to chase my dreams and to shoot for the stars. Your free spirit has always been a source of inspiration to me. Thank you for your bottomless curiosity about the world which nurtured in me the desire to travel far and wide and explore the most remote places on earth. Mum, what I love the most about how you raised me is that you always emphasized growing as a person and helping others. You also taught me to be fearless—and that is such an amazing gift to bestow on any child.

I am also so thankful for the support of my wonderful siblings, Nathalie and Guillaume, despite living so far away from each other and me, you both are always very present and you are such a positive force in my life—I love being your big sister.

A note of gratitude goes to my ex-husband, Mike Amour, who is the wonderful father of my two older children, Yasmine and Malcolm. Thank you for being a big influence in my life; for being a mentor to me in so many ways; and for raising our two beautiful children together despite our divorce. You are the best ex-husband I could have ever asked for.

I'm eternally grateful too, to my Papa, who sadly is no longer with us, but who was larger than life and still lives on in my heart every day. Dearest Papa, you taught me discipline, tough love, manners, respect and so many other important values that have helped me succeed in life and become the person I was meant to be.

Furthermore, when I think back about when I really found the courage and desire to embark on the project of putting together a book about my expeditions, my first thought goes to my WOAM and HER Planet Earth partners and teammates. Firstly, *Wild Wisdom* would not have been possible without them and the story I told is just one version of the experience we all had together.

Right off the bat, I must acknowledge the vital importance of my WOAM co-founders, Valerie Boffy and Karine Moge, who have been along with me on this formative journey, every step of the way. Thank you for founding WOAM with me and for growing it into a meaningful global sisterhood. We have gone through so much together, struggles and successes, that is a true and lasting friendship indeed.

A huge thank you must also go to all my WOAM and HER Planet Earth teammates and partners who are my most precious tribe. I am so grateful to know each and every one of you and to have you in my life, there are too many of you to name but I want to acknowledge: Milena Nikolova, Patricia Jones, Catherine Zaccaria, Jenny Laing, Maggie Cooper, Selina McCole, Vittoria Zipoli, Virigina Perez, Barbara Fras, Corinna Lim, Enkhtur Maini, Iza- Menni Laaberki, Jen Randall, Linda Baigrie, Nadege Winter, Veronica Landry, Winnie Wong, Ana Fong, Sue Fuller-Good, Pritika Gupta, Sharon Wang, Susan Bauer, Adelene Fong, Grace Moshi, Lisa Crosswhite, Rachel Kelly, Sarissa Rodriguez Schwartz, Tanya Watia, Mouna Aouri, Aline Abramczyk, Karine Lewkowicz, Ada Loi, Anastasia Mitnika-Gonta, Nadège Winter, Jakki Harrison, Stella Chow, Foana Fong, Celine Hivet, Veronica Landry, Sakshi Soni, Marjolein Van Paridon, Winnie Wong, Sarah, Tara Derakshan, Adelaida (Adel) Hassan, Savana Peetoom, Maida de Vega-Pierret, Lisa Crosswhite, Jasvinder Kaur, Dr Grace Moshi, Sarissa Rodriguez Schwartz, Karin Majdalany, Adelene Fong, Rachel Kelly, Charmian Grove, Christine Mills, Erin Sandral, Neena Ali, Alexandra Pijuna-Tinker, Selina McCole, Chin Fee Chen, Devika Tay, Linda Woodford, Paige Okun, Hermine Matzer van Bloois, Jacqueline Lee Detert, Michelle Martins, Sandra Lim, Muriel Bauer, Isabelle de Lovinfosse, Jelena Krstajić, Lisa Montford, Marine Debatte, Quitterie Marque, Sandra Marichal, Victoria Great, Winnie Tang, Celine Thibault, Denise de Castro,

Gordana Miladinovic, Pinky David, Nicole Tan, Catarina Galvao, Calina Ow, Lorraine Santos, Marja O'Donnell, Maria Beitia, An Nguyen, Simon Yehuda, Sylvia Chim, Thaddeus Lawrence, Anne Stauffer, Carole Enckhaute, Christine Hart, Erika Switzer-Masiero, Isabelle Ma, Isabelle Valentine, Sabina Wong, Alex Hollombre, Ann Michelle, Dora Lui, Jecca Baillie, Lynda Williams, Meryam Omi, Paulette Baldie, Satbir Walia, Vanessa Gibbons, Claire Floriet, Katrine Friis Olsen, Maysoune Ghobash, Ann Gacutan, Candina Weston, Haylena Krishnamoorthy, Fleur Eve Le Foll, Judith Von Prockl, Loreto Rincon, Sharlyn Stafford, Fanny Lecarpentier, Kristine Zeigler, Robert Baigrie, Paul Spackman, Brita Fernandez Schmidt and Elisa Fernandez.

To Sir Robert Swan, a man I have so much admiration and respect for, you continue to inspire us all to dream, not simply because you are the first person to walk to both the North and South Poles, but because you have dedicated your entire life to the preservation of Antarctica. Through the incredible work of your 2041 Foundation, you have kept pushing tirelessly for the promotion of recycling, renewable energy and sustainability, as a way to combat the destructive forces of climate change. For all that you do and for all that you represent, you are a true hero in my eyes, and to so many people around the world. Thank you for writing the foreword of my book, you have my deepest gratitude and sincere recognition.

Writing a book about the story of your life is a surreal process. I'm forever indebted to the team at Penguin Random House SEA for their editorial help, keen insight and ongoing support in bringing my stories to life. It is because of their efforts and encouragement that I have this beautiful legacy to pass on to a greater audience.

And finally, to my four children. You are the light of my life and the reason I get up in the morning. Words cannot express how much happiness you give me every day. Thank you for your unconditional love. I am so thankful to have you in my life.

REFERENCES

'Among the poorest in the world and richest culturally—EU protects rights of Indigenous Peoples', *European External Action Service, EEAS 2018*, https://eeas.europa.eu/headquarters/headquarters-homepage/49097/among-poorest-world-and-richest-culturally—eu-protects-rights-indigenous-peoples

'Antarctic Treaty Full Version', Cool Antarctica Website, (https://www.coolantarctica.com/Antarctica%20fact%20file/science/antarctic_treaty.php

'Girls' Education', *UNICEF*, https://www.unicef.org/education/girls-education

'Forming a Relationship with Mother Earth', *National Park Service NPS.gov 2019*, https://www.nps.gov/subjects/tek/index.htm

'Student protest, Paris 1968', *British Library Newspaper Archive*, 1968, https://www.bl.uk/learning/timeline/item108278.html

'Success runs deep: The Story of the Philippines' Araneta Family', *Primer.com.ph*, 2016, https://primer.com.ph/business/2016/10/06/success-runs-deep-the-story-of-the-philippines-araneta-family/

'The World Health Report 2001: Mental Disorders affect one in four people', *World Health Organization*, 2001, https://www.who.int/news/item/28-09-2001-the-world-health-report-2001-mental-disorders-affect-one-in-four-people

'*Thérèse of Lisieux*', *saintsressource.com*, http://saintsresource.com/therese-of-lisieux

'Typhoon Rita 1972' (Wikipedia) https://en.wikipedia.org/wiki/Typhoon_Rita_(1972)?fbclid=IwAR3hJncKU-11TqXlTfnJv4e7of4lR5VpF3zjMjvHj0ZGSczGFUg5H1blHUM

'Volunteering, Health and Wellbeing', *Volunteer Scotland*, 2018, https://www.volunteerscotland.net/for-organisations/research-and-evaluation/publications/volunteering-health-wellbeing/

'Why Diversity and Inclusion Matter (Quick Take)', *Catalyst.org*, 2020, https://www.catalyst.org/research/why-diversity-and-inclusion-matter/#easy-footnote-bottom-7-6361

'Why Diversity Matters', *McKinsey & Company*, 2015, https://www.mckinsey.com/business-functions/organization/our-insights/why-diversity-matters

'Why Invest in Indigenous Lands?', *World Resources Institute 2016*, https://www.wri.org/resources/data-visualizations/why-invest-indigenous-lands

'Women representation on boards of Top 100 SGX-listed companies up 20% from a year ago to hit 14.7%: Diversity Action Committee', *Council of Board Diversity*, 2020, https://www.councilforboarddiversity.sg/wp-content/uploads/2022/03/2022-03-22-CBD-NewsRel-Womens-participation-on-Sg-boards-reaching-20-at-top-companies-30-at-statutory-boards.pdf

Aronson, Brad, *Human Kind*, LifeTree Media, 2020.

Baker, Colin, *Foundations of Bilingual Education and Bilingualism*, Multilingual Matters, 2011.

Bhatia, Tej K., *The Handbook of Bilingualism and Multilingualism*, Wiley-Blackwell, 2014.

Bonini, Sheila and Steven Swartz, 'Profits with purpose: How organizing for sustainability can benefit the bottom line', McKinsey & Company, 2014, https://www.mckinsey.com/~/media/McKinsey/Business%20Functions/Sustainability/

Our%20Insights/Profits%20with%20purpose/Profits%20 with%20Purpose.ashx

Boynton, Andy, 'Unilever's Paul Polman: CEOs Can't Be "Slaves" to Shareholders', *Forbes*, 2015, https://www.forbes.com/sites/ andyboynton/2015/07/20/unilevers-paul-polman-ceos-cant-be-slaves-to-shareholders/#3ad53db5561e

Cashman, Kevin and Kari Browne, 'The Profit vs. Purpose Debate . . . in Real Time', *Korn Ferry*, 2020, https://www. kornferry.com/insights/articles/profit-vs-purpose-technology

Cheong, Brian, 'How Chopard Made Sustainable Luxury Its Top Priority', *Tatler Magazine*, 2019, https://my.asiatatler.com/ style/how-chopard-made-journey-to-sustainable-luxury-its-top-priority-ethical-gold

Chouinard, Yvon, *Some Stories: Lessons from the Edge of Business and Sports*, Patagonia, 2019.

Chua, Joyce, 'Meet The Woman Who Started The First Social Stock Exchange In The World', (herworld.com, 2019), https://www. herworld.com/women/women-now/social-entrepreneur-inequality-women-empowerment-she-is-more/

Colman, Mark, *Make Peace with Your Mind: How Mindfulness and Compassion Can Free You from Your Inner Critic*, New World Library, 2017.

Coupe, Stuart, *Living with Wildlife: Sustainable Livelihoods for Park-Adjacent Communities in Kenya*, Practical Action, 2002.

de Houwer, Annick, 'The Cambridge Handbook of Bilingualism', Cambridge University Press, 2018.

de Saint-Exupery, Antoine, *Wind, Sand and Stars*, Harcourt, 2002.

Divinagracia, Dinggol Araneta, 'The Araneta Clan in Cyberspace', the *Araneta Clan Blogpost*, 2006,

Evleth, Donna, *France Under the German Occupation, 1940–1944: An Annotated Bibliography*, Greenwood Press, 1991.

Ferrazzi, Keith and Tahl Raz, *Never Eat Alone*, Currency, 2014.

Firth Murray, Anne, *From Outrage to Courage*, Common Courage Press, 2013.

Frankl, Viktor, *Man's Search for Meaning*, Beacon Press, 2006.

Gan, Tammy, 'Project Drawdown: 76 Solutions to Reverse Global Warming', *Green is the New Black* website, 2020, https:// greenisthenewblack.com/project-drawdown/

Go, Julian, *The American Colonial State in the Philippines: Global Perspectives*, Duke University Press Books, 2003.

Golovnev, Andrei V., *Siberian Survival: The Nenets and Their Story*, Cornell University Press, 1999.

Grosjean, François and Ping Li, *The Psycholinguistics of Bilingualism*, Wiley-Blackwell, 2013.

Hawken, Paul, *Drawdown: The Most Comprehensive Plan Ever Proposed to Reverse Global Warming*, Penguin Books, 2017.

Heath, Robert, 'The Kobe earthquake: some realities of strategic management of crises and disasters', *Disaster Prevention and Management*, Vol. 5, No. 5. MCB UP Ltd., 1995, pp. 11–24. https://www.emerald.com/insight/content/doi/10.1108/ 09653569510100965/full/html

Hirasuna, Delphine, *The Art of Gaman*, Penguin and Random House, 2005.

Holmes, Ryan, *Vietnam Travel Guide 2019: Soon Doong Cave: The Biggest Cave of the World*, Independently published, 2019.

Horne, Alistair, *A Savage War of Peace: Algeria 1954–1962*, NYRB Classics, 2006.

http://thearanetaclan.blogspot.com/2006/06/first-araneta-family-grand-reunion.html

Hunt, Vivian, Dennis Layton and Sara Prince, 'New research makes it increasingly clear that companies with more diverse workforces perform better financially', *McKinsey and Company*, 2015, https:// www.mckinsey.com/business-functions/organization/our-insights/why-diversity-matters

Kelion, Leo, 'Apple's 2030 carbon-neutral pledge covers itself and suppliers', *BBC*, 2020, https://www.bbc.com/news/technology-53485560

Keller, Greg, 'Maurice Herzog, French mountain climber, dies at 93', the *Washington Post*, 2012, https://www.washingtonpost.com/local/obituaries/maurice-herzog-french-mountain-climber-dies-at-93/2012/12/16/27d44e82-4613-11e2-8e70-e1993528222d_story.html

Korda, Michael, *Hero: The Life and Legend of Lawrence of Arabia*, Harper Perennial, 2011.

Kristof, Nicholas D. and Sheryl WuDunn, *Half the Sky: Turning Oppression into Opportunity for Women Worldwide*, Vintage, 2010. Lamb, Christina, *Our Bodies Their Battlefield*, William Collins, 2020.

Legrand, Louis, *The Tale of Two Wolves*, CreateSpace Independent Publishing Platform, 2017.

Lim-Lange, Crystal and Dr Gregor Lim-Lange, *Deep Human, Practical Superskills for a Future of Success*, Singapore: Epigram Books 2019.

Lövin, Isabella, 'Gender must be at the heart of climate action', Eco-Business, 2017, https://www.eco-business.com/opinion/gender-must-be-at-the-heart-of-climate-action/

McChrystal, Stanley, Gen., *Teams of Teams*, Portfolio, 2015.

Mercado, Monina Allarey, *People Power: The Greatest Democracy Ever Told the Philippine Revolution of 1986 (An Eyewitness to History)*, James B. Reuter, 1986.

Milliken, William, Dr, 'The Yanomami are Great Observers of Nature', *SurvivalInternational.org* 2019 https://www.survivalinternational.org/articles/3162-yanomami-botanical-knowledge

Morgan, Conway Lloyd, *Starck*, Universe Publishing, 1999.

Myers, Anthony, '"Cocoa for generations": Mars to launch new sustainability strategy', *confectionarynews.com*, 2018, https://www.confectionerynews.com/Article/2018/09/19/Mars-to-launch-new-cocoa-sustainability-strategy

Ndungu, Lucy, 'How we can overcome the COVID-19 pandemic together', *UNDP.org*, 2021, https://www.undp.org/content/undp/en/home/blog/2021/how-we-can-overcome-the-covid-19-pandemic-together.html

Nic, 'What NGOs can learn from startups about failing', *Stuff.co.za*, 2015, https://stuff.co.za/2015/05/06/what-ngos-can-learn-from-startups-about-failing/

Nisen, Max, 'How Nike Solved Its Sweatshop Problem', Businessinsider.com, 2013, https://www.businessinsider.com/how-nike-solved-its-sweatshop-problem-2013-5

Nurgaiv, Aisholpan, *The Eagle Huntress: The True Story of the Girl Who Soared Beyond Expectations*, Little, Brown Books for Young Readers, 2020.

NVPC Knowledge and Insights Team, 'Subjective Wellbeing Survey 2013 Findings', *Cityofgood.sg*, 2013, https://cityofgood.sg/resources/subjective-wellbeing-survey-2013-findings-2/

O'Toole, Laura L., *Gender Violence, 3rd Edition: Interdisciplinary Perspectives*, NYU Press, 2020, https://nyupress.org/9781479820801/gender-violence-3rd-edition/

Pavitt, Nigel, *Samburu*, Kyle Cathie Ltd, 2001.

Peal, Elizabeth and Wallace Lambert, 'The relation of bilingualism to intelligence', *American Psychological Association*, 1962.

Roberts, Andrew, 'Churchill: the "cry-baby" war hero', *History Extra*, 2020, https://www.historyextra.com/period/second-world-war/churchill-the-cry-baby-war-hero/

Rodham Clinton, Hillary, 'Remarks from the United Nations Fourth World Conference on Women', *Beijing China*, 1995, https://www.un.org/esa/gopher-data/conf/fwcw/conf/gov/950905175653.txt

Salawitch, Ross J., Timothy P. Canty, Austin P. Hope, Walter R. Tribett, Bran F. Bennett, *Paris Climate Agreement: Beacon of Hope*, Springer, 2017.

Salbi, Zainab, *Between Two Worlds*, Gotham Books, 2005.

Sanders, Julia, Dr, *Rwandan Genocide: The Unspeakable Evils of Ethnic Cleansing and Genocide in Rwanda*, Independently published, 2017.

Sinek Simon, *Leaders Eat Last: Why Some Teams Pull Together and Others Don't*, Penguin Random House LLC, New York 2017.

Taleb, Nassim Nicholas, *Antifragile: Things that Gain from Disorder*, Penguin Books, 2012.

Tanuvi Joe, 'Eat Just Serves Cultured Meat to Diners at 1880 Restaurant Singapore In A World First', *green queen* Website, 2020, https://www.greenqueen.com.hk/eat-just-serves-cultured-meat-to-diners-at-1880-restaurant-singapore-in-a-world-first/

The 2019 United Nations Global Compact Accenture Strategy CEO Study on Sustainability, 'The decade to deliver, a call to business action', *United Nations Global Compact—Accenture Strategy*, 2019, https://d306pr3pise04h.cloudfront.net/docs/publications%2F2019-UNGC-Accenture-CEO-Study.pdf

Thornton, Grant, 'Philippines top for gender diversity at senior level according to Grant Thornton', *Consultancy Asia*, 2018, https://www.consultancy.asia/news/511/philippines-top-for-gender-diversity-at-senior-level-according-to-grant-thornton

Wagner, Christine G., *The Power of Natural Mentoring: Shaping the Future for Women and Girl*, CWC Publishing, 2020.

Women for Women International UK, website: https://womenforwomen.org.uk/about-us/our-story

Yee, Amy, 'Gazing Into Danakil Depression's Mirror, and Seeing Mars Stare Back', the *New York Times*, 2017, https://www.nytimes.com/2017/01/30/science/danakil-depression-ethiopia.html

Zandan, Noah and Lisa Shalett, 'What Inclusive Leaders Sound Like', *Harvard Business Review*, 2020, https://hbr-org.cdn.ampproject.org/c/s/hbr.org/amp/2020/11/what-inclusive-leaders-sounds-like